Women in Parliament:

Beyond Numbers

A Revised Edition

Handbook Series

The International IDEA Handbook Series seeks to present comparative analysis, information and insights on a range of democratic institutions and processes. Handbooks are aimed primarily at policymakers, politicians, civil society actors and practitioners in the field. They are also of interest to academia, the democracy assistance community and other bodies.

© International Institute for Democracy and Electoral Assistance 2005
Applications for permission to reproduce or translate all or any part of this publication should be made to:
Publications Office
International IDEA
SE -103 34 Stockholm
Sweden

International IDEA encourages dissemination of its work and will promptly respond to requests for permission to reproduce or translate its publications.

Graphic design by: Trydells Forum
Cover Illustrations by: Anoli Perera, Sri Lanka
Printed by: Trydells Tryckeri AB, Sweden
ISBN: 91-85391-19-0

Women in Parliament:
Beyond Numbers

A Revised Edition

Editors: Julie Ballington and Azza Karam

Contributors: Julie Ballington, Elisa Carrio, Nestorine Compaoré, Drude Dahlerup, Frene Ginwala, Mala N. Htun, Kareen Jabre, Azza Karam, Joni Lovenduski, Richard E. Matland, Sheila Meintjes, Nina Pacari, Sonia Palmieri, Khofifah Indar Parawansa, Elizabeth Powley, Shirin Rai, Amal Sabbagh, Nadezhda Shvedova, Mariette Sineau and Lena Wängnerud.

With a foreword by Ellen Johnson Sirleaf, President of the Republic of Liberia.

Contents

Section 2. Overcoming Obstacles

3. Enhancing Women's Political Participation:
Legislative Recruitment and Electoral Systems

List of Tables, Figures and Boxes

Annexes

Foreword

Women's presence in parliaments around the world is a reality that is impacting on the social, political and economic fabric of nations and of the world. Yet, their access to these important legislative structures, learning how to work within them, and the extent to which they impact on and through them, remain serious challenges. It is critical, for the sake of ensuring fully functional democratic institutions, and total respect for the human rights of all, that these challenges be targeted and overcome. A concerted effort is needed to target all stages of women's political participation, from the moment they decide they want to run for public office, through each step till they reach that designated office, and thereafter to ensure that as members of parliaments, they have the means and needed resources to impact positively and constructively on the advancement of their nation.

This Handbook is a testament to the efforts of many courageous and determined women the world over, to stand shoulder to shoulder with their male compatriots in the construction of representative, just and peaceful polities. The handbook is at once an overview, an analysis and a guide, focused on the obstacles faced by women, the means of overcoming them, the modalities of impacting on and through legislative structures, and the varied and rich experiences available around the world from which to learn.

Each moment we live through is a turning point in history, each event a symbol of what is transpiring. This Handbook is one such event in a rapidly changing, and ever interesting, moment in our global human development.

ELLEN JOHNSON SIRLEAF
President
Republic of Liberia

Ellen Johnson Sirleaf, President of the Republic of Liberia, is the first elected female President of an African country. She was sworn in as President on 16 January 2006

Foreword to the Original 1998 Version

Frene Ginwala

We reproduce here the Foreword written by Frene Ginwala, former Speaker of the National Assembly of South Africa, for the first edition of *Women in Parliament: Beyond Numbers*. Frene Ginwala then reflects on what has happened since in her Afterword.

The 1998 Foreword

The seed of democracy lies in the principle that the legitimacy of the power to make decisions about peoples' lives, their society and their country should derive from a choice by those who will be affected. For many centuries the basis of this legitimacy was limited and many were excluded from making a choice: slaves, those without property or formal education, those not 'civilized' or not part of the dominant culture or religion in society, people of colour, of a particular racial or ethnic group, indigenous peoples of countries conquered and annexed through superior weaponry—and overwhelmingly, women.

The franchise was won through struggles within societies, and the right to self-determination of subject peoples through anti-colonial and liberation struggles in many countries. Today most of those previously excluded have won the right to both choose and be members of institutions of governance. Universal franchise in free and fair elections has become recognized as a minimum standard for democratic societies.

However, in new and established democracies alike, it has become clear that universal suffrage did not in itself lead to the establishment of representative legislatures. Many sections of the population continued to be excluded, mainly the rural poor and the least educated, and still, women. Overall, the proportion of women in legislatures is exceedingly low. The question is why and does it matter? Why should it matter; what difference does it make whether women are in legislatures and other institutions of governance or not?

The seed of democracy lies in the principle that the legitimacy of the power to make decisions about peoples' lives, their society and their country should derive from a choice by those who will be affected.

It is important to appreciate that the issue is not only about numbers. If policy decisions and laws are to be made for the benefit of all members of society, then the

14

extent to which the decision-making body is able to take into account the experience of as broad a spectrum of that society as possible, will be the gauge of the degree to which its decisions will be appropriate and meet the needs of the entire society rather than those of a particular group or groups.

While the debate about enfranchisement of women and participation of women in decision making often focuses on issues of justice, equity and human rights, the representation of women and the inclusion of their perspective and experience into the decision-making process will inevitably lead to solutions that are more viable and satisfy a broader range of society. That is why women should be part of the process and why it matters: all of society benefits as we find better and more appropriate solutions for our problems.

The challenge goes beyond ensuring the election of larger numbers of women into the legislatures. Patriarchy, subordination of women, and the deep-rooted perception that the public domain is reserved for men and that the social contract is about the relationship between men and government and not citizens and government, come together to exclude women—notwithstanding rights guaranteed in law and the political rhetoric of good governance and participatory democracy.

In many countries, women continue to have difficulty in exercising their right to vote due to cultural, religious, patriarchal and economic impediments. Women have and continue to face difficulty in entering institutions of governance; political parties fail to choose them as candidates, and the electorate reflects and acts on the gender stereotypes in society by choosing men. Once in the institution, women have faced new obstacles that constrain their capacity to function.

Conscious that the oppressed must help themselves, large numbers of women participated in the struggle for the liberation of South Africa, and as co-combatants were able to integrate into its theory the liberation of women. Continued involvement in the negotiations by women ensured that the new South Africa has a constitution that is gender-sensitive and provides a unique legal framework for genuine and effective equality. However, in common with women in other countries we found that the existence of rights in law does not automatically mean that women are able to claim and exercise these rights. Patriarchy and the subordination of women that is structured into society, as well as cultural and religious practices remain with us.

Institutions of governance like all other institutions have developed in patriarchal societies and have been shaped by the assumptions of unequal gender relations, and on the basis of who (men) should operate within those institutions.

In South Africa, the building blocks of the society we inherited are impregnated with racism and patriarchy, and so are the institutions. We need to use them to improve the material and social conditions we found, but we recognize that they need to be radically transformed. Their culture, values, organization and style were designed to perpetuate inequality and preserve privilege: objectives which are diametrically opposed to our own. Unless transformed, these institutions will either co-opt and swallow any blacks or women who enter or frustrate them into resignation.

We have been fortunate in having a political leadership that recognizes that women are needed to make the radical changes that are necessary and that in turn the presence of women within the institutions will enable them to change the structures of power of which they are a part, making it easier for those who follow. The South African experience is one of many around the globe.

This handbook is a tool. It proposes no one solution, but accepts that our situations vary though we share common aims. It presents us with information on the methods that have been used elsewhere, and those that are now available to us.

This handbook is a tool. It proposes no one solution, but accepts that our situations vary though we share common aims. It presents us with information on the methods that have been used elsewhere, and those that are now available to us. It draws on the shared experience of women as well as men working as activists, researchers, and politicians; as individual groups and organizations, and as local, regional and global actors.

Most importantly, it focuses on what women need to do. This is not to support those who believe society's responsibility ends with the enactment of equality or anti-discrimination legislation, and then it is up to individual women. Rather it is to recognize that in any society and situation it is those most affected who must act to bring about change. Those who are privileged benefit, even unconsciously from a system that marginalizes others. Hence they cannot be depended upon to make the changes that will remove their privileged status. It is up to us, the women.

In any society and situation it is those most affected who must act to bring about change. Those who are privileged benefit, even unconsciously from a system that marginalizes others. Hence they cannot be depended upon to make the changes that will remove their privileged status. It is up to us, the women.

As we go into the 21st century globalization brings both opportunities and new challenges. In the period leading up to the Nairobi conference in 1985 women came together to overturn the assumptions that confined them to the private sphere and tried to define their concerns as purely social and divorced from the political and economic conditions in society. Women in the developing countries united and secured recognition for the link between equality, development and peace. The Programme of Action adopted at Beijing is based on the recognition that the development of women is integral to the development of society and further that political and civil rights are inseparable from economic and social rights.

When we look back two decades or even half a century, we see the tremendous progress we have made. Looking forward into the new millennium we see how much further we have yet to travel, but we can do so with confidence in our ability to write women's story as one that brought justice, peace and security for all humankind.

Afterword

Experience has shown that the greater representation of women at the highest levels of governance has made a difference in raising awareness, changing agendas and providing a national gender-sensitive legal framework. In emerging democracies it is now generally accepted that special provision should be made to ensure the participation of women, while many long-established democracies still lag behind. To build on our gains we need to strategize on ways of deepening representation into local government and other institutions of state.

But, even as we celebrate incremental progress, we should be wary of complacency. Beyond parliaments there are powerful institutions which remain male bastions, including the private sector, the judiciary, and the multilateral institutions. In the United States only 0.7 percent of chief executive officers (CEOs) are women; in Europe not a single women is among the 25 highest-paid CEOs; in the UK there are no women on the boards of 65 percent of quoted companies. The recent Norwegian example of intervening to ensure that all companies have at least two women on their boards by 2006 is an initiative which could be followed elsewhere.

Last and most importantly, full equality for women has not been sufficiently mainstreamed into the Millennium Development Goals, and some specific issues of concern to women have been largely ignored. There are targets related to the elimination of gender disparity in primary and secondary education by 2005 and at all levels by 2015, and also related to improving maternal health. It is vital that in the struggle to achieve the MDG targets, women ensure that our gains and the further development of our agenda are not ignored.

October 2005

Preface

The International Institute for Democracy and Electoral Assistance (International IDEA), an intergovernmental organization with member states across all continents, seeks to support sustainable democracy in both new and long-established democracies. Drawing on comparative analysis and experiences, IDEA works to bolster electoral processes, enhance political equality and participation, and develop democratic institutions and practices. It is particularly important that these institutions are inclusive and responsive if there is to be effective governance, benefiting a wide spectrum of groups in society. In this context, IDEA is committed to promoting the participation and representation of women in political life.

Increasing women's participation in politics and securing their access to political life is of particular importance to democratic development and sustainability. Efforts to promote and increase women's political participation have taken place all around the world and brought together women from different political, social and cultural groups with the common aim of reaching the goal of gender equality. In some countries the process of reaching equal representation of women in political institutions and parliament has taken a long time—for example, in the Nordic countries—while in other countries the transition to democracy has contributed to a more rapid development and the overall change in society has opened 'windows of opportunity' to promote women's participation in political life. However, no matter what the contextual differences, the struggle to reach a higher representation of women in parliament and to let the women elected make a greater impact has met stiff resistance and required a strong group of women negotiating for their rights as equal members of the society. Women all over the world have mobilized across political lines and from the standpoints of different social and cultural status and ethic affiliations to reach the goal of gender equality. The hard work has paid off and there have indeed been positive changes in most regions of the world: the average number of women in parliament has increased from 11.8 percent in 1998 to nearly 16 percent in 2005; but there is still a long way to go to reach the Beijing Platform for Action target of 30 percent women in decision-making positions. It is therefore of great importance to continue to enhance the tools that are available to women and continue the debate regarding women's political participation. This means not only increasing the number of women represented in parliament but also moving 'beyond numbers' and looking at ways of increasing the effectiveness of the women who are elected and the impact of women elected to powerful positions.

To this end, the new *Women in Parliament: Beyond Numbers* Handbook is published. It identifies the obstacles to winning election to parliament that women face, and provides suggestions and options for overcoming them. It also seeks to move beyond numbers, by identifying the ways in which women can impact on political processes through their participation in decision-making bodies. The Handbook gathers together knowledge and practical experience from all around the world and draws upon women's experiences from different regions in their struggle for gender equality in politics.

The original version of this Handbook was published in English in 1998, and since its initial publication IDEA has become aware of the overwhelming interest in its being made available in other languages to assist those advocating for change in different regions. From 2002 to 2003, IDEA therefore produced 'regional' translations of the Handbook, not only updating and translating the text but adding case studies from the particular regions. Regional versions of the Handbook are available in Spanish, French and Indonesian, and an abridged version is available in Russian.

This Handbook would not have been possible without the ground-breaking and excellent contributions of many individuals. Azza Karam was the driving force behind the production of the original Handbook in 1998, and we are grateful to her for her advice, editorial assistance and guidance provided to International IDEA over the past years. Julie Ballington was the Programme Officer in charge of the IDEA Women in Politics project between 2001 and 2005, and is responsible for this revised version and the regional versions. Without her professionalism, experience and extensive contacts the different versions of the Handbook would not have been possible. We thank both Julie Ballington and Azza Karam for the hard work, dedication and editorial prowess which have brought this Handbook to fruition.

We thank all the authors—Julie Ballington, Elisa Carrio, Nestorine Compaoré, Drude Dahlerup, Frene Ginwala, Mala N. Htun, Kareen Jabre, Azza Karam, Ellen Johnson-Sirleaf, Joni Lovenduski, Richard E. Matland, Sheila Meintjes, Nina Pacari, Sonia Palmieri, Khofifah Indar Parawansa, Elizabeth Powley, Shirin Rai, Amal Sabbagh, Nedezhda Shvedova, Mariette Sineau and Lena Wängnerud—who made this Handbook possible with their contributions and assistance with updates in this volume. We also acknowledge the authors who contributed to the other versions of the Handbook and are grateful for them for sharing their knowledge and experiences from the different regions.

Several committed and skilled consultants and staff members have pulled this publication together. Our sincere thanks go to Eve Johansson, our talented copy editor, for her consistency and meticulous attention to detail. Yee Yin Yap and Cecilia Bylesjö provided invaluable assistance and support to the editors and authors throughout the process. We also thank those responsible for the production of this Handbook, including the staff in our publications unit, Nadia Handal Zander and John Bellamy.

Lastly, we thank our member states without whose support this publication would not have been possible.

We trust that all our readers, including those involved in the practical work of democracy promotion and advancing women's political participation, will find this an illuminating, up-to-date and thorough guide.

LENA HJELM-WALLÉN
Chair of the Board
International IDEA

Acronyms and Abbreviations

ANC	African National Congress (South Africa)
CEDAW	Convention on the Elimination of All Forms of Discrimination Against Women (1979)
CGE	Commission on Gender Equality (South Africa)
DPD	Dewan Perwakilan Daerah (Regional Representatives' Council) (Indonesia)
DPR	Dewan Perwakilan Rakyat (House of Representatives) (Indonesia)
EISA	Electoral Institute of Southern Africa
IPU	Inter-Parliamentary Union
JMC	Joint Monitoring Committee on the Quality of Life and Status of Women (South Africa)
MMD	Multi-member district
MP	Member of parliament
MPR	Majelis Permusyawaratan (People's Consultative Assembly) (Indonesia)
NGO	Non-governmental organization
PAN	Partido de Acción Nacional (National Action Party) (Mexico)
PC	Parti Communiste (France)
PR	Proportional representation
PRD	Partido Revolucionario Democrático (Party of the Democratic Revolution (Mexico)
PRI	Partido Revolucionario Institucional (Institutional Revolutionary Party) (Mexico)
PS	Parti Socialiste (France)
RPF	Rwandan Patriotic Front
SMD	Single-member district
SNTV	Single Non-Transferable Vote
STV	Single Transferable Vote
UN	United Nations
UNDP	United Nations Development Programme
UNIFEM	United Nations Development Fund for Women
USD	US dollar
WNC	Women's National Coalition (South Africa)

Chapter 1

Chapter 1

Julie Ballington

Introduction

International IDEA was established in 1995—the same year as the world's governments recognized that, despite the widespread transition to democracy taking place in many regions, 'the popular participation of women in key decision-making as full and equal partners with men, particularly in politics, has not yet been achieved'.[1] From its very inception, IDEA believed that women's political participation was, and remains, central to democratic governance. IDEA also recognizes that if the world's established and emerging democracies are to be truly democratic, half of the world's population cannot be excluded from either representation or participation.

To that end, IDEA's Women in Politics programme seeks to collate different methods and models for enhancing women's political participation. By bridging the divide between the academics and practitioners, IDEA aims to provide relevant policy options and data to those working to find practicable solutions to the under-representation of women. While taking into account a global perspective, it tries to ensure that the materials generated also reflect an awareness of and comparisons between the different national, regional and local contexts. This Handbook, *Women in Parliament: Beyond Numbers,* together with a whole series of handbooks that IDEA's Women in Politics programme has produced since 1998, is a testament not only to this philosophy, but also to its persuasiveness among the multitude of people working to achieve similar goals globally, as attested by the need for this second English-language edition. This publication brings to six the total number of handbooks in the series.

1. An Approach to Democracy: Why Include Women?

An essential tenet of any democratic framework is the principle of human rights, including the granting and exercise of the political rights of both men and women. The development of any political agenda that does not include the perspectives, views and experiences of those who will be affected is not credible.

Despite efforts over the centuries by prominent women—and men—the recognition and exercise of women's political, economic and social rights is by no means equal between women and men.[2] Women constitute half of the world's population and comprise 50 percent of the labour force, yet make up 1 billion human beings living in poverty. Decision making and priority setting continue to be largely in the hands of men. Taking into account gendered perspectives and involving both women and men in decision-making processes are a sine qua non of any democratic framework. Hence democracy, by definition, cannot afford to be gender-blind. It must strive towards equality and representation of women and men in decision-making processes and in the opportunities to achieve both these goals.

The equal participation of women and men in public life is one of the cornerstones of the Convention on the Elimination of All Forms of Discrimination Against Women (CEDAW) adopted by the United Nations (UN) General Assembly in 1979, and in force since 1981. Today, more than 20 years since the signing of the convention, 179 countries are party to it and bound to take measures to promote women's participation in decision making and leadership positions.

In 1995, the UN Fourth World Conference on Women held in Beijing generated renewed pressure for the implementation of the CEDAW provisions: the Beijing Platform for Action identified 'inequality between men and women in the sharing of power and decision-making at all levels' and 'insufficient mechanisms at all levels to promote the advancement of women' as two areas of significant concern where action was critical for the advancement of women. This was further expanded to encompass women's participation in post-conflict state building, which finds expression in UN Security Council Resolution 1325 on Women, Peace and Security, passed in October 2000. In the debate introducing Resolution 1325 in 2000, UN Secretary-General Kofi Annan stated that 'peace is inextricably linked to equality between women and men ... maintaining and promoting peace and security requires equal participation in decision-making'.[3]

2. A Decade On: Incremental Progress the World Over

Ten years on since IDEA's founding in 1995, and seven years since the original *Women in Parliament: Beyond Numbers* Handbook was published in 1998, the picture regarding women's political participation has slowly changed. Overall the past decade has seen modest progress with regard to women's presence in national parliaments.

While in 1995 women accounted for 11.3 percent of members of parliament, this figure has increased to nearly 16 percent in 2005.[4] More than 30 women have served as heads of government and/or state since 1995, and in October 2005 27 women presided over houses of parliament.[5] Globally, women now hold more elective offices than ever before.[6]

Table 1: Women in Parliament in 2005, by Region of the World

Region	Single House or Lower House	Upper House or Senate	Both Houses Combined
Nordic countries	40.1%	–	40.1%
Europe—OSCE member countries including Nordic countries	18.9%	16.5%	18.4%
Americas	18.7%	18.5%	18.6%
Europe—OSCE member countries excluding Nordic countries	16.8%	16.5%	16.8%
Asia	15.1%	13.5%	15.0%
Sub-Saharan Africa	14.9%	14.0%	14.8%
Pacific	11.2%	26.5%	13.2%
Arab states	6.7%	5.6%	6.5%
Global average	15.8%	14.7%	15.7%

Source: Inter-Parliamentary Union (IPU), 'Women in National Parliaments: Situation as of 31 January 2005', <http://www.ipu.org>.

Important progress has been made in some regions, notably the Nordic countries, where women's representation averages 40 percent in parliament. The percentage of parliaments that have reached the Beijing target of at least 30 percent women in parliament has increased threefold in the past ten years, to 6 percent.[7] Yet in many parts of the world real gains in women accessing legislatures have not occurred, and largely insurmountable obstacles persist. For example, women are still least represented in the Arab states, where the regional average in lower houses is 6.7 percent. Women also remain woefully under-represented in the parliaments of the Pacific Island states, with an average of 3.2 percent (excluding Australia and New Zealand, where women's representation stands at 24.7 percent and 28.3 percent, respectively).[8]

3. About This Handbook

3.1. Background

The slowly changing face of parliamentary representation was not an inevitable consequence of the broadening of the political space in democratization processes. Rather, it has resulted from sustained mobilization, institutional engineering, political party commitment and greater recognition by the international community of the need for gender equality. This international discourse has been the foundation of concerted efforts to support women's full political participation in the past ten years. Women's activism and mobilization at the country, regional and international level have been pivotal to keeping gender equality firmly rooted on the international agenda. These are the premises on which these chapters and case studies are based.

IDEA produced the first edition of this Handbook in 1998. This second edition was revised and updated in 2005. The original idea behind the publication was that women in public life require accessible and useful information on how to effect political change in decision-making bodies. There is an emphasis on the entire process of participation—from the very beginning to the end—as well as the means of making an impact. Azza Karam explains that 'it is clear that the more active and engaged women are in politics, the more there is a need for a culling and systematization of their experiences in such a way as to elaborate how it is that they make it to these bodies and what they can do once in them'.[9]

The Handbook is therefore a practical tool for overcoming the obstacles women encounter throughout the parliamentary electoral process, providing a number of options on how to bring about constructive change and influence in politics. It is underpinned by IDEA's unique approach to democracy assistance: it seeks to bridge the divide between academia and practitioners, providing strategies for those men and women who are committed to correcting the imbalance in politics. It seeks to answer the following questions: *What are the major obstacles women confront when entering parliament? What are the different ways of overcoming these obstacles and in which structural and political contexts? What are the mechanisms and strategies women can use to influence the parliamentary political process?*

3.2. Target Audiences

This Handbook brings together a variety of authors, and draws on the shared experience of women as well as men working as researchers, politicians and activists at the local, regional and global levels. The Handbook is targeted to a wide range of actors working to promote the participation and representation of women in political structures. This includes first and foremost women members of parliament and those campaigning for elected office. Also targeted are members of civil society, including activists, academics, researchers, journalists, and other stakeholders working to advance women in politics.

3.3. Regionalizing Outreach

Since its initial release in English in 1998, there has been incredible interest and demand for the *Women in Parliament: Beyond Numbers* Handbook from those advocating for change around the world. Responding to ongoing requests for the translation of the Handbook into different languages, International IDEA has produced the following regional versions: French (2002); Indonesian (2002); Spanish (2002) and Russian (abridged in 2003). There are more than 25 country case studies from all regions of the world. The different regional versions of the book are fully downloadable on the International IDEA web site.

4. Outline of the Handbook

The provision of comparative information and strategies for practitioners seeking to increase women's participation in political institutions is central. The barriers that women face in reaching parliaments have been defined as falling into two main categories: attitudinal and socio-economic factors, and political and institutional factors. Although the socio-economic and ideological factors cannot be ignored, much emphasis has been placed on the political and institutional factors that influence the levels of representation of women, and these can, and very often do, change over a short period of time.

Key themes in this Handbook include:

- the effect of socio-economic and cultural biases and overcoming the challenges in winning election to parliaments;
- the central role that political parties and electoral systems play;
- increasing women's access to decision-making bodies through the use of special measures such as quotas; and
- looking beyond the question of numbers to enhancing the effectiveness of women politicians in transforming the institution of parliament and effecting policy changes.

The information presented in this Handbook brings together the available expertise and data on the subject and also highlights areas where further research and training need to be undertaken. Thus, it is not the final tome on how women MPs can impact on the political process, nor is it primarily a research instrument. Although it incorporates the views and analyses of researchers, the Handbook is designed primarily for practical purposes, providing strategies and ideas that can be used for further action.

As already mentioned, the issue of impacting on politics necessarily involves first looking at the problems women face in getting into parliament and the mechanisms they have used to overcome these obstacles. All too often, women who want to enter politics find that the political, public, cultural and social environment is not conducive to their participation. In **chapter 2** Nadezhda Shvedova identifies the problems that affect the political participation of women, categorized into political, socio-economic and psychological factors.

Women in Parliament clearly highlights the effect that institutions have on women's access to parliament. In **chapter 3** Richard E. Matland illustrates the consequences of different electoral systems. While they alone do not determine the level of representation of women, electoral systems are important because they can be, and regularly are, changed. Chapter 3 also highlights the impact of political parties as they assume the primary responsibility for candidate nomination. Parties are entrusted with perhaps the most strategic responsibility in a democracy—to prepare and select candidates for election and to support them in positions of leadership and governance.

Because of the obstacles that women face in the electoral process, special measures have been implemented to promote their presence in parliament and other elected positions. Today, quotas are one of the most effective mechanisms to ensure women direct access to political power. In **chapter 4** Drude Dahlerup examines quota systems and how they have come to play a critical role in increasing the representation of women. It provides the various arguments for and against the use of quotas. The introduction of quotas in the past ten years has met with some success. In other instances, quotas have not resulted in an increase in the number of women in politics or in their empowerment. This chapter therefore provides comparative examples of the implementation in countries of quotas around the world.

It is relatively easy to enumerate the various challenges regarding women's political participation, but it is much harder to appreciate the strengths women have and the positive differences they have made in their chosen professions. The second theme of the Handbook shifts the focus to how women can move 'beyond numbers' in parliament to make an impact on the political process. In **chapter 5** Azza Karam and Joni Lovenduski outline how women can reform the inherent 'institutional masculinity' which characterizes most legislatures by implementing a 'rules strategy'. They suggest a framework for thinking about and acting on the question of how women can enhance their parliamentary decision-making power, and identify three key areas: learning the rules, using the rules and changing the rules. The chapter presents strategies that have been tried and those that can be tried in the future, and argues for the importance of looking 'beyond the numbers'.

IDEA always strives to identify and deal with different national realities. Indeed, a great many contexts are presented in this Handbook—different political, social, economic and cultural contexts, as well as countries in transition, developing democracies and established democracies, all of which have their own impact on women's participation. In order to highlight these diversities, **case studies** from different regions of the world are included on all of the issues being discussed. Each case study reflects not only the diverse social, political and cultural situation in each country, but also the commonalities in terms of women's needs and expectations and, in some cases, achievements. Eleven national and regional case studies are presented, including Argentina, the Arab States (Jordan, Lebanon and Yemen), Asia (Bangladesh, India and Pakistan), Burkina Faso, Ecuador, France, Indonesia, Latin America (regional comparison), Rwanda, South Africa and Sweden. A 12th case study on the work of the Inter-Parliamentary Union (IPU) is also presented. The IPU has a long and distinguished record of working with women parliamentarians. The presentations do not advocate one particular approach over another, but rather cover the range of alternatives and best practices. In this way women and men can be informed about the issues and prepared to take action suited to their particular situation.

The Handbook aims to bring together information presented by researchers, politicians and activists working to advance gender equality in decision-making bodies. A great many views and issues are covered and strategies proposed. In **chapter 6,** Azza Karam synthesizes the material presented in the Handbook by providing an overview of the needs identified by women parliamentarians, summarizing the strategies that have been successfully adopted to make inroads within parliament, and affirming the long march to success that women have led and societies have collectively undertaken over many decades.

The Handbook is an attempt to collate information presented by researchers in the field, as well as the practical experiences of women activists, and organizations working on promoting women's participation in parliaments. Both the individuals and the institutions span the local and the international. The Handbook therefore embodies an attempt to bring together a great many threads simultaneously. Certain generalizations tend to be made in an effort to trace commonalties in experiences and results, but even so the specificity of each local circumstance, while respected and taken into account, remains difficult to capture in its entirety.

5. The Future Agenda

In each country the methods may be different, but very few governments around the world will deny that women's participation in the political system needs to be increased and enhanced as part of an overall evolution of the democratic process. Drawing on facts, lived realities, combined insights and experiences, IDEA hopes that this Handbook will contribute to the creation of a critical mass and the forging of strategic alliances necessary for making a difference to the broader political process— and that this information reflects the realities of women east, west, north and south.

Ultimately, the success of any endeavour is the sum total of the efforts of all those who contribute to it, and all societies are called upon to engage in an inevitable process of making our world a better place, with all key agents involved to the best of their abilities. This is where women's entry into and success in the political sphere is headed, and this Handbook is an attempt to salute all the women—and men—who have worked in the past, and who are still part of this important journey, in these interesting times.

Notes

[1] United Nations, 1995. 'Fourth World Conference on Women Platform for Action', 1995, article 15, <http://www.un.org/womenwatch/daw/beijing/platform/plat1.htm>.

[2] United Nations Development Programme (UNDP), 1995. *Human Development Report 1995: Gender and Human Development.* Oxford and New York: Oxford University Press.

[3] Whittington, S., 2004. 'UN Goals for Gender Mainstreaming', Paper presented at the conference on Women and Post-War Reconstruction: Strategies for Implementation of Democracy Building Policies, Florida International University, Miami, March.

[4] The statistics regarding the number of women in parliaments in this handbook are taken from the Inter-Parliamentary Union's Women in National Parliaments database at <http://www.ipu.org>. We have endeavoured to use consistently the statistics from 31 January 2005 unless otherwise specified. See also the case study on the Inter-Parliamentary Union (IPU) in this Handbook.

[5] As of 31 October 2005. See IPU, 'Women Presiding Officers of Parliaments', <http://www.ipu.org>.

[6] The global average number of women in parliament of 15.7 percent as of 31 January 2005 had increased to 16.1 percent as of 31 October 2005.

[7] See the case study on the Inter-Parliamentary Union in this handbook.

[8] IPU, 2005. 'Women in National Parliaments: Situation as of 31 January 2005', <http://www.ipu.org>.

[9] Ballington, Julie, 2005. 'Ten Years of Progress: Enhancing Women's Political Participation', in International IDEA, *Ten Years of Supporting Democracy Worldwide.* Stockholm: International IDEA.

Chapter 2

Chapter 2

Nadezhda Shvedova

Obstacles to Women's Participation in Parliament

Women around the world at every socio-political level find themselves under-represented in parliament and far removed from decision-making levels. As mentioned in chapter 1, in 2005, women hold barely 16 percent of parliamentary seats around the world. The factors that hamper or facilitate women's political participation vary with level of socio-economic development, geography, culture, and the type of political system. Women themselves are not a homogeneous group; there are major differences between them, based on class, race, ethnicity, cultural background and education. The exclusion of women from decision-making bodies limits the possibilities for entrenching the principles of democracy in a society, hindering economic development and discouraging the attainment of gender equality. If men monopolize the political process, passing laws which affect society at large, the decision-making process does not always balance the interests of the male and female populations. As noted in the Millennium Development Goals, women's equal participation with men in power and decision making is part of their fundamental right to participate in political life, and at the core of gender equality and women's empowerment.[1] Women have to be active participants in determining development agendas.

Women who want to enter politics find that the political, public, cultural and social environment is often unfriendly or even hostile to them. Even a quick glance at the current composition of political decision makers in any region provides evidence that women still face numerous obstacles in articulating and shaping their own interests. What are the obstacles women face in entering parliament? How can women better cope with these hindrances? In this chapter we take the first step towards increasing women's parliamentary representation and effectiveness by identifying the common problems that women face. We categorize the problems into three areas: political, socio-economic, and ideological and psychological (or socio-cultural). In the chapters that follow, we identify some of the strategies to overcome these obstacles and analyse what women can do once they enter parliament.

1. Political Obstacles

> Men dominate the political arena; men formulate the rules of the political game; and men define the standards for evaluation. The existence of this male-dominated model results in women either rejecting politics altogether or rejecting male-style politics.

At the beginning of the 21st century, over 95 percent of all countries in the world have granted women the two most fundamental democratic rights: the right to vote and the right to stand for election. New Zealand was the first country to give women the right to vote, in 1893; and Finland was the first to adopt both fundamental democratic rights in 1906. There are still a few countries that deny women both the right to vote and the right to stand for elections.[2]

In theory, the right to stand for election, to become a candidate and to get elected is based on the right to vote. The reality is, however, that women's right to vote remains restricted, principally because the candidates are mostly male. This is true not only for partial and developing democracies, but for established democracies as well. The low level of women's representation in some European parliaments should be considered a violation of women's fundamental democratic right and, as such, a violation of their basic human rights. This unequal rate of representation in legislative bodies signifies that women's representation, rather than being a consequence of democratization, is more a reflection of a status quo.

In most countries de jure difficulties exist, either by virtue of laws being enacted and not followed or by virtue of laws not even existing in the first place. To achieve gender balance in political life, it is necessary to ensure that commitment to equality is reflected in laws and national policies. 'The rising force of women organized at all levels of society throughout the world has given greater impetus to the 30 percent target for women in political positions originally promoted in 1995. Introducing quotas for electoral seats is considered an important strategy.'[3] Indeed, positive action is a necessary tool to maintain at least 30 percent of women at all levels of decision making.

The Argentinean law on quotas, for example, requires all parties to nominate women to 30 percent of electable positions on their lists of candidates. Such a law can effectively facilitate the election of women to legislative bodies. When such laws are rescinded there is evidence that women's representation is affected. A case in point is Bangladesh where, following the expiry of the quota law in April 2001, the number of women members of parliament (MPs) dropped from 10 to 2 percent in the October 2001 election. On the contrary, in Rwanda, the 2003 elections demonstrated a significant increase in the number of women elected to the National Assembly.

Among all national parliaments, Rwanda is now closest to reaching equal numbers of men and women: 48.8 percent of seats are held by women, surpassing even the proportion in the Nordic countries. This is largely because of a constitutional quota which reserves 24 of the 80 seats in the lower house for women. Women in the Rwandan upper house are also guaranteed 30 percent of the seats.[4]

Research indicates that political structures can play a significant role in women's recruitment to parliament. The system of elections based on proportional representation (PR), for example, has resulted in three to four times more women being elected in countries with similar political cultures, for example, Germany and Australia. Generalizations such as this are valid so long as there are cultural similarities, that is similar levels of social and economic development, between countries. In Russia, this generalization is not applicable because of the different and evolving political culture—specifically, the weakly developed party system, the existence of many parties and blocs (until 2003), the lack of confidence many women have to contend with, and the tendency of political parties to marginalize women's interests. A voter's political literacy (the capacity to make coherent choices and decisions when voting, which is clearly not only dependent on level of formal education) plays a significant role, as does the political will to improve the situation.

Among the political obstacles that women face, the following feature prominently:

- the prevalence of the 'masculine model' of political life and of elected government bodies;
- lack of party support, for example, limited financial support for women candidates, limited access to political networks, and the more stringent standards and qualifications applied to women;
- lack of sustained contact and cooperation with other public organizations such as trade (labour) unions and women's groups;
- lack of access to well-developed education and training systems for women's leadership in general, and for orienting young women towards political life; and
- the nature of the electoral system, which may or may not be favourable to women candidates.

1.1. The Masculine Model of Politics

Men largely dominate the political arena; largely formulate the rules of the political game; and often define the standards for evaluation. Furthermore, political life is organized according

> Political life is organized according to male norms and values, and in some cases even male lifestyles.

to male norms and values, and in some cases even male lifestyles. For instance, politics is often based on the idea of 'winners and losers', competition and confrontation, rather than on systematic collaboration and consensus, especially across party lines. It may often result in women either rejecting politics altogether or rejecting male-style politics. Thus, when women do participate in politics, they tend to do so in small numbers.

'The most interesting aspect of the Swedish Parliament is not that we have 45 per cent representation of women, but that a majority of women and men bring relevant social experience to the business of parliament. This is what makes the difference. Men bring with them experience of real life issues, of raising children, of running a home. They have broad perspectives and greater understanding. And women are allowed to be what we are, and to act according to our own unique personality. Neither men nor women have to conform to a traditional role. Women do not have to behave like men to have power; men do not have to behave like women to be allowed to care for their children. When this pattern becomes the norm then we will see real change.'

Birgitta Dahl, former Speaker of Parliament, Sweden

Differences between men and women also appear with respect to the content and priorities of decision making, which are determined by the interests, backgrounds and working patterns of both sexes. Women tend to give priority to societal concerns, such as social security, national health care and children's issues.

The male-dominated working pattern is further reflected in the parliamentary work schedule, which is often characterized by lack of supportive structures for working mothers in general, and for women MPs in particular. In addition to their party and constituency work, and serving on different committees, women parliamentarians are called upon to network within their parties, at multi-party levels and with women outside parliament. Furthermore, they have to play the socially prescribed nurturing roles of mother, wife, sister and grandmother. Currently, most parliamentary programmes and sitting times are not adjusted to take into consideration this dual burden that women carry. Many women MPs struggle to balance family life with the demands of work that often involve late hours, much travelling and few facilities.

> In addition to their party and constituency work, and serving on committees, women parliamentarians are called upon to network within their parties, at multi-party levels and with women outside parliament.

1.2. Lack of Party Support

Women play important roles in campaigning and mobilizing support for their parties, yet they rarely occupy decision-making positions in these structures. In fact, fewer than 11 percent of party leaders worldwide are women.

Although political parties possess resources for conducting election campaigns, women rarely benefit from these resources. For example, many parties do not provide sufficient financial support for women candidates. Research indicates that a large pool of women candidates, combined with sufficient financial resources, can significantly increase the number of women elected. This is discussed further in chapter 3.

The selection and nomination process within political parties is also biased against women in that 'male characteristics' are emphasized and often become the criteria in selecting candidates. An 'old boys' club' can inhibit and prevent women from integrating themselves into their party's work. This in turn impacts on the perception of women as viable candidates on the part of those who provide money for election campaigns. In addition, women are often not placed in winnable positions on party lists. Women's participation is therefore better realized when there are quotas with a placement mandate. In Sweden, for instance, most political parties use 'zipper' lists where women's and men's names alternate on the party lists, resulting in 45.3 percent women in parliament.

Table 2: Women Presidents or Speakers of Parliament

1945–97	As of 28 February 2005
In 52 years of world parliamentary history, only 42 of the 186 countries with a legislative institution have, at one time or another in recent history, selected a woman to preside over parliament or a house of parliament: this has occurred 78 times in all. The countries concerned are 18 European countries, 19 countries of the Americas, 3 African countries, 1 Asian country and 1 country in the Pacific region. 24 of the 42 countries concerned had a bicameral parliament, and the presidency was entrusted to a woman a little more often in the upper house than in the lower house.	Only 22 women preside over one of the houses of the existing parliaments, 70 of which are bicameral. This means 8.6% of the total of 255 posts of presiding officers of parliament or of one of its houses. The countries concerned are: Antigua and Barbuda (House of Representatives and Senate); Bahamas (Senate); Belgium (Senate); Belize (House of Representatives); Colombia (Cámera de Representantes); Dominica (House of Assembly); Estonia (Riigikogu); Georgia (Sakartvelos Parlementi); Greece (Vouli Ton Ellinon); Grenada (Senate); Hungary (Orszaggyules); Jamaica (Senate); Japan (Sangiin); Latvia (Saeima); Lesotho (National Assembly); Moldova (Parlamentul); the Netherlands (Eerste Kamer de Staten-General); San Marino (Consiglio grande e generale); South Africa (National Assembly and National Council of Provinces); Trinidad and Tobago (Senate); Uruguay (Cámera de Representantes).

Source: Inter-Parliamentary Union (IPU), 2005. 'Women Speakers of National Parliaments: History and the Present. Situation as of 28 February 2005', available at <http://www.ipu.org/wmn-e/speakers.htm>.

'It is very difficult for a woman to make up her mind to enter politics. Once she makes up her own mind, then she has to prepare her husband, and her children, and her family. Once she has overcome all these obstacles and applies for the ticket, then the male aspirants against whom she is applying make up all sorts of stories about her. And after all this, when her name goes to the party bosses, they do not select her name because they fear losing that seat.'

Sushma Swaraj, MP, India

1.3. Cooperation with Women's Organizations

During the last decade women's parliamentary representation in long-standing democracies has increased. One of the critical reasons for this rise is the impact of women's organizations both inside and outside political parties. Women's organizations were well aware of the effect of single-member electoral districts on women's candidacies. They worked with political and government institutions to secure electoral changes to facilitate women's nomination and election. This strategy resulted in increasing women's representation within legislative bodies.

'As women parliamentarians, we need to share our experiences. This in itself will inspire women. We will not feel that we are alone in this game, and other women will not feel isolated from the process. At every opportunity, at every forum, each and every time we must share information, ideas, and knowledge. We must make sure that women are the most informed people within society.'

Margaret Dongo, former MP, Zimbabwe

However, in new democracies there is less contact and cooperation between women politicians and women's organizations or other broad interest organizations such as trade and labour unions. This due either to lack of awareness of the potential benefits of this networking function or to lack of resources to invest in such contacts.

Although governments might declare their commitment to democratic forms of change, it is nevertheless unrealistic to expect governments alone to secure women's rightful place in all spheres of society. Civil society in general, including non-governmental organizations (NGOs) and women's groups, must play a role in advancing women's representation. Faith-based women's organizations and unique outreach networks are also critical allies.

Women also must think carefully about their own goals, strategies and tactics. It is important to help women already in parliament to deliver on their promises and to equip them with the necessary skills and strategies to ensure that issues raised by women are taken into account in the debate and the decision making that take place in parliament. In order to empower women and enable them to participate in politics, it is necessary to extend the scope of women's participation at the grass-roots level and in local elected bodies. This also constitutes an important step towards confidence-building and facilitates the sharing of experiences.

The main mission of the women's movement is to inculcate the right type of confidence and assertiveness among them. It needs leaders who can express proper ideological messages and inspire confidence. New ways of thinking and acting, educational activities, research about women's status, and means of communication among women's organizations are needed. The challenge for women is to build a society according to a paradigm that reflects their values, strengths and aspirations, and thereby reinforce their interest and participation in political processes.

1.4. Electoral Systems

The type of electoral system in a country plays an important role in women's political representation. (This issue is discussed in detail in chapter 3.)

> 'We have several explanations for the high presence of women in the Nordic parliaments. One is the proportional electoral system. In Finland, there is a proportional list but the individual choice of the voters also comes into play. Another explanation is to be found in ideological debates in the country. In this area in Scandinavia, politics is, so to speak, in the lead. The business world is falling behind, and the academic world lags behind as well. We have not enough women university professors, and women are also poorly represented in the trade unions.'
>
> *Bjorn von Sydow, Speaker of the Swedish Riksdag*

2. Socio-Economic Obstacles

Socio-economic conditions play a significant role in the recruitment of women to legislatures in both long-standing and new democracies. The social and economic status of women in society has a direct influence on their participation in political institutions and elected bodies. For example, researchers point to the correlation between women's legislative recruitment and the proportion of women working outside the home, as well as the percentage of women college graduates. According to some researchers, socio-economic conditions take second place to electoral systems in women's legislative recruitment within established democracies.

The economic crisis in the so-called 'developing democracies' has intensified the risk of poverty for women. Poverty, like unemployment, is increasingly being feminized.

Box 1. The Effect of Development and Culture on Women's Representation

One of the most important characteristics of society that correlate with women's representation levels is a country's state of development. Development leads to a weakening of traditional values, decreased fertility rates, increased urbanization, greater education and labour force participation for women, and attitudinal changes in perceptions regarding the appropriate role for women—all factors that increase women's political resources and reduce existing barriers to political activity.

One characteristic of development that has proved particularly important for women's representation in Western countries is higher rates of women's participation in the labour force. Moving out of the house and into the workforce appears to have a consciousness-raising effect on women. Greater development increases the number of women who are likely to have formal positions and experience, for example in labour unions or professional organizations.

Culture is related to development, and as development increases women's standing in society relative to men becomes more equal. On the other hand, two countries could be quite similar in terms of development, but women may have come substantially further in terms of equality in one country than in the other.

While culture consistently has been believed to be important, it has been difficult to test directly for an effect. As a possible proxy for culture, in some recent research I developed a measure using a cluster of variables, specifically the ratio of women's literacy to men's literacy, the ratio of women's labour force participation to men's labour force participation, and the ratio of university-educated women to university-educated men.* The assumption was that when women approach men in levels of literacy, workforce participation, and university education—and thus become men's equals in the social spheres—they are more likely to be seen as men's equals in the political sphere, and therefore their representation will increase. This hypothesis holds, as the cultural measures described correlate very strongly with women's representation.

It is important to note that, while research tracking women's representation in established democracies has been quite successful at identifying causes for variations, attempts to model women's representation in developing countries have been much less successful. Factors driving variations in representation in the developed world are clearly understood, but we have a much poorer understanding of representation in developing countries. In the latter, none of the variables deemed significant among established democracies, nor several other plausible variables, are found to have a consistent effect.**

These findings indicate that there is a minimum level of development (including women's labour force participation) that is needed to create the foundation for other variables, such as electoral systems, to have an effect. Without that basis, the factors that assist women in gaining representation in more developed countries simply have no effect. It appears that in most less developed countries the forces aligned against female political activity are so great as to permit only minimal representation. As development increases, however, cultural changes start to occur. In addition, more women start to acquire the resources needed to become politically powerful—such as education, experience in the salaried labour force, and training in the professions that dominate politics. This leads to the formation of a critical mass. When the number of women with the necessary resources becomes substantial, they then start to become an effective interest group demanding greater representation and influence in decision making. Development is a crucial part of this process.

Richard E. Matland

* Matland, Richard E., 1998a. 'Women's Representation in National Legislatures: Developed and Developing Countries'. *Legislative Studies Quarterly.* Vol. 23, no. 1, pp. 109–25.
**— 1998b. 'The Two Faces of Representation'. Paper presented at the European Consortium for Political Research workshops in Warwick, UK, 23–28 March.

In addition to lack of adequate financial resources, the socio-economic obstacles impacting on women's participation in parliament are:

- illiteracy and limited access to education and choice of professions; and
- the dual burden of domestic tasks and professional obligations.

> 'The two most overwhelming obstacles for women in entering parliament are lack of constituents and lack of financial resources. Women move from their father's home to their husband's home . . . They are like refugees. They have no base from which to develop contacts with the people or to build knowledge and experience about the issues. Furthermore, they have no money of their own; the money belongs to their fathers, their husbands or their in-laws. Given the rising cost of running an effective campaign, this poses another serious hurdle for women in the developing world.'

Razia Faiz, former MP, Bangladesh

2.1. The Feminization of Poverty and Unemployment

In 2004, the overall share of women in total paid employment was above 40 percent worldwide.

> 'One of the most striking phenomena of recent times has been the increasing proportion of women in the labor force . . . In 2003, out of the 2.8 billion people that had work, 1.1 billion were women . . . However, improved equality in terms of quantity of male and female workers has yet to result in real socioeconomic empowerment for women, an equitable distribution of household responsibilities, equal pay for work of equal value, and gender balance across all occupations. In short, true equality in the world of work is still out of reach.'[5]

Despite the increase in women's employment rates, many of the economic gains made by women in industrially developed countries since the 1960s are in danger of being eroded, which seems to be in part a result of the restructuring of both the global and the domestic economies.

At the same time, in the majority of countries women's unpaid labour activity amounts to twice that of men, and the economic value of women's unpaid labour is estimated to be around one-third of the world's economic production (or 13 trillion USD).[6] In all countries a significant gap exists between the status of women and that of men. Surveys carried out in the late 1990s reveal increasing gender discrimination in salaries, recruitment, promotion and dismissal, as well as growing professional segregation and the feminization of poverty. According to United Nations statistics, 1.8 billion persons in the world live in poverty and 70 percent of them are women. The gender gap in earning is registered all over the world: a woman's average wage is equal to 75 percent of a man's average wage (not including an agricultural worker's salary). The economic crisis in countries with so-called 'developing democracies' has intensified the risk of poverty for women, which, like unemployment, is likely to be increasingly feminized.

Women are major contributors to national economies through both their paid and their unpaid labour. As far as the latter is concerned, rural women's input and their role as a significant electorate should not be underestimated. Although the importance of women's biological and social roles is clear, their input in all spheres of life often goes unrecognized. Eradicating poverty will have a positive impact on women's increased participation in the democratic process. The economic empowerment of women, along with education and access to information, will take women from the constraints of the household to full participation in politics and political elections.

2.2. The Dual Burden

In most countries women carry a disproportionate share of domestic work. Their participation in politics is further constrained by poverty and lack of education and access to information. It must be recognized that it is difficult for women to participate in political life when their major concern is survival and they have no choice but to spend much of their time trying to meet the basic needs of families. This is accentuated by the increase in the number of female-headed households (which stands at 25 percent worldwide), particularly in developing countries, where this is partly a result of ongoing conflicts.

In addition to that, however, some women may have full-time jobs as wives and mothers as well as other full-time careers (e.g. as teachers, lawyers or doctors). Becoming an MP in these conditions might then be considered a third full-time job.

> 'Women believe that entering parliament means choosing between a private life or a public life. This is not the case. Instead, women should view their life as a continuum. They should decide what they want to achieve in life and prioritise these goals in chronological order. There is a certain right time to achieve each of these goals, whether it is becoming a wife, mother, professional or a parliamentarian. Life is long and women can achieve many things.'

> *Anna Balletbo, former MP, Spain*

2.3. Education and Training

> 'It's very difficult for women to talk, to argue, to press for their concerns. How can we encourage women to talk and to express themselves? Maybe the woman in the hut has a lot to say, but we have to encourage her to talk—not about politics, but about her problems, her life, issues that concern her. The answer is education. Education has led many women in my society to join political parties or participate in political activities. Education is the most important channel for encouraging women to speak out.'

> *Rawya Shawa, Member of the former Palestinian Legislative Council*

Literacy rates in developed countries are about 99 percent, as opposed to 84 percent in less-developed countries. There is no consistent correlation between literacy rates and women's political representation, but many candidacy nomination procedures require a minimum level of literacy. This prevents women from registering as candidates for elections. In addition to basic education, many women lack the political training required to participate effectively in the political arena. An expansion of the pool of women who are qualified for recruitment to political careers is therefore needed.

This can be done by giving women access, from an early stage, to work patterns that are conducive to political leadership, such as special training in community-based or neighbourhood organizations.

Common understanding of the concerns of women, gendered political awareness-raising, lobbying skills and networking are important for the process of training women for political careers. To that end, women's leadership programmes play a special role since they provide the opportunity for links to be made with wider groups of women and diverse politicians; and they are very often the only occasions when women can be prepared for a political career in parliament and encouraged to aspire to such a career. Special attention should be given also to the involvement of young women and the importance of collaborating with men.

3. Ideological and Psychological Hindrances

The ideological and psychological hindrances for women in entering parliament include the following:

- gender ideology, cultural patterns, and predetermined social roles assigned to women and men;
- women's lack of the confidence to stand for election;
- women's perception of politics as a 'dirty' game; and
- the way in which women are portrayed in the mass media.

3.1. Traditional Roles

'Women have tried to enter politics trying to look like men. This will not work. We have to bring our differences, our emotions, our way of seeing things, even our tears to the process.'

Anna Tibaijuka, Professor, Tanzania

In many countries, traditions continue to emphasize women's primary roles as mothers and housewives and to restrict them to those roles. A traditional strong, patriarchal value system favours sexually segregated roles, and 'traditional cultural values' militate against the advancement, progress and participation of women in any political process. Societies all over the world are dominated by an ideology of 'a woman's place'. According to this ideology, women should only play the role of 'working mother', which is generally low-paid and apolitical. In addition, in some countries, men even tell women how to vote.

This is the environment, in which a certain collective image of women in traditional, apolitical roles continues to dominate, which many women face. The image of a woman leader requires that she be asexual in her speech and manners, someone who can be identified as a woman only through non-sexual characteristics.

Often it is supposed to be unacceptable or even shameful in the mass consciousness for women to be open about their feminine nature. In fact, the more authoritative and 'manly' a woman is, the more she corresponds to the undeclared male rules of the game. That is why some women politicians in general have to overcome the difficulty of feeling uncomfortable in the political field, as though they are somewhere where they do not belong, behaving in ways that are not natural to them.

Often women internalize many of these ideas and end up frustrated when they cannot match this almost impossible image. This sense of frustration is inextricably tied to a woman's sense of having to be apologetic either for her own womanhood or for betraying her sense of womanhood. Until they reconcile (or make the choice between) certain collective images, dominant stereotypes, and their own feminine nature, their lives will be difficult

> When a woman becomes a politician she does not cease to be a woman. It is this womanhood which should be placed first, since it contains different creative potentials and intellectual strength.

and it will be hard for them to accommodate these clashing expectations. A woman should be prepared for the fact that when she becomes a politician she does not cease to be a woman. It is this womanhood which should be placed first, since it contains different creative potentials and intellectual strength. The ability to make decisions and implement them is not a gender-specific trait, but a common human one; in other words, it is as natural for a woman to hold power as for a man to hold power.

3.2. Lack of Confidence

Lack of confidence is one of the main reasons for women's under-representation in formal political institutions, whether parliaments, ministries or political parties. With confidence and determination women can reach the highest levels in the political process. That is why women should believe in themselves and should do away with the widespread perception that men have to be their leaders. Women are equal to and have the same potential as men, but only they can fight for their rights. Women are very good campaigners, organizers and support-mobilizers, but fear sometimes prevents women from contesting elections and from participating in political life.

3.3. The Perception of Politics as 'Dirty'

In some countries, women perceive politics as a 'dirty' game. This has jarred their confidence in their ability to participate in political processes. In fact, such a perception is prevalent worldwide. Unfortunately, this perception reflects the reality in many countries. Although the reasons for this differ, there are some common trends.

The basis of passive corruption can be explained by an exchange between the advantages and benefits of the public market (e.g. legislation, budget bills) and of the economic market (e.g. funds, votes, employment), which seek financial gains by escaping competition and by fostering monopolistic conditions. In addition to this, a significant increase in the cost of election campaigning has become obvious, and this in turn increases the temptation to use any source of money that becomes available.

Corruption can have many faces. Bribery and extortion in the public sector, as well as the procurement of goods and services, are key manifestations of it. Although new democracies need time to establish themselves and to develop roots, corruption has spread further in countries where the process of political and economic transformation is taking shape in the absence of civil society, and where new institutions are emerging. However, in many places where the changes in the political and economic system have already taken place, the market economy has become enmeshed in the 'law of the jungle', the mafia and corruption.

Moreover, hypocrisy is an increasingly common feature in countries with established centralist and authoritarian regimes. There are 'rules of survival' in an economy of persistent scarcity which stand in stark contrast to the ideas officially proclaimed by the state. In poor countries the financing of political parties and the survival of an independent press remain major unresolved problems for the development of democratic functions.

> In some countries, corruption and organized crime scare women and provoke their fears of losing members of their families, all of which militates against their political involvement or their standing for elected bodies.

The high cost of bribery and extortion for a society has been recognized. Many governments and business leaders have expressed their desire to curb and eliminate corruption. But this is not an easy task; corruption is rooted in the system by some parties who continue to pay bribes. Corruption inevitably results in the creation of favourable conditions and opportunities for the existence of the most negative manifestation of organized crime. These factors combine to scare women and provoke their fears of losing members of their families, all of which militate against their political involvement or their standing for elected bodies.

Although the perception of corruption may not always be a fair reflection of the actual state of affairs, it is itself having an impact on women's attitude towards a political career. Is it a coincidence that countries where corruption occurs on only a small or a moderate scale seem to have a higher rate of women's representation in elected bodies? For example, Norway, Finland, Sweden, Denmark and New Zealand are perceived as the least corrupt, and in these countries women MPs make up between 30 percent and 45.4 percent of the total number of MPs, that is, between five and ten times more than in countries where corruption scores higher.

Women who have made the decision to stand for election should take all these circumstances into consideration and be ready to resist the corruption 'disease'. Corruption requires secrecy, whereas democracy breeds increased transparency resulting from political pluralism, freedom of the press, and the rule of law. By ensuring the real participation of the people and the establishment of efficient countervailing measures, democracy can contribute to curbing corruption.

Market forces cannot replace the rule of law. Economic liberalization should contribute to reducing the phenomenon of corruption, although this will not occur automatically. A regulated market economy will reduce the opportunities for corruption. Hence, it remains important to have the political commitment and the will to eliminate corruption by prioritizing this on the political agenda. Women can contribute a great deal to this process.

3.4. The Role of the Mass Media

The mass media deserve to be called the fourth branch of power because of their influence on public opinion and public consciousness. The media in any society have at least two roles: as a

> The mass media tend to minimize coverage of events and organizations of interest to women.

chronicler of current events; and as an informer of public opinion, thereby fostering different points of view. Often, the mass media tend to minimize coverage of events and organizations of interest to women. The media do not adequately inform the public about the rights and roles of women in society; nor do they usually engage in measures to promote or improve women's position. Most of the world's media have yet to deal with the fact that women, as a rule, are the first to be affected by political, social and economic changes and reforms taking place in a country—for example, they are among the first to lose their jobs. The fact that women are largely alienated from the political decision-making process is also ignored by the media.

The media can be used to cultivate gender biases and promote a stereotype about 'a woman's place', helping conservative governments and societies to put the blame on women for the failure in family policy, and to reinforce the idea that women are responsible for social problems, such as divorce and the growth of minor crime, getting worse. Another widespread trend in the mainstream media is to depict women as beautiful objects: women are identified and objectified according to their sex, and are made to internalize certain notions of beauty and attractiveness which relate more to a woman's physical capacities than to her mental faculties. Such an approach encourages the long-standing patriarchal stereotype of the 'weaker sex', where women are sexual objects and 'second-class' citizens.

Admittedly, the mass media also tell stories about women politicians and about businesswomen and their successes, but this kind of coverage is rare and infrequent. The presentation of topics such as fashion competitions, film stars, art and the secrets of eternal youth is more typical. Not surprisingly, such views hardly promote women's sense of self-worth and self-respect or encourage them to take on positions of public responsibility.

> If there is a lack of proper coverage of women's issues and the activities of women MPs, this contributes to a lack of public awareness about them which in turn translates into a lack of constituency for women MPs. The mass media still need to recognize the equal value and dignity of men and women.

The role of the mass media in an election process cannot be emphasized enough, and we do not yet have adequate global and comparative research. Practically speaking, if there is lack of proper coverage of women's issues and the activities of women MPs, this contributes to a lack of public awareness about them, which in turn translates into a lack of constituency for women MPs. The mass media still need to recognize the equal value and dignity of men and women.

4. Summary

The 20th century saw women gain access to political, economic and social rights. All these achievements are leading to important changes in women's lives but, while women have partly succeeded in combating discrimination based on gender, disparities still remain in many fields. At the beginning of the 21st century, women continue to face both old and new challenges, particularly intra- and interstate conflicts and terrorism. The persisting challenges include:

- balancing work and family obligations;
- segregation into lower-paid jobs;
- inequality of pay between men and women;
- the feminization of poverty;
- increases in violence against women; and
- exclusion from post-conflict peace negotiations and rehabilitation and reconstruction efforts.

Despite the removal of legal barriers to women's political participation in many countries, governments remain largely male-dominated. Various factors influence women's *access to decision-making bodies,* including:

- lack of party support, including financial and other resources to fund women's campaigns and boost their political, social and economic credibility;
- the type of electoral system as well as the type of quota provisions and the degree to which they are enforced;
- the tailoring of many of these institutions according to male standards and political attitudes;
- the lack of coordination with and support from women's organizations and other NGOs;
- women's low self-esteem and self-confidence, endorsed by certain cultural patterns which do not facilitate women's access to political careers; and
- the lack of media attention to women's contributions and potential, which also results in the lack of a constituency for women.

Obstacles vary according to the political situation in each country. Yet regardless of the political context, in all countries women need to be able to compete on a level playing field with men. Among the *indicators of success of women's* participation in politics are the following:

- the introduction of political, institutional and financial guarantees that promote women's candidacies to ensure the equal participation of female nominees in electoral campaigns;
- designing legislative regulations for implementing effective quota mechanisms;
- the creation of educational programmes and centres designed to prepare women for political careers; and
- the development of and support for schools (or centres) for the training of women for participation in electoral campaigns.

Excluding women from positions of power and from elected bodies impoverishes the development of democratic principles in public life and inhibits the economic development of a society. Men, who do not necessarily support women's political participation, dominate the majority of governing institutions. Thus it remains imperative to emphasize that women must lead the process to organize and mobilize their networks, learn to communicate their interests with their male counterparts and different organizations, and push for mechanisms to enhance their representation.

Positive action measures should be taken to assure representation that reflects the full diversity of societies, with the target of the 'gender-balanced' legislative body. To that end, the following two chapters look at two of the most significant mechanisms which have been used to overcome many of the obstacles to women's legislative representation: namely, electoral systems and quotas.

Notes

[1] 'Promote Gender Equality and Empower Women', Millennium Development Goals, available at <http://www.developmentgoals.org/Gender_Equality.htm>.

[2] Inter-Parliamentary Union (IPU), 2004. 'Women in Parliaments 2003'. Release No. 183, 1 March, available at <http://www.ipu.org/press-e/gen183.htm>.

[3] Tinker, Irene, 2004. 'Many Paths to Power: Women in Contemporary Asia', in Christine Hünefeldt, Jennifer Troutner and Peter Smith (eds). *Promises of Empowerment: Women in Asia and Latin America.* New York: Rowman & Littlefield.

[4] IPU 2004, op. cit. See also the case study in this Handbook.

[5] Emphasis added. See International Labour Organization (ILO), 2004. 'Global Employment Trends for Women 2004', p. 1, available at <http://kilm.ilo.org/GET2004/DOWNLOAD/trendsw.pdf>.

[6] United Nations Population Fund (UNPF), 2000. 'Lives Together, Worlds Apart: The State of World Population 2000'. New York: UNPF.

References and Further Reading

Fraser, Arvonne and Irene Tinker (eds), 2004. *Developing Power: How Women Transformed International Development.* New York: Feminist Press at the City University of New York

International Labour Organization (ILO), 2004. 'Global Employment Trends for Women 2004', available at <http://kilm.ilo.org/GET2004/DOWNLOAD/trendsw.pdf>

Inter-Parliamentary Union (IPU), 1989. *Reports and Conclusions of the Inter-Parliamentary Symposium on the Participation of Women in the Political and Parliamentary Decision-Making Process.* Reports and Documents, no. 16. Geneva: IPU

— 2003. 'The Convention on the Elimination of All Forms of Discrimination Against Women and Its Optional Protocol', in *Handbook for Parliamentarians.* Geneva: IPU

— 2004. 'Women in Parliaments 2003', Release no. 183, 1 March, available at <http://www.ipu.org/press-e/gen183.htm>

— 2005. 'Women Speakers of National Parliaments: History and the Present. Situation as of 28 February 2005', available at <http://www.ipu.org/wmn-e/speakers.htm>

Matland, Richard E., 1998a. 'Women's Representation in National Legislatures: Developed and Developing Countries'. *Legislative Studies Quarterly.* Vol. 23, no. 1, pp. 109–25

— 1998b. 'The Two Faces of Representation'. Paper presented at the European Consortium for Political Research workshops in Warwick, UK, 23–28 March

Norris, Pippa and Joni Lovenduski, 1995. *Political Recruitment: Gender, Race and Class in the British Parliament.* Cambridge: Cambridge University Press

'Promote Gender Equality and Empower Women', Millennium Development Goals, available at <http://www.developmentgoals.org/Gender_Equality.htm>

Reynolds, Andrew, Ben Reilly and Andrew Ellis, 2005. *The New International IDEA Handbook of Electoral System Design.* Stockholm: International IDEA

Shvedova, N. A., 1994. 'A Woman's Place: How the Media Works Against Women in Russia'. *Surviving Together.* Vol. 12, no. 2

— and W. Rule, 1996. 'Women in Russia's First Multiparty Election', in Wilma Rule and Norma Noonan (eds). *Russian Women in Politics and Society.* Westport, Conn. and London: Greenwood Press

Tinker, Irene, 2004. 'Many Paths to Power: Women in Contemporary Asia', in Christine Hünefeldt, Jennifer Troutner and Peter Smith (eds). *Promises of Empowerment: Women in Asia and Latin America.* New York: Rowman & Littlefield

United Nations Population Fund (UNPF), 2000. 'Lives Together, Worlds Apart: The State of World Population 2000'. New York: UNPF

Case Study: The Arab States

The Arab States: Enhancing Women's Political Participation

Amal Sabbagh

The Arab region, long characterized by political activity, whether in its anti-colonial movements, its own regional and internal conflicts, or the various wars it has witnessed, still lags far behind other regions in the world when it comes to the political status of its women. The Arab world is ranked by the United Nations Development Programme (UNDP) as the second-lowest region in the world on the Gender Empowerment Measure, and by the Inter-Parliamentary Union (IPU) as the lowest region in terms of percentage of women in parliaments. The political status of Arab women is therefore a critical issue.

Space only allows for a broad presentation of the situation. This case study first provides an overview of the Arab region and focuses on the political status of women. A cautionary point should be made here: although there are many common socio-economic and political factors influencing the development of the Arab countries, each state's response to these factors is unique and depends on the internal dynamics within each country. Hence, when discussing Arab women, it should be remembered that the Arab world is not a homogeneous region and there is no single archetype for Arab women. In the second section, an overview of the key challenges that confront women in achieving decision-making positions is presented, drawing on experiences from three countries: Jordan, Lebanon and Yemen. The third section of the case study describes some of the mechanisms that have been used to tackle the challenges and promote Arab women's participation in parliaments, and suggests others that might be appropriate for the region.

A. Overview

The Arab region stretches from the Atlantic Ocean in the west to the Arabian Gulf and Indian Ocean in the east, comprising 22 states that are currently members of the

Arab League. Although there are wide variations among these countries, their Arab Islamic cultural heritage and common language have preserved a distinctive character for the region and its peoples. This section outlines the major factors that shape the socio-economic and political environment in the region and then focuses on the political status of Arab women.

Factors that Shape the Socio-economic and Political Environment

More than other regions, the Arab region is defined by a complex set of issues, including but not limited to the Arab–Israeli conflict and its repercussions, unstable economic conditions and trends, population-resource imbalances, undemocratic internal governance systems and environmental stress. Civil societies across the region are in different stages of development, but generally do not fulfil the role civil society has in other regions.

The Political Sphere

The four Arab–Israeli wars that took place in 1948, 1956, 1967 and 1973, as well as the three consecutive conflicts that took place in the east of the Arab world— the Iran–Iraq war in the 1980s, Iraq's invasion of Kuwait in 1990 and the war that ensued, and most recently, the war launched by the coalition forces on Iraq and its subsequent occupation—have all taken their toll on the Arab world. Certainly, their impact on the different countries has varied depending on various factors such as proximity to the region of conflict and the number of refugees residing in each country. Nevertheless, these regional events have had a grave influence on civil and political rights.

The Arab 'freedom and democracy deficit' has gained much attention since the publication of the first *Arab Human Development Report* in 2002.[1] This fact has been highlighted for some time now by the Freedom House ratings of political rights and civil liberties in different countries of the world. During the past ten years, none of the Arab states has been classified as free. There are only seven Arab countries that are categorized as partly free, and the remaining 15 are categorized as not free.[2] Since 11 September 2001 it has been noted that the issues mentioned above 'have remained the same or worsened, and new stresses and strains have been superimposed on the region'.[3] It is further noted that many countries of the region have witnessed a regression in their human rights and political conditions, greater state control of citizens and sometimes even more repression.

Explanations for this abound in the Arab region. These range from unfavourable domestic conditions and underlying cultural, political and economic factors, on the one hand, to proposing that external pressures from the West, and more pointedly from the United States, have not been enough to cause a shift in democratic trends in the region, on the other.[4]

The Socio-economic Sphere

Although other regions of the world have moved towards democracy as their economies have developed (with improved services in terms of education, health and urbanization), the Arab region had until recently not shown such a tendency, despite having achieved noticeable increases in most socio-economic indicators. Arguments put forward to explain the situation have focused on the political culture of the region, highlighting tribalism as one of the predominant factors in shaping a context that is not conducive to greater freedom and democracy.

Tribalism has also been branded as a major factor hindering the development of a vibrant civil society in the Arab region. Yet one could equally argue that the inability of civil society to cater to the socio-political needs of citizens has led them to cling more to their tribal identities as a more plausible means of fulfilling their needs.

In the economic sphere, the Arab states are usually perceived as rentier states. Nonetheless, international indicators illustrate that, although most of the Arab states' economies are not embedded in industrial modes of production, they do vary between oil-rich countries, human resource-rich countries, and countries that are very poor on all indicators.

The issue of poverty continues to require further research in the Arab world. Only a few countries have officially established national poverty lines.[5] Yet the fact that several countries have had to undergo structural adjustment programmes, which entailed subsidy cuts and the curtailing of services in previously heavily state-controlled economies, has meant that there was no 'alternative, capable and dynamic private sector. Hence, the withdrawal of the state in many countries created a vacuum in the social services sector'.[6]

The Political Status of Women in the Arab Region

In a region witnessing such political ferment and grave socio-economic conditions, Arab women have had to create their own path into the public sphere. Women's participation in the labour force in the region is generally low, but their political participation—whether in appointed or in elected positions—is even lower. The regional average women's participation in Arab states is currently below 7 percent, less than half the world average. There have been some breakthroughs during the past decade in both quantitative and qualitative terms, as well as in terms of more concerted efforts to achieve increased participation, yet the obstacles such efforts face appear to be much greater than they are in other regions. The difficulties faced in aligning national legislation with the stipulations of the Convention on the Elimination of All Forms of Discrimination Against Women (CEDAW) in Arab states that have ratified the agreement stand out as the most striking example of the underlying tensions that exist regarding the advancement of women.

Patriarchy

Patriarchy is still a major force hindering Arab women's advancement. A combination of patriarchy, conservative religious interpretations and cultural stereotyping has built a very strong psychological barrier among Arab populations regarding women's participation in the public sphere. The hierarchical, patriarchal tribal structure of several Arab societies may be another factor that contributes to this state of affairs. Ultimately, an acceptance of the status quo and possibly an unconscious fear of change have become a major challenge that has to be dealt with. Hisham Sharabi's concept of neopatriarchy[7] in the region aptly describes the conditions of patriarchy in Arab society that have been reinforced and sustained in more modernized forms. Sharabi contends that the drive towards modernity in the region has strengthened the patriarchal norms and values; hence he views the oppression of women as the cornerstone of the neopatriarchal system and their liberation as an essential condition for overcoming it.

Religion

Islam has often been cited as the main culprit behind the slow/incremental development of the status of women in the region. Delving into the various interpretations of Islam and Islamic feminism is beyond the scope of this case study; suffice it to state that Islam has not deterred women in non-Arab Islamic countries such as Indonesia, Bangladesh and Pakistan from reaching top elected positions. It can also be added that some Islamist political parties in the Arab world have promoted their women members as parliamentary candidates. One can question whether Arab non-Muslim women have had better chances than their Arab Muslim sisters, or whether they all face similar challenges in their quest to improve their lot and advance their political careers. It has been rightly pointed out that 'what is at issue is not so much the religion per se, but a broader aspect of neopatriarchy… it is not culture alone that impacts on women's political participation, but a whole host of other factors combine to render the situation as it is'.[8]

The Public–Private Divide

Arab social norms and attitudes which have eulogized women's role in the private sphere while creating barriers to their participation in the public one remain an important obstacle. The World Bank sees gender roles and dynamics within the household as being shaped by a traditional gender paradigm that presumes that the most important contribution women can make is to family and society, as homemakers and mothers. While the World Bank put this paradigm forward to explain the low rates of female participation in the labour force, it can easily be applied to explaining their low rates of participation in political life or public life in general. This gender paradigm is based on four elements:

1. 'The centrality of the family, rather than the individual, as the main unit of society. This emphasis on the family is seen as justification for equivalent, rather than equal, rights . . '.

2. 'The assumption that the man is the sole breadwinner of the family'.

3. 'A "code of modesty" under which family honour and dignity rest on the reputation of the woman. This code imposes restrictions on interaction between men and women.

4. 'An unequal balance of power in the private sphere that affects women's access to the public sphere. This power difference is anchored in family laws.'[9]

Hence the paradigm presumes that the man's responsibility for supporting and protecting his wife and family justifies his authority over his wife's interaction in the public sphere and control over it. This stress on women's primary role in the private sphere to the detriment of their role in the public sphere has actually jeopardized their access to full citizenship rights. Recently, it has been rightly pointed out that 'on paper in many states, women are declared to be citizens, but there are many social rights and benefits that remain inaccessible to women except through the medium of the family'.[10] While women in many Arab states have acquired their full political rights as citizens, unless they acquire their full social and economic rights, their practice of citizenship will remain curtailed.

Recent research on Arab women's political participation has concluded that 'women are not active in politics because politics is not a safe and secure place', calling for a focus on human security to ensure that women can participate freely without threats and coercion.[11] While such a new angle for analysing Arab women's political participation could lead to certain improvements in women's levels of participation, it is rather simplistic to think that this would be enough to turn the tables and bring women's participation to its full measure.

Discourses

Despite certain improvements in the conditions of women in the region, a challenge has re-emerged more recently in that attempts to empower women are viewed with suspicion, as part of a 'Western agenda'. In the 1990s this claim came as a response to international conferences that highlighted women's human rights. The establishment of the US–Middle East Partnership Initiative (MEPI) towards the end of 2002, and later the announcement of the Greater Middle East Initiative submitted to the Group of Eight industrialized countries (G8) Summit, only served to reinforce such apprehensions. In an attempt to prove that reforms should come from within, the Arab heads of state at their Tunis Summit (May 2004) committed themselves to 'promote the role of women, consolidate their rights, encourage their effective participation in development and their role in the political, economic, social and cultural fields'.[12] This was the very first reference to women in the history of Arab summits.

Women's Movements

The patriarchal order that the Arab states share permeates civil society and is an obstacle to civil society becoming a major force for social change. Unlike other regions of the world, in the Arab world the women's movements have not been credited with helping women's advancement. Rather, women's organizations have been criticized for adopting patron–client patterns of leadership, thus emulating the patriarchal patterns found in their societies at large.[13]

With the exception of some scattered incidents when women activists or women's movements took the lead, most attempts at widening the scope of Arab women's participation in public life have been led by 'state feminism', a term coined by Mervat Hatem in the early 1980s. Ranging from literacy programmes to legal amendments in personal status laws that outlaw certain practices sanctioned by religion (e.g. outlawing polygamy in Tunisia), state feminism cannot be criticized for not benefiting women. The major criticism targeted at it is that its programmes served as part of 'broader state building and/or regime consolidation processes. Women were instruments or tools, and their "liberation" was part of a larger project of reinforcing control within a series of states that continued to be dominated by what are generically referred to as patriarchal structures'.[14] Certainly, earning international recognition has been a key factor for motivating Arab states to create mechanisms that advance women's status even if the impact of this process could contradict traditional patriarchal structures. However, the pace of change has not been rapid enough to warrant a showdown between such structures and governments.

Electoral Practices

Closely linked to the issue of the 'Arab freedom and democracy deficit' raised earlier are the electoral laws in force in Arab countries and the electoral processes that ensue. In the case of women, the questions that arise are how gender-sensitive processes and legislation are, and more importantly, whether they can be gender-sensitized in settings that tend to be non-democratic or in nascent democracies. The linkage between patriarchal societies, levels of democratization and the political status of women is very intriguing indeed, yet, regrettably, it has not been adequately researched in the Arab region. The electoral systems in Arab countries vary, but apart from the few cases where quota systems have been applied they are not generally women-friendly.

Arab Women's Participation in Legislatures

Mirroring the dialectical relationship of the various factors reviewed above, Arab women's representation in legislatures is the lowest in the world, with the world average standing at 16 percent while in the Arab world (excluding the Pacific region) it is only 6.5 percent.[15] In contrast to most other regions of the world, in the Arab countries women have generally been better represented in the upper houses of national parliaments than in the lower houses. This could be explained by the fact that most upper houses in the Arab region are appointed.

It is evident from table 3 that the percentage of women in Arab legislatures has not yet reached the Beijing Platform for Action target of at least 30 percent in any country, which makes it difficult for those women who are present in national parliaments to effect any changes in legislation to benefit women. According to the ranking of countries in terms of women's representation, illustrated in table 3, the Arab countries do not fare well, with the exception of Iraq at 31 percent and Tunisia at 22.8 percent. Syria is in 71st position with 12 percent and Djibouti in 78th position, with 10.8 percent women, followed by Algeria and Jordan, while the Gulf states of Bahrain, Saudi Arabia and the United Arab Emirates share the lowest rank, i.e. 0 percent women.

There are two issues worth highlighting. First, despite certain positive amendments to legislation in various Arab countries, legal discrimination still remains a major obstacle to women's advancement. In one Arab country (Saudi Arabia) they still do not have the suffrage. More commonly, in laws governing social security, pensions, income tax, inheritance and criminal matters, women are not treated equally, nor do they enjoy all the benefits men do. The linkage between such discrimination and the low participation of women in legislatures, even in countries that have given women the full suffrage, has not been fully researched or recorded.[16]

The second issue is that of the electoral processes within each country. Although this paper does not review electoral processes fully, but focuses more on the various types of obstacle that hinder women from political participation, electoral processes as such have certain elements that do discriminate against women. This is exacerbated by the fact that the conditions in which elections are held seem to constantly shift and change within each country in response to internal and/or regional developments. Additionally, there are certain cases where electoral laws are passed as provisional laws, hence not allowing for public or parliamentary debate about the legislation. This does not allow for the planning and lobbying that are required to overcome any gender discrimination inherent in such processes.

Table 3: Women's Representation in Arab Legislatures, 2005

Country	Lower/Single House				Upper House				IPU Rank (1)
	Election Year	Total No. of Seats	No. of Women	% Women	Last Elections	Total	No. of Women	% Women	
Algeria	2002	389*	24	6.2	2003	144*	4	2.8	105
Baahrain	2002	40*	0	0	2002	40***	6	15	126
Comoros	2004	33	1	3.0					119
Djibouti	2003	65*	7	10.8					78
Egypt (2)	2000	454	11	2.9	2001	264**	18	6.8	120
Iraq	2005	275	87	31.6					15
Jordan	2003	110*	6	5.5	2003	55***	7	12.7	109
Kuwait	2003	65*	0	0					126
Lebanon	2000	128*	3	2.3					122
Libya	1997	760**							
Mauritania	2001	81*	3	3.7	2002	56**	3	5.4	117
Morocco	2002	325*	35	10.8	2003	270**	3	1.1	78
Oman	2003	38*	2	2.4	2001	58***	9	15.5	121
Occupied Palestinian Territories (OPT)	1996	85*	5	5.9					
Qatar	2002	35***	0	0					
Saudi Arabia	2001	120***	0	0					126
Somalia									
Sudan (3)	2000	360	35	9.7					85
Syria	2003	250*	30	12.0					71
Tunisia	2004	182*	21	22.8					27
United Arab Emirates (UAE)	1996	40***	0	0					126
Yemen	2003	301*	1	0.3					126

Notes:

(1) Ranked by descending order of the percentage of women in the lower/single house in 183 countries.

(2) 444 members elected, 10 appointed by the head of state.

(3) 270 directly elected, 35 representatives of women, 26 representatives of university graduates and 29 representatives of trade unions.

* Members are elected through direct elections.

** Members are elected through indirect elections.

*** Members are appointed by the head of state.

Sources: Compiled from information available on the Inter-Parliamentary Union (IPU) web site, 'Women in National Parliaments', <http://www.ipu.org>, for all countries except Iraq, Oman and Qatar, which were compiled from information available on the Arab Inter-Parliamentary Union (AIPU) web site, <http://www.arab-ipu.org/>. Information on the OPT available on the Palestinian Legislative Council web site, <http://www.pal-plc.org>.

The Arab States: Enhancing Women's Political Participation

B. Key Challenges at the National Level

This section identifies key challenges that confront women seeking decision-making positions, specifically in parliaments. In addition to the political environment outlined above, this section discusses the specific obstacles faced, such as the role played by political parties, tribalism, the women's movement and financial constraints, which are the key obstacles. Undeniably, mature and organized political parties have a crucial role in the political development of a given country and in preparing candidates to participate actively in decision making. Tribalism, often criticized for hindering women's advancement, appears to be co-opting any opportunities for women to its own advantage. Similarly, the role played by women's movements is expected to be a key factor in promoting women's access to decision making. Finally, financial capacity plays a crucial role in mobilizing resources to support any candidate.

Since the number of countries in the region makes it impossible to look at each country's electoral process individually, three countries will be highlighted here: Yemen, Lebanon and Jordan. It is important to note that, in addition to the regional conflicts mentioned above and their various impacts on each Arab state, both Yemen and Lebanon have had their own internal conflicts, which have ultimately shaped the political, economic and social contexts in these countries. Although these cases may not be representative of the entire region, they reflect issues that have resonance with neighbouring countries.

During the past 15 years, Yemen and Lebanon have had three national elections each, and Jordan has had four. The participation of women as candidates in these elections is summarized in table 4, which shows that in Yemen and Lebanon women's participation remains limited but Jordan has witnessed shifts and developments over the four elections, with a marked increase in 2003, attributed to the introduction of six reserved seats for women.[17]

Yemen

Table 4 illustrates the decline in the number of women in the Yemeni Parliament, to just 0.3 percent in 2003.[18] Different factors have contributed to this situation.

Illiteracy. The illiteracy rate among Yemeni women (76.1 percent)[19] is the highest in the region, which affects not only the processes of voter registration and voting, but also political awareness of the importance of electing women. However, the higher educational levels of women in Lebanon and Jordan have not yielded better results for women's broader participation in those countries.

Mobility. This is an important factor limiting women's opportunities to participate in Yemeni elections. Table 4 shows that the number of women candidates standing for elections has nearly halved since 1997. This is attributed to the stipulation introducedin the General Election Law, No. 13 of 2001, which states that an independent candidate has to be supported by at least 300 people from his or her constituency.

Table 4: Women's Participation in National Elections in Yemen, Lebanon and Jordan: As Candidates

Country	Election Year	No. of Women Candidates	Percentage of Women to Total Candidates	No. of Successful Women Candidates	Percentage of Women in Lower House
Yemen	1993	41	1.3	2	0.7
	1997	19	1.3	2	0.7
	2003	11	0.6	1	0.3
Lebanon	1992	n/a	n/a	n/a	n/a
	1996	10	n/a	3	2.3
	2000	11	n/a	3	2.3
Jordan	1989	12	1.86	0	0
	1993	3	0.18	1	1.3
	1997	17	3.24	0	0
	2003	54	7.06	6	5.5

Source: Mashhur, Huriya, 2005. 'Political Participation by Yemeni Women', in International IDEA and Arab NGO Network for Development (ANND), *Building Democracy in Yemen: Women's Political Participation, Political Party Life and Democratic Elections.* Stockholm: International IDEA and ANND.

This was a difficult requirement for all candidates to fulfil, but is probably more so for women, who cannot afford to travel far and are less well known within their communities.[20]

The political parties. While political parties seem to have thrived in post-unification Yemen, women formed only 2 percent of their membership when they were established following unification in 1990. The major political parties do have token representation of one or two women in their higher echelons (either on the executive board or in the highest decision-making body of the party, which usually constitute around 20 persons), with the exception of the Socialist Party, which had four women in its 29-member political bureau in 2003. Reported reasons for this vary from women themselves refraining from party work to women feeling that 'they are not given serious tasks except to mobilize women to vote during elections'.[21]

Women who stood for the 2003 elections argued that they were not given any kind of financial or moral support for their campaigns. While traditional forces openly resisted women's participation, the resistance of the political parties was not so straightforward, but indirectly they pressured women not to stand. The ruling party, the General People's Congress (GPC), fielded only one woman candidate, whereas the Socialist Party (which was previously the ruling party in the People's Democratic Republic of Yemen (South Yemen) and was then noted for its pro-women policies) fielded two. Furthermore, their electoral platforms in 2003 did not commit these parties to support women to stand for election.

Tribalism. Exacerbating these factors, Yemeni women still have to confront the traditional forces of tribalism. Many have admitted that the regressive trend in women's participation has been a result of 'tribalism, its value system and its view of women. Even political parties, which should have effected change since they represent modernizing influences within the state, were themselves an extension of the tribe and of the tribal attitude that resists any advancement in the status of women'.[22]

Lebanon

As a result of the 2000 election, only 2.3 percent of parliamentary representatives are women. This is explained by different factors, including the following.

The political parties. The results of the three successive parliamentary elections do not reflect the advancement of Lebanese women in several other areas, such as education, the economy and culture. The civil war can be blamed for stunting the political advancement of women in various ways. Prior to the civil war, women were quite active in the political parties, and even during the war certain parties specifically sought women's participation. Recently, however, the situation has regressed, and women's wings or sections in the 18 political parties have in some instances been reconstituted as non-governmental organizations (NGOs). 'Some civil society actors feel that women's sections of political parties have in effect been marginalized and "pushed aside" into these NGOs, and thus it is more an indication of the lack of incorporation of women into party politics than genuine attention to women's issues.'[23]

Men dominate the leadership of political parties, and among six major parties women's participation at the highest levels of decision making ranges from zero to 10 percent.[24] According to personal testimonies, women face difficulties within the political parties, they question the internal democracy of the parties, and they argue that there is an obvious division of labour based on gender within the parties' general activities.[25] In addition, financial constraints stifle women aspirants, and without party and financial support electoral campaigns become prohibitively expensive.

Patronage and family ties. Although tribalism does not exist in Lebanon, the political scene is governed by other factors that carry within them similar patriarchal overtones, including powerful families that have dominated political life. In short, the system governing Lebanese politics could be termed a sectarian, family-based system. The effect on women's political participation has been negative and is often criticized.

Lebanese women parliamentarians have been branded as the women 'dressed in black'.[26] The first two women to enter parliament, in 1963 and much later in 1992, 'inherited' their seats—the first from her father, and the second from her assassinated husband—thus explaining the black mourning dresses they wore. The current situation is not much improved, since the women parliamentarians have not had political careers as such, but their socio-political status is still derived from a male politician, either deceased or alive.[27] Yet it can also be argued that women politicians in Lebanon, given the more liberal family structure within Lebanese society, might have had sufficient exposure, especially in politically influential families, to ideologies, know-how and techniques to support them in their future political careers.

Jordan

The 2003 elections showed a marked increase in women's parliamentary representation, from zero to 5.5 percent. This was attributable to the adoption of six reserved seats for women in the parliament, which were introduced to overcome the barriers to women's participation.

Tribalism. Tribalism is a major force in both Jordanian politics and society. It is interesting to note in this respect that, of the six 'winners' of the reserved seats for women, five had the support of their tribes and were fielded as 'tribal candidates', while only one was a partisan candidate. In contrast to the situation in Yemen, where tribalism is seen as debilitating to the advancement of women, the quota system seems to have suited smaller tribes whose male candidates would not have stood a chance in open competition with candidates of larger tribes. Some simple calculations assured the smaller tribes that the quota system would give them much better opportunities; hence they used it to their advantage.

The political parties. With the resumption of political liberalization in 1989 and the passing of a new political party law, Jordan now has 32 registered political parties. The membership of women in these parties does not exceed 8 percent, and there are very few women in the higher echelons. An analysis of the discourse of political parties and gender equality has revealed that their general commitment to the advancement of women is very much of a token nature, since none of the parties appears to grasp the nature and magnitude of such issues, and they address major challenges such as poverty, unemployment, health and education in a totally gender-blind fashion.[28]

Women's linkages. After the election of six women through reserved seats, an emerging challenge is the relationship between women members of parliament (MPs) and the women's movement. It is argued that women MPs are an 'obstacle' in securing gender equality and are not articulating women's interests in society.[29] While this charge points to an important challenge, there are certain structural and financial deficiencies that put women MPs at a disadvantage, including the view that MPs' role in Jordan is much more tilted towards being a 'service MP'.[30] This reflects what most critics of Jordanian MPs maintain—that they do not fulfil their proper legislative roles as they seem more preoccupied with securing special services from government (e.g. high-level appointments or cash assistance to a poor family) for their constituents.

Equally challenging is the question what the women's movement is doing to ensure the increased political participation of women. The symbiotic relationship between women's movements and legislatures that characterizes several Western democracies is non-existent in Jordan, or is rather of a hostile nature, as the Jordanian press has reported over the years.[31] Traditionalist parliamentarians have invoked 'preserving our cultural norms and traditions' against the onslaught of the 'Western agenda'. The relationship between women MPs and the women's movement did not begin cordially either: MPs criticized some women leaders, and women activists stated that the women MPs were not fulfilling their aspirations.[32] While there is no research on the Jordanian women's organizations to corroborate the patron–client patterns cited earlier, some expert views are highly critical of the Jordanian model, stating that the six reserved seats are being used by women not for the advancement of women in general but for self-advancement or other self-serving interests.[33]

C. Mechanisms to Promote Arab Women's Participation in Parliaments

The above examples provide a snapshot of some of the main obstacles facing women in three Arab states. In contrast to Lebanon and Yemen, Jordan has maintained a stable internal political environment with no internal conflicts. Nonetheless, the three countries share similarities when we look at the role of women in public life. Furthermore, whatever the contextual and historical differences between the political parties in each country, it is clear that the position of political parties, being crucial to women's political empowerment, has fallen short of realizing that role.

It is clear that in the Yemeni case illiteracy rates pose a specific dilemma. Certainly, while this issue may not appear as forcibly in other countries, it is clear that specific measures to address such constraining factors are essential if the inclusion of all members of society is to be ensured.

Electoral systems have not been touched upon in detail in this paper because of space limitations but are discussed in detail in chapter 3.

In sum, the factors that hinder the promotion of Arab women in the public domain are complex and intertwined. The small windows of opportunity available vary between countries, and consequently there is no blueprint for the promotion of women that can be applied across the Arab world, given the different contexts and experiences of each country. However, the examples given here illustrate certain common obstacles that are shared by women, and to a lesser extent some mechanisms or general recommendations that could be implemented to overcome these obstacles. The following section addresses four groups of recommendations: general strategies that target women's advancement (grouped into state-level and political party actions); and specific recommendations about electoral processes, categorized into pre-election measures and measures during elections.

General Recommendations and Mechanisms
State Level

The non-democratic systems or nascent democracies in the Arab world need further political liberalization. In the Arab world such attempts have not always been conducive to women's advancement,[34] yet one cannot underestimate the benefits of democratization in patriarchal structures that prevail not only in the state apparatus but also within families and societies at large.

With further democratization, it could be assumed that the legal impediments facing Arab women should be amended, and that Arab states parties to CEDAW[35] will undertake a major overhaul of their legislation to align it more closely with the stipulations of CEDAW. This would overcome the lack of full citizenship rights for women that prevails over the whole region, as highlighted in the United Nations Development Fund for Women (UNIFEM) *Progress of Arab Women 2004.*

The opportunity to capitalize on existing high-level political will, which seems to have had a significant impact on women's political participation, is one that should not be ignored. In Jordan, the support came from the king and other members of the royal family. In Yemen, the support came from the major political parties, while in Lebanon it came from leading male politicians. Other examples underlining the key role of such support, although not discussed here, include Tunisia and Morocco, where positive changes to the legislation became possible. Obviously, in patriarchal settings such support needs to be constantly drawn upon and women's movements should continue to create strategic alliances with these policy makers.

The establishment of national mechanisms could be viewed as a factor facilitating women's participation, despite views that they are tools of 'state feminism'. The Jordanian National Commission for Women, the oldest in the Arab world, and the Yemeni Women National Committee have become more effective over the years. The much younger Lebanese equivalent may play a significant role in the forthcoming elections.

A final observation is that the relationship between women politicians and the women's movement must be further developed into a mutually collaborative one. Mechanisms to improve and enhance this relationship need to be further studied and developed.[36] Within the Arab region, examples from North African countries such as Morocco, Tunisia and Algeria can be used to highlight how women politicians responded to legislative amendments demanded by the women's movement. However, given that in most Arab countries women politicians have not yet reached a critical mass, both women politicians and women's movements need to strategize together on how best to effect change within each country's set of priorities, opportunities and challenges.

The Political Parties

As indicated earlier, the political parties' development in general and in relation to the role of women within them needs to be seriously revised and considered. Women's tokenism is much more apparent in the political parties than in state institutions; this is apparent not only in quantitative terms but also in terms of policies, where state policies often appear to be more gender-sensitive than those of the political parties. Hence the political parties need to identify gender issues in their platforms, institutional set-ups and internal procedures.[37]

One country in this case study, Jordan, has been seriously considering giving financial incentives to political parties that engage more women in their party membership and leadership.[38] In countries that adopt proportional representation systems, one strategy might be to give incentives, such as public funding for election campaigns, or providing more air time for campaigning during elections, as has happened in Timor-Leste, to parties that place women in winnable positions on their party list.[39] Another mechanism could be the implementation of quotas for women, with strict sanctions for enforcement.

Electoral Processes
Pre-election Measures
Patriarchal structures are entrenched within the Arab states' social fabric. Certainly there is an immense need to challenge the patriarchal authority in the private and public spheres. As discussed elsewhere,[40] voter education and civic education in general seem to be rather rudimentary and sporadic in the cases reviewed. Projects to design country-specific gender-sensitive programmes have been initiated to overcome this.[41]

Certainly, women's limited political exposure and experience have minimized their chances as candidates. Skills training and individual consultations for women candidates and their campaign managers on issues such as time management, targeting voters, recruiting volunteers, communications, fund-raising, and formulating and implementing field strategies have been used with varying success.[42] Such training programmes could be further developed based on evaluations of previous activities.

The role of the women's movement in supporting candidates has not been as successful as its role in bringing attention to women's issues in general. This could be attributed to various factors such as legislation that prohibits all NGOs from dealing with political issues, or patriarchal structures such as tribalism or political families, whereby women's support for candidates is automatically geared towards the family candidate. These factors, together with the impermeability of patriarchal structures within the political parties themselves, also inhibit the women's movement in pressuring the political parties to nominate more women.

Measures During Elections
Taking socio-economic and cultural specificities into account in electoral legislation has paid dividends in a country like Yemen. To overcome the illiteracy barrier, symbols or logos were adopted for each candidate on the ballot papers. Establishing women's committees in each electoral district charged with the registration of female voters and

overseeing polling on election day also facilitated women's roles as voters and increased their turnout rates.[43] Both Yemen and Jordan have separate polling stations for men and women, which respects the traditional tendencies in those societies. Additionally, in the 2003 elections, Jordan allowed voters to use any polling station within their district, rather than specifying a polling station for each voter. This provided easier access for women voters, whose freedom of movement is more restricted.

In the case of Yemen, the provision introduced in the 2003 elections that requires each independent candidate to have the endorsement of 300 voters in order to register seriously hindered women.[44] Such procedures constitute indirect discrimination against women and need to be eliminated.

The representation and inclusion of women in electoral commissions is expected to have an influential impact on women's political advancement. Yemen had only one woman on the 1993 electoral commission and none on subsequent ones. Jordan had only one woman on the women's quota subcommission in 2003 (which is responsible for counting the votes and announcing the winners of the quota seats). The committee which drafted the suggested quota mechanism had an equal representation of men and women, yet women have not served on the electoral commission proper. Ensuring equal representation of women in electoral commissions may facilitate the process.

Finally, one should note that sex-disaggregated statistics regarding election processes are not easily available in many Arab countries. If such statistics were made available this could facilitate the process of improving women's participation by highlighting the strengths or weaknesses of electoral arrangements from a gender perspective.

D. Conclusion

'The women's movement…is the detonator which will explode the neo-patriarchal society from within. If allowed to grow and come into its own, it will become the permanent shield against patriarchal regression, the cornerstone of future modernity.'[45]

It is often the case that discussions on the political status and representation of Arab women tend to highlight the difficulties and challenges at the expense of presenting the more positive aspects or breakthroughs that have occurred during the last ten to 15 years. This positive momentum is gaining strength; even over the short time span of writing this case study, changes were taking place that promise a more prominent role and presence for Arab women. If Arab societies are to benefit fully from the winds of political reform that are currently sweeping the region, then women have to become an active part of these processes by asserting their full potential as the harbingers of a better future.

Notes

1 United Nations Development Programme (UNDP), 2002. *Arab Human Development Report 2002: Creating Opportunities for Future Generations.* New York: UNDP, p. 2.

2 According to Freedom House ratings, the 'partly free' countries are Bahrain, the Comoros, Djibouti, Kuwait, Jordan, Morocco and Yemen. The category of 'not free' includes Algeria, Egypt, Iraq, Lebanon, Libya, Mauritania, Oman, the Occupied Palestinian Territories (both Israeli- and Palestinian Authority-administered), Qatar, Saudi Arabia, Somalia, Sudan, Syria, Tunisia and the United Arab Emirates. Freedom House, 2004. *Freedom in the World 2004: Freedom in the World Country Ratings,* available at <http://www.freedomhouse.org/research/freeworld/2004/countryratings/>; and *Freedom in the World 2004: The Annual Survey of Political Rights and Civil Liberties,* <http://www.freedomhouse.org/research/survey2004.htm> (accessed 27 October 2004).

3 Khouri, Rami, 2004. 'Politics and Perceptions in the Middle East after September 11'. Social Science Research Council/Contemporary Conflicts (accessed 27 October 2004) available at <http://conconflicts.ssrc.org/mideast/khouri/pf> (accessed 26 October 2004).

4 Gambill, Gary C., 2003a. 'Explaining the Arab Democracy Deficit: Part I'. *Middle East Intelligence Bulletin.* Vol. 5, no. 2, February/March, available at <http://www.meib.org/articles/0302 me.htm>; and Gambill, Gary C., 2003b. 'Explaining the Arab Democracy Deficit: Part II'. *Middle East Intelligence Bulletin.* Vol. 5, no. 2, February/March, available at <http://www.meib.org/articles/0303 me1.htm> (both accessed 26 October 2004).

5 Karam, Azza, 1999. 'Strengthening the Role of Women Parliamentarians in the Arab Region: Challenges and Options', available at <http://www.pogar.org/publications/gender/karam1/karama.pdf>.

6 Ibid.

7 Sharabi, Hisham, 1988. *Neopatriarchy: A Theory of Distorted Change in Arab Society.* New York: Oxford University Press.

8 Karam 1999, op. cit.

9 World Bank, 2003. *Gender and Development in the Middle East and North Africa: Women in the Public Sphere.* Washington, DC: World Bank, pp. 8–9.

10 United Nations Development Fund for Women (UNIFEM), 2004. *Progress of Arab Women 2004.* Amman: UNIFEM Arab States Regional Office, p. 126.

11 Ibid., pp. 271, 287.

12 Hamzeh, Alia, 2004. 'Leaders Adopt Reform Plan'. *Jordan Times,* available at <http://www.jordanembassyus.org/05242004001.htm> (accessed 24 October 2004).

13 Joseph, Suad, 1997. 'The Reproduction of Political Process Among Women Activists in Lebanon: "Shopkeepers" and Feminists', in Dawn Chatty and Annika Rabo (eds). *Organizing Women.* Oxford: Berg, pp. 51–81.

14 Brand, Laurie A., 1998. *Women, the State, and Political Liberalization: Middle Eastern and North African Experiences.* New York: Columbia University Press, p. 10.

15 Inter-Parliamentary Union (IPU), 2005. 'Women in National Parliaments: Situation as of 31 January 2005', available at <http://www.ipu.org>.

[16] Linkages between legislation (covering such areas as family laws, social security, etc.) and labour force participation are discussed in World Bank 2003, op. cit. One can draw comparisons between constraints on labour force participation and political participation.

[17] A more detailed review of women and the electoral processes in these countries can be found in Sabbagh, Amal, 2004a. 'Electoral Processes in Selected Countries of the Middle East. A Case Study'. Presented at UN Expert Meeting: Enhancing Women's Participation in Electoral Processes in Post-conflict Countries, Office of the Special Adviser on Gender Issues and Advancement of Women (OSAGI) and Department of Political Affairs Expert Group Meeting, New York, January, available at <http://www.un.org/womenwatch/osagi/meetings/2004/EGMelectoral/epl-sabbagh.pdf>.

[18] Mashhur, Huriya, 2005. 'Political Participation by Yemeni Women', in International IDEA and the Arab NGO Network for Development (ANND), *Building Democracy in Yemen: Women's Political Participation, Political Party Life and Democratic Elections*. Stockholm: International IDEA and ANND.

[19] UNDP 2002, op. cit., p. 151.

[20] Mashhur, Huriya, 2003. [Political participation of Yemeni women]. San'a: National Women's Committee (unpublished report, in Arabic), p. 7.

[21] Ibid., p. 15.

[22] Ibid., p. 14.

[23] Centre for Research and Training in Development (CRTD), 2003. 'Gender Profile of Lebanon 2003', available at <http://www.crtd.org> (accessed 12 January 2004).

[24] Ibid.

[25] Bizri, Dalal, 2000. [Democracy and women's political participation], in Hussein Abu Rumman (ed.), [Arab women and political participation]. Amman: al-Urdon al-Jadid Research Centre, p. 342 (in Arabic).

[26] CRTD 2003, op. cit.

[27] International Union of Local Authorities (IULA), 2003. 'Focus: Women in Local Government in the Middle East', available at <http://www.iula-int.org/iula/web/news.asp?L=ENJD=168> (accessed 16 December 2003).

[28] Sabbagh, Amal, 2004b. [Women in the discourse of Jordanian political parties]. Amman: Jordanian National Commission for Women (unpublished paper, in Arabic).

[29] *al-Ghad*, 2004. [Women parliamentarians an obstacle in achieving women's interests in society]. No. 69, October, pp. 3, 8.

[30] Sabbagh, Amal, 2004c. [Cooperation between elected women and women leaderships in Jordan]. Paper submitted to the Noor Al-Hussein Foundation Fourth National Forum for Rural Women, 7 October (unpublished paper, in Arabic).

[31] *al-Arab al-Yawm*, 2003. [Women's victory in the governorates embarrasses women of Amman]. No. 2227, 7 July, p. 2; *ad-Dustour*, 2003a. [Al-Khoulu' battle resumes in Parliament]. No. 12966, 31 August, p. 16; *ad-Dustour*, 2003b. [Immediately required: A women's party]. No. 12904, 30 June, p. 21; *ad-Dustour*, 1999. [Parliament likely to reject amendment to article 340 of Penal Code]. no. 11589, 15 November, p. 17; *al-Ghad*, 2004; and *Jordan Times*, 2000. 'Press Stays Away from House Debate on Elections

Law: Deputy Says Women's "Honour" Could Be "Jeopardized" If They Are Elected to Parliament'. No. 7607, 15 November, p. 3.

[32] See *al-Bilad*, 2003. [Adab Saud opens files and reveals all]. No. 524, 10 September, p. 5; *al-Arab Al-Yaum*, 2003; and *ad-Dustour*, 2003.

[33] Focus group discussion attended by the author on 4 August 2004. The discussion was held at the Jordanian National Commission for Women to discuss means of implementing the National Plan of Action which was adopted at the National Conference on Political Development and Jordanian Women.

[34] Brand 1998, op. cit., pp. 256–8.

[35] Sixteen of the 22 Arab countries have so far acceded to or ratified CEDAW. These are: Algeria, Bahrain, Comoros, Djibouti, Egypt, Iraq, Jordan, Kùwait, Lebanon, Libya, Mauritania, Morocco, Saudi Arabia, Syria, Tunisia and Yemen. All of these countries have made reservations on certain articles of the Convention. (UNIFEM 2004, op. cit.)

[36] See Karam 1999, op. cit., and Sabbagh 2004b, op. cit.

[37] Sabbagh 2004b, op. cit.

[38] *al-Arab al-Yawm*, 2004. [Daoudieh: Parties are national institutions that will be supported]. No. 2596, 14 July, p. 23.

[39] United Nations, Office of the Special Adviser on Gender Issues and Advancement of Women (OSAGI), 2004. UN Expert Meeting: Enhancing Women's Participation in Electoral Processes in Post-conflict Countries. OSAGI and Department of Political Affairs Expert Group Meeting, New York, January, available at <http://www.un.org/womenwatch/osagi/meetings/2004/EGMelectoral/finalreport.pdf>.

[40] Sabbagh 2004a, op. cit.

[41] The 2004 National Conference on Jordanian Women and Political Development developed the National Plan of Action focusing on the importance of designing such curricula with the participation of major stakeholders such as women's NGOs and political parties. The Jordanian Prime Minister, Faisal al-Fayez, endorsed this Plan of Action at the close of the conference on 1 August 2004 and preparations are under way to start with the design of each measure outlined in the Plan of Action. The role of women's NGOs will not be limited to the design of these programmes but will also include their delivery. Jordanian National Commission for Women (JNCW), 2004. National Plan of Action. 'Political Development and Jordanian Women: Discourse and Mechanisms'. JNCW: Amman. 3 July–1 August.

[42] Sabbagh 2004a, op. cit.

[43] Mashhur, 2005, op. cit.; and Colburn, Martha, 2002. *Gender and Development in Yemen*. Bonn: Friedrich-Ebert Stiftung.

[44] Mashhur, 2005, op. cit.

[45] Sharabi 1988, op. cit., p. 154.

Further Reading

Arab Inter-Parliamentary Union (AIPU). 'State of Qatar', available at <http://www.arab-ipu. org/members/majles.asp?Maj=12>; and 'Sultanate of Oman', available at <http://www. arab-ipu.org/members/majles.asp?Maj=29>
(accessed 24 October 2004)

ad-Dustour, 2004. [Daoudieh: Criteria for party support and funding based on objective standards]. No. 13280, 14 July, p. 2

Inter-Parliamentary Union (IPU), 2004. 'General Information about Parliamentary Chambers', available at <http://www.ipu.org/parline-e/reports/> and <http://www.ipu. org/wmn-e/classif.htm> (accessed 24 October 2004)

Palestinian Legislative Council (PLC). 'The Elections', available at <http://www.pal-plc. org/english/about/elections.html> (accessed 24 October 2004)

Case Study: Ecuador

Ecuador:
Unfinished Business.
The Political Participation
of Indigenous Women

Nina Pacari

Out of a total population of about 500 million, Latin America has some 40 million indigenous people. Among the countries with a predominantly indigenous population are Guatemala, Bolivia and Ecuador. In Guatemala, the indigenous population has been estimated to account for anywhere from 43 to 70 percent of the population; in Bolivia 80 percent of the population are indigenous, most of them living in poverty. In Ecuador, approximately 45 percent of the population are indigenous, and also suffer profound inequities. Of the rural population, 90 percent are indigenous and almost all are living in extreme poverty.[1]

In Latin America, political participation by indigenous women is a recent phenomenon. While there are cases that show that women in general have advanced according to both quantitative and qualitative measures, such progress is very tentative where indigenous women are concerned. In general in Latin America, and in Ecuador in particular, the history of the encounters and clashes that the indigenous peoples have had with the political system has provoked harsh discrimination against indigenous women and led to their exclusion.

In the early 1980s, the women's movements in Ecuador focused on proposing legislation that would be favourable to women without taking into account the ethnic and cultural reality or the growing need for gender-sensitive approaches. It was thought at that time that a change in legislation would translate into concrete and immediate results in the actual situation of women. Experience, however, has shown otherwise. While there have been changes in the civil, labour, criminal, electoral and even constitutional laws, a major democratic deficit remains, with repercussions for the process of constructing national citizenship, especially in a multicultural setting such as Ecuador.

This case study analyses the participation of indigenous women in the Ecuadorian Congress, beginning with a general overview of the political participation of the indigenous peoples. It also identifies some of the most important lessons learned, key challenges, and strategies for seeking the inclusion and full political participation of indigenous women in public affairs.

Background

In contrast to women who face a male-dominated patriarchal political system, the indigenous peoples find themselves face to face with a *mono-ethnic political system*[2] that excludes diversity of identity. Both systems, the patriarchal and the mono-ethnic, work to the detriment of indigenous women.

In general, the indigenous populations in Latin America, who are the bearers of a rich 1,000-year-old culture, have maintained their forms of social, economic, political, religious and cultural organization. During the 1990s, they began to be recognized as social actors in their own right, coming onto the political stage as part of the response to the global movement to include and vindicate the rights of indigenous populations.

At present, the indigenous peoples are recognized throughout the region as political actors who make proposals regarding not only land claims and the effective recovery of indigenous land rights but also structural changes in the model of the state and the representative political systems. In addition, the indigenous populations have called into question the formal democracy that excludes them not only from political participation but also from equitable economic development. In order to participate politically and become agents of change, the indigenous peoples have had to participate in the political life of the countries in the region under the legal and regulatory frameworks provided by the legislation in each country. In some cases, such as Ecuador, they have won reforms that have promoted their participation.

In the area of constitutional provisions, there have been two important experiences in Latin America regarding indigenous participation. A comparative analysis of the constitutions of the region reveals that only Colombia recognizes what can be called an 'ethnic quota'. Under the Colombian constitution, the indigenous peoples can have two representatives in the Senate, elected in a special nationwide electoral district by indigenous communities.[3] Notwithstanding this important advance, no indigenous woman has been elected senator. In Nicaragua, the recognition and creation of the autonomous regions has led to indigenous women having access to the legislature. The political development of indigenous organizations and the legal framework that creates the current autonomous regime for some regions require the political parties to include indigenous persons on their lists, especially indigenous women.[4]

In the case of Ecuador, in 1994 the indigenous movement, through the Confederación de Nacionalidades Indígenas del Ecuador (CONAIE, Confederation of Indigenous Nationalities of Ecuador), proposed a constitutional amendment according to which there would be one additional legislator per province, to be elected by the indigenous peoples. The Congress did not accept the proposal. Later, in

1996, a proposal to allow the participation of independent movements in elections, in addition to the political parties, was approved. Ever since, the indigenous movement has channelled its electoral participation by fostering the formation of the Movimiento de Unidad Plurinacional Pachakutik–Nuevo País (Pachakutik Movement for Multinational Unity–New Country) political movement. This movement came on to the political scene in the 1996 elections, when it had eight legislators (four of them indigenous, none of whom were women) elected out of a total of 82 members. In addition, it saw 13 of its candidates, seven of them indigenous, elected to mayoral posts.

In other countries such as Bolivia, Peru and Guatemala, the indigenous peoples have participated in elections by forming alliances with political parties. Support for the cause of indigenous peoples has run counter to the agenda of the political parties. In the 1990s, in an effort to overcome these difficulties, indigenous groups formed short-term and issue-based alliances with political parties. In Bolivia, for example, the indigenous political party Túpak Katari established a programmatic alliance with a neo-liberal political party, and was able to have an indigenous vice-president and approximately three indigenous legislators, including an Aymara woman, elected.

In general, experience of the participation of indigenous peoples in politics is a recent phenomenon. Not all experiences have been positive, but they have made it increasingly possible to develop new perspectives that promote regional and social transformation that affords indigenous women an increasingly prominent role.

Women's Political Participation

The Ecuadorian constitution of 1929 was the first in Latin America to give literate women the right to vote. Ecuador has a unicameral legislature, and since the return to democracy in 1978 it has elected, in the first round, 'national' and 'provincial' deputies using closed lists and the secret, universal and direct ballot. In 1998, the members of the National Constitutional Assembly (established in 1997 as a result of the overthrow of the then president, Abdalá Bucaram) amended the constitution (article 99 on the electoral system) to incorporate a proportional representation (PR) system with open lists.

The past decade has seen a significant increase in women's participation in all spheres of Ecuador's political life. From 5.3 percent in 1998, women's overall representation at different levels jumped to a high of 24.8 percent in 2000.[5] Of the members elected to Congress in the 1998 elections, 13.2 percent were women (16 of 121 legislators), and this number increased to over 20 percent in 2000 as more women alternates replaced principal legislators, either permanently or intermittently. In addition, it should be noted that for the 1998–2000 term, one indigenous woman was elected vice-president of the Congress, and in August 2000, for a brief period, a woman who was not indigenous was elected president of the National Congress. In the 2002 elections to Congress, 17 of the (now) 100 legislative seats (17 percent) were won by women, with 19 women alternates.

Case Study: Ecuador

Ecuador: Unfinished Business. The Political Participation of
Indigenous Women

This change in the level of women's participation in Congress reflected in part three legal reforms advocated by the women's movement:

- the Ley de Amparo Laboral, or Quota Law, of 1997, which established a minimum quota of 20 percent women on the party lists for electoral districts in which more than one person was to be elected (applied in the November 1998 elections);
- the constitutional reform of 1998, which provides for the equitable participation of men and women in elections (article 102); and
- the reform of the electoral law, or the Political Participation Law of 2000, which set quotas for women on political party lists. The quota is to increase by 5 percent with each successive election, from a minimum of 30 percent and up to the point where equitable representation is reached, at 50 percent. Article 102 of the constitution guarantees the political participation of women in the following terms: 'The State shall promote and guarantee the equitable participation of women and men as candidates in the elections, in the directing and decision-making bodies in the public sphere, in the administration of justice, in the oversight organs, and in the political parties'. Under this constitutional guarantee, amendments were made to the electoral law in February 2000. Article 58 of the Political Participation Law now states: 'The lists of candidates in the elections in which more than one person is to be chosen shall be submitted with at least 30 percent women for the candidates for office and 3 percent for the alternates, on an alternating and sequential basis; this percentage shall be increased in each general election, by an additional 5 percent, until equality of representation is attained. Ethnic–cultural participation shall be taken into account'. Other provisions of the same law specify the details of the process of registering candidates, ensuring that the spirit of the provision is respected.[6]

While the electoral law was a real legal gain and presented challenges regarding the equal participation of women—insofar as it requires all the parties and political movements to include a certain percentage of women in the lists on an alternating and sequential basis—in practice the Tribunal Supremo Electoral (TSE, Supreme Electoral Tribunal) hindered its proper application by issuing an instruction for the local and provincial elections of May 2000 regarding the placement of women candidates on the lists. As a result, women were relegated to the last positions, thus contradicting the law's mandate on 'alternation and sequencing'.[7] Ahead of the 2004 provincial elections, the TSE handed down a decision on how electoral lists should be made up to the leaders of the political parties and the candidates. However, in direct contravention of the law, the parties did not fulfil the legal requirements regarding the alternation and sequencing of women candidates' names on the lists, thus obstructing the enforcement of the placement mandate, and women were relegated to low positions on the party lists. The TSE did not report on this in its report to the nation but committed itself to review the instruction in response to the demands of various women's organizations.

As of 2004, the tribunal had not carried out this commitment; on the contrary, it has proposed a reform to include the said instruction in the electoral law.

Provincial Elections

Despite the legal gains in terms of women's participation in elections, the benefits for indigenous women are still imperceptible. Although the law indicated that the parties and political movements should take ethnicity and culture into account in the 2000 and 2004 provincial elections, the political parties did not include any indigenous or black women on their lists. In the elections of 2000, 952 men (92 percent) and 80 women (8 percent) were included in the list for mayoral posts. Of the total number of candidates, 106 were presented by the Pachakutik Movement, of whom only seven were women, none of them indigenous. In the 2004 elections to provincial assemblies, 129 women candidates participated, nine of whom were proposed by the Pachakutik Movement, giving a small but positive boost for women's participation. However, only 13 women, three of whom are from the Pachakutik Movement, won and now serve as mayors.

To summarize, the political parties in Ecuador do not display a clear focus on or interest in the participation of indigenous women. At the same time, because of the exclusionary and hegemonic nature of the traditional political parties, indigenous peoples, and particularly indigenous women, do not display any keen interest in participating in them and have channelled their incipient participation accordingly—almost exclusively through the Pachakutik Movement.

The Participation of Indigenous Women

Discrimination against women in politics hits indigenous women harder than other women. Compared to women's overall political gains, the presence of indigenous women in public office as a result of popular election is disappointingly small. In the lists of principal legislators for elections to the Congress for the period 1998–2002, there was just one Quichua woman, from the Pachakutik Movement, while the list of alternates included just one indigenous woman, in 12th position, for the Izquierda Democrática political party. In reality no indigenous women are principal legislators or even alternates.

It is difficult to understand how it is, even in the Pachakutik Movement, that women in general and indigenous women in particular have not participated more or played a more prominent role. One possible explanation is women's lack of education and training. Another important factor is the conditions in which indigenous women become involved in politics—generally in the face of profound socio-political and economic difficulties and disadvantages, which effectively deter them from politics.

Lessons Learned

From the political and social standpoint, indigenous women are fostering procedural and substantive changes, and generating novel forms of citizen participation and of transparent and collective administration. In addition, more attention is being given to the gender and generational agenda, ethnic and cultural issues, ecological identity, and the concept of integral development promoted by local governments.

The reality in which indigenous women find themselves from the moment they become candidates, as well as when they are elected, poses enormous challenges to the process of enhancing the dynamics of women's political work, renewing political leadership and promoting the inclusion of women in politics. Experience so far points to some important lessons.

1. *There is a lack of a common women's agenda framed in a single political project.* The experience in Congress shows that when economic policy matters are discussed there is no consensus regarding gender implications because the ideologies of the political parties determine agendas and voting patterns. On issues related to women's rights or families' rights, for example, it has been possible to reconcile different points of view, but this has not happened with respect to proposals in other areas, especially the economy.[8]

2. *Few indigenous women seek nomination as candidates.* In general, the political parties did not include any indigenous or black women on their candidate lists.

3. *There is a structural problem of illiteracy.* The indigenous movement participated in elections for the first time in 1996. In the light of the expectations surrounding this participation, an exit poll was performed to look at the quality and effectiveness of the indigenous vote. The first results indicated that 80 percent of the indigenous voters aged between 45 and 55—the vast majority of them women—did not know how to vote, as they were illiterate.

4. *There is a lack of training to improve the quality of women's performance in government.* The indigenous leadership, particularly of indigenous women, will find it difficult to survive without an improvement in the current level of participation in government. Weaknesses are apparent in administrative, legal, and technical matters.

5. *The indigenous movement lacks solid political experience.* Indigenous participation in politics is dispersed, and therefore in this context the gender agenda and the inclusion of women do not appear to have been accorded priority.

6. *The potential strength of the indigenous movement is not reflected in election results.* Although the indigenous movement has a strong organizational basis and in recent years has gained the ability to bring considerable social pressure to bear, this is not reflected in the electoral results of the Pachakutik Movement. Its weight as a social movement is not translated automatically into gains in electoral politics, which affects the capacity of indigenous women to participate through this channel.

7. A political culture of consensus is lacking. This delays timely decision making and has an impact on the effectiveness of performance in government.

Key Challenges

Several challenges must be addressed in order to achieve women's participation in politics, and especially the participation of indigenous women.

1. The first fundamental challenge is to achieve equality not only in the drawing up of the lists but in actually winning elections, and to strike a balance between gender equity and a democratic outlook based on social equality. Women should be on the lists in positions in which they can actually be elected, and not just for adornment.

2. The second challenge is the need to link the entry of women into politics with the consolidation of democracy and the promotion of an economy that offers new prospects for development. Women's participation becomes essential to building a political project that would entail profound changes in the structure of patriarchal power, which is exclusionary and mono-culturalist.

3. The third challenge is to train women for participation by means of ongoing educational efforts by which women can expand their knowledge and increase their self-esteem.

4. A fourth challenge is to incorporate a gender perspective into party by-laws and programmes. The party directive according to which 'one cannot take the floor until authorized by the party whip', a common practice in Latin American parliaments, must be overcome.

5. It is essential to promote the political participation of indigenous women. They often have to fight racism and display their capacity for initiative, knowledge of the issues, and the tenacity to face conflict and break down stereotypes. This task should be carried out by designing and adopting public policies that help bring about the transformation of society, and society's recognition of the plurality of cultures and ethnic groups.

6. Finally, a challenge is to continuously sensitize male candidates and society in general to the importance of including gender issues in the government programmes and electoral platforms.

Strategies

Forging citizenship through participation is one of the fundamental strategies for addressing poverty and corruption, for bringing about equitable and multi-ethnic development, and for ensuring political and social equality. In terms of discrimination against indigenous women in politics, partnerships can help overcome the discrimination, exclusion and mono-culturalism that have predominated in Ecuador.

One strategy involves the need to develop solid groups to support women legislators. These could be constituted initially by women parliamentarians around the Committee on Women, Youth, Children and the Family, which brings together women from various political parties. It is critical to develop caucuses to support women's participation within the political parties, the indigenous movement, and organized social sectors in order to incorporate women's interests in their by-laws and programmes. Women, including indigenous women, are bearers of a different perspective on politics. In effect, by incorporating issues such as gender and respect for multiculturalism, women are contributing to a transformation of traditional norms and of politics itself.

Moreover, women legislators should maintain close coordination with the social organizations from which they have come and with their constituencies. Distancing themselves from these constituencies weakens women's interventions, and indeed those of a party as a whole. These linkages should be maintained to respond consistently and transparently to popular demands, and to ensure that the electorate performs its proper role in the system of checks and balances.

Conclusion

In Latin America, major constitutional reforms are needed to ensure indigenous representation in the legislatures. Indigenous representatives could be elected in special electoral districts at the national level. This could be combined with the general elections held in each of the countries, through either the political parties or the political movements, as in Ecuador, especially since the Ecuadorian Congress, as currently constituted, does not have any indigenous legislators other than those elected from the Pachakutik Movement. The indigenous peoples' demand for one additional legislator in each province who is elected by the indigenous peoples is therefore just, necessary and urgent for democratizing the political system and the current make-up of the Congress. In other words, we must work to build inclusive and multi-ethnic democracies.

Change in the systems of representation combined with a redistributive economy would result in a major improvement of the quality of democracy, transforming our societies and improving the participation of critical social constituencies, such as women. In the case of indigenous women, the strength of their identity will be one of the fundamental pillars for expanding their influence to bring about public policies consistent with their reality, and to design a social project that promotes change and a political project aimed at democratizing the exercise of power. At the congressional or local levels, we have had the opportunity to show that indigenous persons, and especially women, are prepared to effectively assume roles in the public administration, serve in parliament on an equal footing, ethically and by bringing forward proposals, and demonstrate that we are fully prepared to debate and propose solutions to national problems.

Notes

1   United Nations Development Programme (UNDP), 2001. 'Informe sobre Desarrollo Humano' [Report on human rights]. Quito: UNDP (see in particular the chapter on Ecuador, pp. xxiv and xxv); and Ordóñez, Aylin, 2000. 'Acceso a la Justicia y Equidad' [Access to justice and equity]. San José: Inter-American Institute of Human Rights, with support from the Inter-American Development Bank (IDB).

2   The political system does not cease to be mono-ethnic simply by allowing the participation of an indigenous person. More critical than the number of indigenous candidates is the integration of indigenous democratic forms into national legislation. As an example, rather than secret, universal and direct suffrage, indigenous elections are public and collective.

3   Constitution of Colombia, article 171: 'The Senate of the Republic shall be made up of 100 members elected in a nationwide electoral district. There will be two additional senators elected in a special national electoral district by indigenous communities . . .'.

4   Mirna Cunninhan is one of the most outstanding Miskitu parliamentarians. As of 2002, she was also president of the University of the Northern Atlantic Autonomous Region, known as the Indigenous University, in Nicaragua.

5   In 1998, elections were held for the posts of president, vice-president, 20 national deputies and 101 provincial deputies to Congress. In the 2000 elections, local and provincial authorities were elected, that is, mayors, prefects, and members of the local councils and provincial assemblies.

6   Article 59 of the electoral law provides: 'In elections in which three representatives are to be elected, at least one woman candidate shall be registered as principal and one as alternate; in those in which four to six representatives are to be elected, at least two women as principals and two as alternatives; in those in which seven to nine representatives are to be elected, at least three women as principals and three as alternates; in elections of 10 to 12 representatives, at least four women as principals and four as alternates; and so on. In elections in which two representatives are to be elected, one of the principal candidates preferably shall be a woman, and likewise for the alternates. This proportion shall increase by the percentage indicated in the previous article, until egalitarian representation is achieved.'

7   The Coordinadora Política de Mujeres (Political Coordinating Body of Women) challenged the constitutionality of the instruction in the courts, as a result of which the Supreme Electoral Tribunal recognized that it was arbitrary and undertook to work together with the women's organizations to draw up the instructions for the 2002 elections.

8   In some proceedings in Congress, such as the passing of the law establishing the Deposit Guarantee Agency, the women who belong to right-wing political groupings ended up voting for a law that has been notorious in Ecuador.

Case Study: Indonesia

Enhancing Women's Political Participation in Indonesia

Khofifah Indar Parawansa

The history of representation in the Indonesian Parliament is one of a long process of women's struggles in the public sphere. The first Indonesian Women's Congress in 1928, which prompted the emergence of an increased women's nationalist activism, is a turning point in history because of the role the Congress played in improving opportunities for Indonesian women to participate in all aspects of development. Women played a major role, in the armed services and generally in the public sphere, during the struggle for independence up to and after 1945.

However, after independence, along with the homecoming of men from the war, patriarchal values broadly re-emerged, as did the perception that the role of women was to manage the household. In the first general election of 1955, women made up 6.5 percent of those elected to the Parliament. Since this election, women's representation has ebbed and flowed, peaking at 13.0 percent in 1987. After the first general election of the reform era, in 1999, women made up 8.8 percent of the elected representatives, rising to 11.3 percent in 2004.

The under-representation of women in the Indonesian Parliament is due to a range of obstacles. This case study presents the history of women's participation, the various obstacles faced by Indonesian women gaining access to political institutions, and strategies to increase their representation in politics.

The National Context

Under normal political circumstances, general elections in Indonesia are held every five years. The first general election was held in 1955, ten years after Indonesia achieved independence from colonialism under the Soekarno presidency. From 1955 onwards, changes in the way in which general elections were conducted altered the numbers of political parties participating in the elections and brought about a different pattern of women's representation within the political parties. The 1955 election was recognized as democratically acceptable: several candidates came from women's organization affiliated with the wide range of political parties which contested the election, and 17 women were elected to the legislature.

The second election was not held because the Constituent Assembly, which had been charged with amending the 1945 constitution, was unable to complete its task, and President Soekarno issued a decree in July 1959 that returned Indonesia to the terms of the 1945 constitution. At this point, Indonesia became a 'guided democracy'. The transition to the New Order of President Soeharto took place without an election. General elections were held in the New Order era in 1971, 1977, 1982, 1987, 1992 and 1997. In the New Order elections, with a system under which a single party was dominant, women's representation was determined by the party's national-level elites. The candidates were all chosen by and beholden to the national-level elites; some of them had close relationships with the party elites. Under the closed-list proportional representation (PR) electoral system, candidates were not necessarily involved actively in election campaigns, and there was often little relationship between those who were elected and their constituents.

The end of authoritarianism and the transition from the Soeharto government to that of B. J. Habibie in 1998 was followed by an early election in 1999. For this election, the electoral process underwent significant changes, and the recruitment of party candidates for the legislature, including women, required the approval of the regions, specifically the regional party officials (although this did not apply to representatives from the armed forces and the police, who served as legislators until September 2004). The majority of the women elected in 1999 participated actively in the electoral process, through community advocacy, discussions, speeches and other party activities associated with the election campaign.

After the 1999 election, Abdurrahman Wahid was chosen as the new president by the Majelis Permusyawaratan (MPR, People's Consultative Assembly) but was subsequently replaced by his deputy, Megawati Soekarnoputri, in 2001. During these two presidencies, a major process of constitutional amendment took place, under which Indonesia changed from an integrationist state in which the MPR was the single highest institution of the nation to a conventional presidential system with separation of powers. As a result, Indonesia held elections for the national legislature and for provincial and district legislatures in 2004, accompanied by the first election for the newly established second chamber of the legislature, the regional Dewan Perwakilan Daerah (DPD, Representatives' Council). These elections were followed by Indonesia's first-ever direct presidential election, conducted in 2004 using a Two-Round system.

The DPD, which is an upper house with limited powers, was elected using the Single Non-Transferable Vote (SNTV). At first sight surprisingly, there is a higher proportion of women representatives in the DPD than in the legislature (the Dewan Perwakilan Rakyat, DPR, House of Representatives): there are 27 women out of 128 (21 percent) in the DPD compared with 11.5 percent in the DPR. The DPD, however, is unlike the national and local legislative bodies in that individual candidates, not political parties, are the participants in DPD elections. In some areas, women candidates clearly attracted support from women voters.

The new election law for the 2004 general elections made two important changes which could affect women's representation in the national and regional/district legislatures. The first was the introduction of a limited open-list system, in which voters could vote for a party and also a candidate from that party, and a candidate who received a predetermined number of individual votes would be elected even if not placed high enough on the party list. In practice, however, few candidates were able to poll enough individual votes for this to make a significant difference.

Much more important was the new provision requiring parties to 'bear in their hearts' the desirability of 30 percent of nominated candidates being women, which can be described as a 'maybe quota'. Although this was not imperative, and in addition it contained no provisions about the position of women on party lists, many parties did attempt to fulfil the requirement to propose 30 percent women candidates in their lists for elected bodies at all levels. This is an important first step, but needs to be strengthened and its enforcement made mandatory.

The requirement of 30 percent representation did not come only from women activists' awareness of the importance of legislation to improve women's representation in politics. Its origin also lay in the response of some parties in the legislature first to the consideration of the amendment to the constitution (although the constitution does not address the issue, either in its original or in its revised form), and then in debate on the new political party law of 2002. Although these attempts were not successful, they did motivate various non-governmental organizations (NGOs) in favour of the expansion of women's representation to bring together and to approach and pressure the legislators working on the bill for the new election law. It was these movements that led to the agreement (article 65(1) of the election law, UU12/2003) that each political party participating in the election should bear in its heart the desirability of a minimum of 30 percent of women in each region for the national, provincial and district-level legislators in their lists of electoral candidates.

Representation of Women in the Legislatures (DPR, MPR, DPD)

In addition to the 1945 constitution and its amendments (completed in 2002), the policy basis for the functioning of the government was determined by the elaboration of the 1945 constitution that had been developed by the MPR in the Garis-Garis Besar Haluan Negara (GBHN, Broad Guidelines of State Policy). From 1988, these guidelines contained provisions regarding the role of women, and there has in addition been a junior Ministry for Women's Affairs (latterly for Women's Empowerment). In the 1999 Broad Guidelines, it was declared that the empowerment of women would be conducted through a twofold strategy. First, improvements would be made in the position and role of women in the nation and state, through national policies formulated and implemented by institutions responsible for gender equality and justice. Second, improvements would be made in the quality, role and independence of women's organizations, in continuing efforts to empower women and safeguard the prosperity and well-being of the family and society. These guidelines applied to all state agencies, including the executive (the president), the judiciary (the Supreme Court), the legislature (DPR/MPR) and the state audit agency (Badan Pemeriksa Keuangan, BPK). Under the amended constitution, the Broad Guidelines no longer exist: they have been replaced by the president's vision and mission.

It is not, however, the provisions of legislation that hinder women's access to legislatures. In reality, the representation of women in legislative bodies at both the national level and the provincial and district levels (in the regional and District People's Representative Assemblies (DPRDs)) is still relatively low. In 1999, approximately 6 percent of the members of provincial DPRDs and fewer than 5 percent of the members of district DPRDs were women. Accurate figures for the number of women members of DPRDs are still not available after the 2004 elections—which speaks for itself.

Table 5: Women in Formal Political Institutions in Indonesia, 2005

Institution	Women		Men	
	Total	%	Total	%
DPD (upper house)	27	21.0	101	79
DPR (constituent assembly)	63	11.5	487	88.5
Supreme Court	8	14.8	40	85.2
State Audit Agency	0	0	7	100
National Election Commission	2	18.1	9	81.9
Governor (provincial level)	0	0	30	100
Mayor/Regent (metropolitan district/regency level)	5	1.5	331	98.5
Civil Service Echelon IV & III*	1,883	7.0	25,110	93.0
Judges*	536	16.2	2,775	83.8
State Civil Court*	35	23.4	150	76.6

* Data based on the speech delivered by the State Minister for the Empowerment of Women, Khofifah Indar Parawansa, 21 June 2001. This estimate is not believed to have changed greatly since 2001.
Source: Data formulated by the Division on Women and the Elections (CETRO), 2001; Profile of DPD Members 2004–2009; and the Secretariat of the Indonesian legislature (DPR-RI).

In the 2004 election, the number of women in the legislature increased by 2.5 percent in comparison with the election of 1999, as table 6 shows.

Table 6: Representation of Women in Indonesia: The House of Representatives (DPR)

	Women		Men	
	Total	%	Total	%
1950–5 (Provisional DPR)	9	3.8	236	96.2
1955–60	17	6.3	272	93.7
Constituent Assembly:1956–9	25	5.1	488	94.9
1971–7	36	7.8	460	92.2
1977–82	29	6.3	460	93.7
1982–7	39	8.5	460	91.5
1987–92	65	13.0	500	87.0
1992–7	65	12.5	500	87.5
1997–9	54	10.8	500	89.2
1999–2004	45	9.0	500	91.0
2004–2009	62	11.3	488	88.7

Note: Based on the 1955 election, the DPR contained 272 representatives, but President Soekarno formed the Constituent Assembly to revise the constitution. This assembly was dismissed by Soekarno in July 1959 because it was deadlocked.

Source: DPR Secretariat, 2001. Data formulated by the Division on Women and the Elections, CETRO, 2002. With this level of representation, the Inter-Parliamentary Union (IPU) places Indonesia in 75th position out of more than 180 countries in terms of women's representation in the legislature (January 2005).

Although there is an increase in the number of women representatives, there is still a tendency for women to hold posts that are traditionally seen as 'soft' (i.e. relating to women's issues), so that the distribution of female members in the commissions of the national legislature reflects traditional patterns for dividing responsibilities between men and women. The highest percentage of women members is found in Commission VIII (religion, social, empowerment of women), followed by Commission X (education, youth, sport, tourism, art and culture), as shown in table 7. Women's representation is relatively low in 'prestige' commissions which deal with economics, poverty and politics, which are significant in determining executive programmes and budget.

While the amended 1945 constitution states that 'all citizens are equal before the law' and that the 'government guarantees freedom of union and association, and to express opinions both orally and writing', nevertheless the low representation of women in politics persists. It is rooted in a patriarchal culture. In spite of positive action measures, such as the quota for women representatives, women are still facing various obstacles in achieving equality with men in all aspects of life.

Table 7: Members of Commissions of the Indonesian Legislature, by Gender, 2005

Commission	Women		Men	
	Total	%	Total	%
I. Defence, International Affairs, and Information	1	2.1	45	97.9
II. Home Affairs, Regional Autonomy, Bureaucracy, and Land Affairs	5	10.2	44	89.8
III. Constitution and Law, Human Rights, and Security	6	13.3	39	86.7
IV. Agriculture, Estate, Forestry, Sea Resources, Fishery and Food	2	4.0	48	96.0
V. Transportation, Telecommunications, Public Works, Housing, Village Development, and Less Developed Region	2	3.8	50	96.2
VI. Trade, Industry, Investment, Cooperatives, Small and Medium-Scale Enterprises, and Public Enterprises	5	9.4	48	90.6
VII. Energy, Mineral Resources, Research and Technology, and Environment	2	3.9	49	96.1
VIII. Religion, Social and Women Empowerment	14	31.1	31	68.9
IX. Population, Health, Manpower, and Transmigration	9	20	36	80.0
X. Education, Youth, Sports, Tourism, Arts and Culture	10	20.8	38	79.2
XI. Finance and National Development Planning, Banking, and Non-bank Institutions	6	10.7	50	89.3
Total (100%)	62		478	

Source: DPR Secretariat, 2002. Data formulated by the Division of Women and the Elections, CETRO, 2002.

Obstacles Preventing Women from Becoming Members of Parliament

There are several factors influencing the patterns of the recruitment of men and women as legislators.[1] They include the following.

- The cultural context in Indonesia is still heavily patriarchal. The common perception is that the political arena is for men, and that it is less preferable for women to become members of parliament.
- The selection of candidates by political parties is usually done by a small group of officials or party leaders, almost always men. In Indonesia awareness of gender equality and justice issues is still low. Male political leaders have a disproportionate influence over party politics and women do not receive much support.

- The media have yet to effectively mobilize the public regarding the importance of women's representation in parliament.
- Despite the existence of women's organizations fighting for the goal of increased representation of women (since 1999), there is little effective networking among these organizations, NGOs and political parties towards this common goal.
- Poverty and the low levels of education of women make it difficult to recruit women who have the political capabilities that would allow them to compete on an equal basis with men. The standard for qualification set by the 2003 electoral law allows candidates with at least a senior high school degree to compete in elections. The women who have the political abilities required tend to engage in advocacy or choose non-partisan roles.
- Women with families often experience obstacles, in particular opposition from their spouses.
- Political activities usually require large investments of time and money, and many women hold positions that are not rewarding financially.
- The large number of political parties contesting elections and winning seats in parliament can affect the level of representation of women. As political parties receive a limited number of seats in the legislature, these tend to be divided among male candidates who tend to be ranked at the top of the party election list.

Strategies to Increase the Representation of Women

First and foremost, the links between women's networks and organizations must be supported and strengthened.

There are currently several major associations of women's organizations. For example, the Kongres Wanita Indonesia (KOWANI, National Council of Women's Organizations of Indonesia) is a federation of 78 women's organizations which cooperates with women from a range of different religions, ethnicities and professional organizations. The BMOIWI (Federation of Indonesian Muslim Women Organizations) is a federation of approximately 28 Muslim women's organizations. The Center for the Political Empowerment of Women is a network of organizations that cuts across party, religious and professional lines and includes approximately 26 organizations. All these networks have significant potential to support increased representation of women in parliament, both in quantitative and qualitative terms, if they and their member organizations work together to synergize their efforts.

Further strategies include:
- increasing the representation of women in political parties by introducing a quota system within political parties and ensuring the accession of women to strategic decision-making positions;
- conducting advocacy with the leaders of political parties to enhance awareness of the needs of a significant voting block;

- enhancing women's access to the media as a tool to rally public opinion;
- empowering women through education, training and increased access to information; and
- introducing a formal quota with enforcement mechanisms to increase the number of women members of the legislature.

The Road Ahead

Since the Habibie administration (1998–9), there has been greater openness in the political system. The number of NGOs has grown and the limitations on the activities of political parties have been lifted. This new atmosphere has benefited women: NGOs active in the area of women's rights have enhanced their activities. During the Wahid administration, the situation improved further. Two political caucuses of women emerged—the Kaukus Perempuan Parlemen (Women's Legislative Caucus) and the Kaukus Politik Perempuan Indonesia (Indonesian Political Women's Caucus).

These associations began to develop a network for women in the parliament, leaders of political parties, leaders of mass organizations, and other stakeholders to increase and strengthen their efforts. In general, these associations lobbied for a legislated quota of at least 20–30 percent for women. The result was the inclusion in the new Electoral Law passed in February 2003 of the provision that political parties 'should bear in their hearts' including women as 30 percent of all electoral candidates. This was something of a victory for the groups that had lobbied hard for quotas, although its implementation has been weak. It was not universally welcomed at the time: then President Soekarnoputri expressed reservations during her Mother's Day address on 27 December 2001, saying that a quota would in fact reduce women's standing, and place an increased burden on women and on the institutions they would occupy.

Finally, aside from the issue of a quota, one pressing issue is that the level of representation of women in parliament could be increased and the aspirations of the community could be better channelled through further revisions to the electoral law. Until now the system in force in Indonesia has been a PR system. Many argue that PR gives women the best opportunity to increase representation, as women can be forwarded for election through the use of candidates' lists (see, e.g., chapter 3 of this Handbook). If women are well represented on these lists in a beneficial ranking, they stand a good chance of being elected. Revisions to the electoral law to ensure this can therefore have a positive impact on the election of women to the Indonesian Parliament in future.

Note

[1] For further detail of some of the obstacles, see Matland, Richard E., 2001. 'Sistem Perwakilan dan Pemilihan Kaum Perempuan: Pelajaran Untuk Indonesia' [Representation and election system for women: Lessons learned for Indonesia], in *Keterwakilan Perempuan dan Sistem Pemilihan Umum* [Women's representation and the electoral system]. Jakarta: National Democratic Institute and State Ministry for Women Empowerment, p. 22.

Further Reading

CETRO (Centre For Electoral Reform), 2002. 'Executive Summary Data dan Fakta Keterwakilan Perempuan Indonesia' [Executive summary of data and facts of women representatives in Indonesia], in *Partai Politik dan Lembaga Legislatif* [Political parties and legislative bodies]. Jakarta

Crouch, Harold, 1982. *Perkembangan Politik dan Modernisasi* [Political development and modernization]. Jakarta: Yayasan Perkhidmatan

Karam, Azza, 1999. 'Kesimpulan Bukan Sekedar Tanda Bukti Representasi' [Conclusion: not only representation—approval'], in International IDEA. *Perempuan di Parlemen, Bukan Sekedar Jumlah, Bukan Sekedar Hiasan* [Women in Parliament: Not just numbers, not just decoration]. Jakarta: International IDEA

Robinson, Kathryn and Sharon Baseel, 2002. 'Women in Indonesia, Gender Equity and Development'. Singapore: Institute of Southeast Asian Studies

Sanit, Arbi, 1985. 'Perwakilan Politik di Indonesia' [Political representation in Indonesia]. Jakarta: CV Rajawali

— 1995a. 'Ormas dan Politik' [Mass organizations and politics]. Jakarta: Lembaga Studi Informasi Pembangunan

— 1995b. 'Sistem Politik Indonesia: Kestabilan Peta Kekuatan Politik dan Pembangunan' [The Indonesian political system: Stability of the political power map and development]. Jakarta: PT Raja Grafindo Persada

'Zaman telah Berubah Sesudah Kartini' [The era has changed since Kartini], 1978. *Tempo* magazine (Jakarta), 29 April

Chapter 3

Chapter 3

Richard E. Matland

Enhancing Women's Political Participation: Legislative Recruitment and Electoral Systems

The following two chapters examine strategies to overcome the obstacles to political participation outlined previously. This chapter focuses on two issues. First, we examine the principal steps involved in the process of recruiting to countries' legislatures. Second, we look at the effect of a country's electoral system. Which electoral systems are best suited to securing the election of women, and why? What specific factors should women be concerned about in the design of electoral systems? By addressing these questions, we hope to provide some insight into the effective and practical strategies that can be used to increase women's parliamentary representation.

1. The Legislative Recruitment Process and its Impact on Women

The legislative recruitment process refers to the process by which individuals move from meeting the legal criteria to serve to actually serving in parliament. The norm in most countries is for political parties to play an important role in this process by identifying possible candidates, selecting them as their official candidates, and putting them forward to the public for election.

For women to get elected to parliament they need to pass three crucial barriers: first, they need to select themselves; second, they need to be selected as candidates by the parties; and, third, they need to be selected by the voters. This process is elaborated in figure 1. While the steps involved in moving from eligible to aspirant to candidate occur in most political systems, the actual process varies dramatically from country to country. In particular, party rules and norms, along with the country's social culture and electoral system, affect the recruitment process at different stages and influence the degree of openness to women candidates.

The stage at which the party gatekeepers actually choose the candidates is the crucial stage for getting women into office.

Figure 1: The Legislative Recruitment System

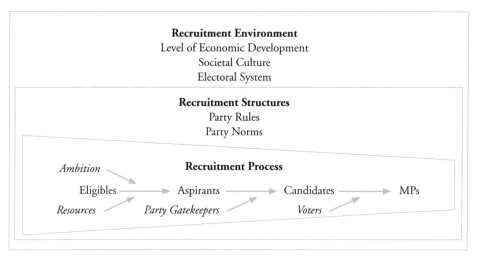

Source: Matland, R. and K. Montgomery, 2003. 'Recruiting Women to National Legislatures: A General Framework with Applications to Post-Communist Democracies', in R. Matland and K. Montgomery (eds). *Women's Access to Political Power in Post-Communist Europe.* Oxford: Oxford University Press, p. 21.

1.1. Selecting Yourself

The first stage consists of a person deciding to stand for elected office. The decision is influenced by personal ambition, resources and opportunities to stand. The decision to stand for office is generally portrayed as the decision of an actor who is rational, but has limited abilities to predict outcomes and estimate the possible benefits and costs of specific actions taken. Such a boundedly rational actor's personal ambition is tempered by an assessment of the resources the candidate can generate to help in the campaign, an estimation of how friendly the socio-political environment will be to the individual's candidacy, and calculations concerning the opportunities to stand for office, that is whether open positions exist. Already at this first stage there are more men than women. Men, across virtually all cultures, are socialized to see politics as a legitimate sphere for them to act in. This leads to men having a greater knowledge of and interest in politics, and greater political ambition. They also have access to more resources. In virtually every country women start out as more than 50 percent of those eligible to serve, but even after just the first step of selecting themselves the system is starting to become skewed towards men.

A women's movement or organizations focusing on women's political empowerment can contribute significantly to an increase in the number of potential women candidates aspiring for office. Even non-political organizations with predominantly women members can play important roles. These organizations can provide women with experience in public settings, help build their self-confidence, and provide a support base if a woman decides to contest an election. Women's organizations can also pressure parties both to address women's issues and to address the question of women's increased political representation. These are important resources a woman can draw on and they make it more likely that she will stand and that the party apparatus will see her as a viable candidate.

1.2. Being Selected by the Party

The second step is to be selected by the party. Selecting candidates is one of the crucial roles played by political parties. Nomination procedures vary across countries and parties and can be distinguished by a number of features, including the breadth of participation and the degree of centralization or decentralization of the process.[1] At one end of the spectrum are processes that provide a broad opportunity for people to participate in a decentralized context, such as primary elections in the USA and all-member party caucuses run by the major Canadian parties. At the other end of the spectrum are systems in which the party leader, national faction leaders, or the national executive choose the candidates. For example, the choosing of candidates by the Liberal Democratic Party (LDP) in Japan is very much under the control of party faction leaders. Depending on which of these procedures is used, party leaders, a broader set of party officials, or a significant portion of party rank and file play the gatekeeper role.

We can also distinguish between patronage-oriented and bureaucratic selection systems.[2] In a bureaucratic system of candidate selection rules are detailed, explicit, standardized and followed, regardless of who is in a position of power. Authority is based on legalistic principles. In a patronage-based system there are far less likely to be clear rules, and even when they exist there is a distinct possibility that they will not be followed carefully. Authority is based on either traditional or charismatic leadership rather than legal–rational authority. Loyalty to those in power in the party is paramount.

Clear bureaucratic procedures for selecting candidates can have a distinct advantage for women.

For women, bureaucratically-based systems that have incorporated rules to guarantee women's representation—that is, quotas—are a significant advantage. In many of the Nordic countries, parties have adopted quotas guaranteeing that either 40 percent or 50 percent of the party's list will be women. This has had a positive effect on women's representation in the Nordic countries (see the case study on Sweden).[3] Even when there are no explicit rules to guarantee representation, clear bureaucratic procedures by which candidates are chosen can have a distinct advantage for women. Clear and open rules provide women with the opportunity to develop strategies to take advantage of those rules. When the rules are unwritten it becomes much harder to devise a strategy to break into the inner circle of power.

Box 2. Candidate Recruitment in Norway

The case of Norway provides one example of how to take advantage of explicit and clear procedures. Norway has a closed-list proportional representation (PR) system.

Nominating starts with party committees in each county recommending a slate of candidates for the party list.* The committee recommendation is sent to a county-wide nominating convention where it must be approved, position by position. Local party members in local meetings choose the delegates to the nominating convention. With these explicit rules, even before quotas existed, it was possible for women to identify crucial decision points around which they could mobilize to press their demands.

This mobilization was aimed first at the committee recommendation stage, and second at the nominating convention stage. Women would start by demanding fair representation from the nominating committee. If the party nominating committee failed to take account of their demands satisfactorily, they would organize local female party members to maximize turnout at the local party organization meetings where delegates were selected. In so doing, they could guarantee that delegates who would vote to ensure representation of women were elected to go on to the country convention. Such a procedure could become highly contentious. Often, merely the threat of mobilization would be sufficient to get party nominating committees to accommodate demands for women's representation in their nominating recommendations, rather than risk having their proposals voted down by the party membership at the nominating convention.

* Valen, Henry, 1966. 'The Recruitment of Parliamentary Nominees in Norway'. *Scandinavian Political Studies.* Vol. 1, no. 1, pp. 121–66; and Valen, Henry, 1988. 'Norway: Decentralization and Group Representation', in Michael Gallagher and Michael Marsh (eds). *Candidate Selection in Comparative Perspective: The Secret Garden of Politics.* London: Sage.

Under any nominating system an important consideration for a party is to present candidates that the party believes will maximize its vote.[4] If certain types of candidates are seen as a liability, gatekeepers will shy away from nominating them. Research reviewing several individual country studies reveals that there is a set of characteristics party selectors look for in possible candidates across all countries. The most widely valued characteristic is the aspirant's track record in the party organization and in the constituency.[5] Perhaps the strongest manifestation of this is the high rate at which incumbents are re-nominated. Even for new candidates, a past history of party participation and activism is important, although not a requirement. Visibility in the community either through one's profession, the holding of public office, or leadership positions in civil society organizations is also highly desirable. Because incumbents and community leaders are often disproportionately male, these criteria can damage women's opportunities.

> **An aspirant's track record in the party and in the constituency is the most widely valued characteristic in potential candidates.**

The stage at which party gatekeepers choose the candidates is the most critical one for getting women into office. It is extremely hard to estimate the proportion of people who make the jump from simply being eligible to actually aspiring to elected office. Polling data show that the percentage of people who say they have considered standing for political office runs from a few percent to close to 20 percent of the population in industrial democracies. We also know that this pool of aspirants is skewed towards men. My estimate would be that in industrialized democracies somewhere between 25 percent and 40 percent of those who aspire to office are female. The important point, however, is that this pool is big enough for parties to be able to elect only women many times over *if they wanted* to. For example, in the 2002 German federal elections, the Sozialdemokratische Partei Deutschlands (SPD, Social Democratic Party) won approximately 20 million votes, which led to its winning 251 seats. Even if only 5 percent of the SPD voters might aspire to political office and of this aspirant pool only 20 percent were women, this would still mean there were 200,000 women in the aspirant pool. To put up a slate of candidates that was exclusively female, the party would have needed only 602 women, well below 1 percent of its total number of female aspirants.

The crucial point is that political parties have the power to compensate for the skewed nature of their pool of aspirants through the use of quotas or other party rules which can lead to greater gender equality. Because the eligibility pool is skewed, if the parties adopt gender-neutral nominating rules the consequence would be a pool of candidates skewed towards men. If the parties use selection procedures that hurt women the pool of candidates will become even more biased towards men than the eligibility pool. Whether party gatekeepers see women as desirable candidates who can help the party win votes will be influenced by a number of factors, including a country's culture as well as its electoral system, as discussed below.

1.3. Getting Elected

The final barrier to becoming a member of parliament (MP) is being chosen by the voters. It is a matter of some dispute whether there is a systematic bias against women at this stage. Most studies of elections in established democracies suggest that voters vote primarily for the party label rather than for the individual candidates.[6] This is certainly true of electoral systems that use closed-list proportional representation (PR).[7] In such cases, there is little reason to see the voters as a serious deterrent to women's representation. The crucial stage of the process under these conditions is actually getting nominated by the party.

While this is most typical, there are countries where the personal vote for the candidate is important (just how important is a matter of considerable debate in political science). Consistently, political scientists have argued that party loyalties, retrospective evaluations of the job done by the regime in power, and views on the prominent political issues of the day will tend to swamp the effect of candidates' sex. As researchers have pointed out, however, even if objectively the individual characteristics of candidates do not matter to the electorate, party officials are convinced that they are important. They will therefore continue to choose candidates carefully with an eye to those who they believe will strengthen the parties' chances of winning votes.[8] The individual candidate is most likely to have some effect on vote totals in countries with plurality/majority, single-member district (SMD) electoral systems. Even in these countries, however, there is considerable evidence that female candidates do as well as male candidates when directly facing the voters.[9]

> **Most voters primarily vote for the party label rather than for individual candidates in established democracies.**

Some PR electoral systems use an open-list ballot or preferential voting, that is, the party nominates many candidates, usually in its preferred order of choice, but the voter has the ability, if he or she wishes, to influence which of the candidates on the party's list should be elected. When voting, the voter first chooses a specific party ticket, but then has the option of supporting a specific candidate by giving that individual a personal vote. How many personal votes it takes to influence the order in which candidates are elected is determined by the election laws and can vary tremendously.[10]

> **Party officials are convinced the individual counts, therefore they will continue to carefully choose candidates who they believe strengthen their party's chances of winning votes.**

Under preferential voting systems such as the Single Transferable Vote (STV) or open-list PR voting systems, being a woman may be an advantage or a disadvantage. To the degree that women organize and actively encourage the striking out of male names and voting for female names, this procedure can produce a surprisingly strong showing by women. A stark example of this occurred in Norway. Norway has open-list PR in local elections at the municipality level. In the early 1970s, women were able to organize a remarkably effective campaign to promote women. In the 1971 local elections, women's representation in several large Norwegian cities rose from approximately 15–20 percent of the city council to majorities on the council. This 'women's coup' became a source of great surprise and pride at women's abilities to take advantage of the electoral structure. It should be noted, however, that there was a counter-reaction in the following election, when many men who felt that striking out male candidates simply because they were men was unfair went out of their way to strike out women candidates. In the following local election and in every local election since, the number of women elected in local elections in Norway has been less than it would have been had there been no personal vote.[11]

While this is only a cursory look at the barriers facing women as they try to move from merely being in the eligible pool of candidates to actually becoming MPs, it should be clear that among established democracies the crucial points are to convince women to stand and to convince the parties to choose women as their candidates.

2. The Effect of Electoral Systems on Women's Representation

When considering women's representation, a crucial factor is whether the electoral system has SMDs where only one legislator is elected in the district, or a multi-member district (MMD) system where several MPs are elected from each electoral district. This distinction tracks quite well, although not perfectly, with the distinction between plurality/majority (majoritarian) and PR systems.

> In the short term, changing a country's electoral system often represents a far more realistic goal to work towards than dramatically changing the culture's view of women.

- In plurality/majority systems the winner is the candidate or party with the most votes, and typically there is only a single winner in each district.
- In proportional systems the electoral system is designed to ensure that the overall votes for a party or coalition are translated into a corresponding proportion of seats in the legislature. If a party wins 20 percent of the votes, it should get approximately 20 percent of the seats in parliament. All PR systems use multi-member districts.[12]

There are several reasons why scholars of politics and women activists emphasize the effect electoral systems have on women's representation. First, the impact of electoral systems is dramatic. As seen in table 8 and figure 2, the differences in women's representation across electoral systems are substantial. Second, and just as important, electoral systems can be, and regularly are, changed. Compared to the cultural status of women in society, or a country's development level (the two other factors known to affect women's representation), electoral rules are far more malleable. Changing the electoral system often represents a far more realistic goal to work towards than dramatically changing the culture's view of women.

Table 8: Percentage of Women MPs Across 24 National Legislatures, 1945–2004.
Plurality/majority (SMD) Systems vs PR/Mixed, Multi-member District Systems

System/Year	1945	1950	1960	1970	1980	1990	1997	2004
SMD	3.05	2.13	2.51	2.23	3.37	8.16	15.42	18.24
MMD	2.93	4.73	5.47	5.86	11.89	18.13	21.93	27.49

Plurality/majority, SMD systems: Australia, Canada, France (from 1960), Japan (to 1990), New Zealand (to 1990), United Kingdom United States.	PR and mixed, MMD systems: Austria, Belgium, Denmark, Finland, France (1945 and 1950), Greece**, Iceland, Ireland, Israel*, Italy, Japan (after 1993), Luxembourg, Netherlands, New Zealand (after 1996), Norway, Portugal**, Spain**, Sweden, Switzerland and Germany (Federal Republic of Germany* prior to 1990).

* Israel did not exist, and the Federal Republic of Germany did not hold elections in 1945. They are therefore not included in the 1945 numbers. They are included for all years following 1945.
** Greece, Portugal and Spain became democratic in the 1970s and are therefore only included in the calculations from 1980.

Key: SMD = Single-member districts systems: only one member is elected in each electoral district.
MMD = Multi-member district system: more than one representative is elected in each electoral district.

© INTERNATIONAL IDEA

Table 8 and figure 2 present data for 24 established democracies over the post-World War II period. They show that women have always had a slight advantage under PR as compared to plurality/majority systems. Until 1970, however, this advantage was very small: the difference in women's representation across the different systems is 3 percent or less. After 1970, however, there is a marked change and there has been a consistent and substantial divergence in women's representation across electoral systems.[13]

In the 1960s and 1970s all of the developed world saw the spread of 'second-wave feminism' (suffrage movements were the first wave feminist movement): women were demanding equal rights on a whole array of issues, among them greater representation in politics. In countries with PR systems, women were able to translate those demands into greater representation. In plurality/majority systems, on the other hand, the same demands were made but they were largely unsuccessful or only very modestly successful.

2.1. The Advantages of PR Systems

The obvious question is why countries with PR electoral systems should show such a strong increase in representation and plurality/majority systems show such a modest effect? There are a number of explanations. First, PR systems have consistently higher district magnitudes, which lead to higher party magnitudes. (District magnitude is the number of seats per district; party magnitude is the number of seats a party wins in a district.) Party and district magnitudes are important because they affect party strategy when choosing candidates. The party gatekeepers, who choose candidates, will have a different set of concerns and incentives depending upon the electoral system.

When district magnitude is one, as it is in almost all plurality/majority systems, the party can nominate one person per district. By definition, the party has no chance to balance the party ticket. In nominating decisions in single-member districts, female candidates must compete directly against all men; and often when nominating a woman a party must explicitly deny the aspirations of the most powerful male politician in the same district. When district magnitude increases, the chance that a party will win several seats in the district increases. When a party expects to win several seats, it will be much more conscious of trying to balance its ticket. Gatekeepers will divide winning slots on the party list among various internal party interests, including, possibly, women's interests.

There are several reasons for this balancing process.[14] First, party gatekeepers see balance as a way of attracting voters. Rather than having to look for a single candidate who can appeal to a broad range of voters, party gatekeepers think in terms of different candidates appealing to specific sub-groups of voters. Candidates with ties to different groups and different sectors of society may help attract voters to their party. A woman candidate can be seen as a benefit to the party by attracting voters without requiring the most powerful intra-party interests represented by men to step aside, as would be required in a plurality/majority system. Conversely, failing to provide some balance, that is, nominating only men, could have the undesirable effect of driving voters away.

A second reason is that within the party balancing the ticket is often seen as a matter of equity. Different factions in the party will argue that it is only fair that one of their representatives should be among those candidates who have a genuine chance of winning. Especially when a women's branch of the party has been established and is active in doing a significant amount of the party's work, women can argue that equity requires that they get some of the slots in winnable positions. A third reason for balancing the slate is that dividing safe seats among the various factions within the party is a way of maintaining party peace and assuring the continued support of the different factions.

Proportional representation systems can also help women because a process of 'contagion' is more likely to occur in these systems than in plurality/majority systems.

Figure 2: Percentage of Women in Parliament: Majoritarian vs PR Electoral Systems

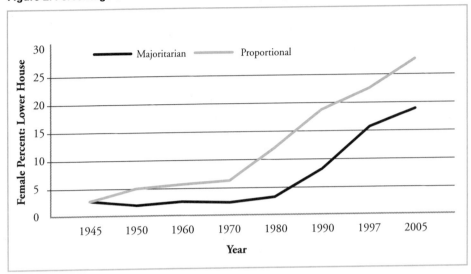

Contagion is a process by which parties adopt policies initiated by other political parties. In this case, once one party starts to nominate women in prominent positions, parties in PR systems will be much quicker to adopt this policy. The cost to a party of responding to the adoption of such a policy by another party or other parties that it is competing with is likely to be lower in PR systems, compared to plurality/majority systems, and the gains may be greater. The costs will be lower in a PR system because the party will have several slots from which to find room to nominate a woman; in plurality/majority systems, where the party has only one candidate, in order to open a space for a woman it might have to deny re-nomination to an incumbent or deny a slot to the male candidate of an internal faction that has traditionally received the nomination. The gains may be greater because in PR systems even a small increase in votes, produced by adding women to the party ticket, could result in the party winning more seats.

To study this question, we looked for contagion effects in Norway and Canada. In Norway, looking for contagion effects in elections prior to the dominant Labour Party adopting quotas, we found that contagion occurred within local districts. The Norwegian Labour Party increased the number of women in winnable positions in exactly those districts where it faced a serious challenge by the Socialist Left, the first party to adopt quotas in Norway. When we tested for a similar effect in Canada—that is, whether the Liberal Party was more likely to nominate women in those districts where the New Democratic Party had nominated women—we found no evidence of such an effect. In other words contagion occurred in the country with a PR electoral system and did not in the country with a plurality/majority electoral system.[15]

More generally it is worth noting that gender quotas as a policy have clearly been contagious in Norway. In 1977, only two parties with less than 4 percent of the parliamentary seats had quotas. By 1997, five of the seven parties represented in the Parliament, with approximately 65 percent of the seats combined, had officially adopted gender quotas.[16]

2.2. Why Some PR Systems are Better than Others

While proportional representation systems are more advantageous for women, not all PR systems are to be equally preferred. There are two particular aspects that can help or hinder women's representation within the broader umbrella of PR systems.

> **Higher district magnitude:** parties have the chance to compete for and win several seats, allowing them to go further down the party lists, where women are usually listed.
>
> **High electoral thresholds:** these discourage the creation of 'mini-parties' which often elect only one or two representatives, usually male.

2.2.1. District Magnitude

As already noted, the driving force behind women doing better in PR systems is the ticket-balancing process which occurs when the party sets up its election list in each electoral district. What is crucial if women are to win seats in parliament is that parties win several seats so that they go deep into the party list when selecting their MPs.

Above, party magnitude was defined as the number of seats a party wins in an electoral district. In designing electoral rules, women will be helped both by having high district magnitudes and by electoral thresholds, because of their effects on average party magnitude. Not surprisingly, there is generally a strong positive correlation between average district magnitude and average party magnitude. As the number of seats per district increases, parties go further down their lists (that is, win more seats) and more parties will have multi-member delegations. Both should increase women's representation. This suggests that women's groups should be supportive of moves to increase the total number of MPs in the parliament and of moves to reduce the number of electoral districts. The limiting case, and the one that may be the most advantageous for women, is that of the whole country being simply one electoral district. There are, of course, other considerations apart from women's representation that are important in evaluating an electoral system, and these considerations in turn may render a proposal to have the whole country as one district unattractive. In many countries, for example, it is often seen as important to guarantee regional representation, in which case some geographic form of districting may need to be accommodated.

The whole country is one electoral district in the Netherlands, which has a comparatively high level of women's representation (37 percent) and in Israel, which has an average level of women's representation (15 percent). One lesson learned from Israel is that electoral systems cannot *guarantee* high representation levels. A second lesson is that having a high electoral threshold, which is the minimum percentage of the vote that a party must have in order to win a seat in the legislature, is important to increasing women's chances. In Israel the level of support needed to win a seat has been extremely low. The low threshold, 1.5 percent, has encouraged the creation of many mini-parties, which often elect only one or two representatives. Overwhelmingly, parties tend to have male leaders, and party leaders inevitably take the first few slots on the list. Women first tend to show up a little farther down the list when the party concerns turn to ensuring ticket balance. If only one or two representatives of a party win election, even though many of its candidates in mid-list positions are women, women are quite likely not to win any representation.

2.2.2. Electoral Thresholds

When designing electoral systems there is a trade-off between representing the voters who choose small parties and increasing the 'descriptive representation' of the legislature by having more women representatives from the larger parties. Data from Costa Rica and Sweden, used to test this hypothesis, confirm the trade-off. Both these countries use electoral thresholds. Simulations show that without thresholds very small parties would have won representation; with thresholds the smaller parties are eliminated, but more women are elected from the largest parties in the country. Women's groups may support proposals to establish the whole country as one electoral district, but it would be an important strategic addendum to make sure that electoral thresholds are included in the proposal.

2.3. Type of Electoral List

Another distinction between different PR systems is that some systems have closed party lists, where the party determines the rank-ordering of candidates, and some have open party lists, where the voters are able to influence which of the party's candidates are elected by means of personal voting. The crucial question is whether it is easier to convince voters to actively vote for women candidates, or to convince party gate-keepers that including more women on the party lists in prominent positions is both fair and, more importantly, strategically wise. I suspect that the answer varies from country to country. It is worth noting that, if effective parliamentary quotas have been adopted, closed lists do help guarantee women's representation.

Figure 3: Why PR Systems are Better for Women

HIGHER DISTRICT MAGNITUDES	CONTAGION
Has higher number of seats per district *(higher district magnitude)*	Party lists present greater opportunities to nominate women
Party can expect to win several seats in each district *(higher party magnitude)*	Greater capacity to promote women when challenged by another party (contagion)
Party more likely to balance ticket by including women *(balancing)*	Party does not have to pay the cost of denying a slot to an incumbent or male candidate in order to nominate a woman

© INTERNATIONAL IDEA

For the initial version of this Handbook, published eight years ago, on the basis of the limited empirical work that had been done up to that point, I cautiously suggested that closed lists were preferable. Since then further research has analysed the effect of the open-list system in several countries. The most recent research indicates that it is not possible to make a general recommendation: the effects of open-list systems on women's representation in fact vary dramatically, depending on the party's supportiveness of women's candidacies.

The open-list system is used in Norway for local elections. In developing their party lists, many of the Norwegian parties strictly follow a principle of making every other candidate a woman. Research finds that voters appear to have a slight preference for male candidates.[17] In other words, in Norway, where the parties are highly supportive of women candidates, preferential voting hurts women. In Poland, on the other hand, my analysis of party parliamentary nominating lists and electoral results found that women do better with voters than they do with the party committees putting together party lists, that is, the preferential vote leads to greater representation of women. Party leaders undervalue women candidates, either because of sexism among members of the selection committees or, possibly, because members of selection committees have a misplaced fear of sexism on the part of the voter.

Furthermore, Gregory Schmidt found in Peru that open-list voting did not disadvantage women. Women activists in Peru ran a campaign urging voters to give their preferential votes to 'one of each' (i.e. pick one man and one woman) and this led to female candidates in open-list voting doing as well as men.[18] Based on a review of this (admittedly limited) research, it would appear that no strong or unambiguous recommendation can be made one way or the other in terms of whether preferential voting helps or hurts women.[19]

It is true, however, that open lists let the parties 'off the hook': they are not responsible for the final outcome. The final outcome rests with thousands of individual voters making individual decisions. If the sum of all those individual decisions is that

105

women are voted down and out of parliament, the parties cannot be held responsible, as they cannot control how their supporters vote. With closed party lists, however, it is clear that it is the party's responsibility to ensure balance in the party delegation. Under these conditions parties could be held responsible for women's representation. If representation fails to grow, women could search out parties that were more willing to consider their demands for representation.

3. Lessons for Expanding Women's Representation

A number of lessons for increasing women's representation can be drawn from the above discussion.

1. Women should organize both inside and outside political parties. Being organized either in interest groups outside or as women's caucuses inside political parties provides valuable experience for women and gives them a power base on which to build if they aspire to office. Political as well as professional groups such as women doctors or women lawyers' associations can play an important role as a recruiting ground for women candidates. Being organized also increases visibility and legitimacy. In addition, in political parties, where women commonly do a considerable amount of the essential party work, it is important to be organized into a women's caucus that can lobby for improved representation.

2. Women should urge parties to set down clear rules for candidate selection. Generally, women will benefit if parties have clear bureaucratic procedures for selecting candidates rather than a system based on loyalty to those in power. When the rules of the game are clear, it is possible for women to develop strategies to improve representation. When the process is dominated by patronage, rules can be unclear and decisions are often made by a limited number of persons, who are almost certainly predominately male.

3. PR systems are better than plurality/majority systems for increasing women's representation. In looking at the countries that are defined as free or partly free by Freedom House, the ten that rank highest in terms of women's representation all use proportional representation electoral systems. Single-member district plurality/majority systems have consistently proved to be the worst possible for women.

4. Some PR systems are preferable to others. Systems that guarantee high party magnitudes through a combination of high district magnitudes and electoral thresholds are expected to be superior for women. Just having a PR system is not sufficient. Ireland, for example, which uses the STV form of PR, has very small district magnitudes (between three and five members) and has lower levels of female representation than plurality/majority systems in countries such as Canada, Australia and the United Kingdom. The optimal system for women is likely to be a PR system where the whole country is one district. As noted earlier, however, this will not always be a viable option, and often there will be good reason to divide the country into several geographically-based electoral districts.

5. Women should carefully evaluate all parts of any proposed electoral system for their possible advantages or disadvantages for women. Even when there is broad agreement on a system based on geographical electoral districts, there will usually be different ways of implementing such a system. Those interested in increasing women's representation should not neglect these alternatives. The existing research suggests that the more seats in the national legislature the better for women, because this will increase party magnitude. When deciding how many geographic districts should be formed, the smaller the number of districts created the better for women, again because this will increase party magnitude. Meier, for example, asserts that much of the significant increase in women's representation that occurred in Belgium was due to a decrease in the number of electoral districts which has led to a significant increase in average party magnitude.[20] In addition, women should be watchful when the number of seats in each electoral district is determined. Often this process results in rural districts being over-represented and urban districts being under-represented. It is in urban districts, where non-traditional roles for women are more common and where there are far more resources for women interested in participating in politics to draw on, that women tend to do well, especially when they arc just starting to make significant gains. Women's groups should watch carefully to see that, when the number of seats per district is determined, the distribution of seats is as close to 'one person, one vote' as possible.

6. While PR systems are better in the long run, immediate results cannot be guaranteed. While changes in the electoral system make greater women's representation more likely, and in the long run there is no question that electoral system changes help women improve their representation levels, an immediate effect is not guaranteed. While PR systems have, on average, higher proportions of women than plurality/majority systems, this is not true for every case. While there are several striking cases of women gaining significant representation in developing countries with PR systems, there are many more cases where no gains have been made despite an advantageous electoral system. The non-effect for the electoral system variable in these countries is an important example of a more general point: while certain institutions or rules may benefit one group or another, an effect will appear only if the group is sufficiently well organized to take advantage of the situation. If not, the institutional arrangement can have no effect on outcomes. The relatively small difference for women's representation between proportional systems and plurality/majority systems for the period 1945–70 well illustrates this point. If the forces interested in women's representation are not effectively organized, then the electoral system is expected to have only a limited effect.

7. Changing the electoral system is only one part of a more comprehensive strategy for improving women's representation. Women need to become active and effective voices within their individual parties and within society as a whole to be able to take advantage of the institutional advantages certain electoral structures provide.

Women have made steady, albeit slow, progress in terms of parliamentary representation, with women now holding nearly 16 percent of seats in lower houses of parliament across the world. Some of that progress has occurred thanks to improvements associated with increased development, education, and incremental changes in women's standing in society. Much of that change has, however, been due to activists becoming more astute to the intricacies of electoral system design and legislative recruitment, and pushing for institutions that maximize women's chances of representation. These processes are complex and often difficult to follow, but when they are understood, as they are increasingly are, gender equality activists can more effectively and successively press their demands for more equitable representation.

Notes

[1] Gallagher, Michael, 1988. 'Conclusions', in Michael Gallagher and Michael Marsh (eds). *Candidate Selection in Comparative Perspective: The Secret Garden of Politics.* London: Sage.

[2] Norris, Pippa, 1996. 'Legislative Recruitment', in Lawrence LeDuc, Richard Niemi and Pippa Norris (eds). *Comparing Democracies: Elections and Voting in Global Perspective.* London: Sage.

[3] While quotas are often credited with being responsible for the lead that Nordic countries have in terms of women's representation, it should be noted that Nordic countries were generally world leaders in this area even before such rules were adopted. Causality may run from being a world leader to adopting rules, rather than the rules causing one to become a world leader. See Dahlerup, Drude and Lenita Freidenvall, 2005. 'Quotas as a "Fast Track" to Equal Representation for Women'. *International Feminist Journal of Politics.* Vol. 7, no. 1, March, pp. 26–48.

[4] Clearly, this is not the only concern and sometimes not even the primary concern. Concern for party unity or intra-party factional fights may from time to time trump the desire to maximize votes, but in the long run parties in democracies are forced to be concerned about winning votes. If they are not they run the risk of disappearing from the political stage.

[5] Gallagher 1988, op. cit., p. 248.

[6] LeDuc, Niemi and Norris 1996, op. cit.

[7] On the different electoral systems referred to in this Handbook, see 'Glossary of Terms', in Reynolds, Andrew, Ben Reilly and Andrew Ellis, 2005. *The New International IDEA Handbook of Electoral System Design.* Stockholm: International IDEA, annex B.

[8] Bochel, John and David Denver, 1983. 'Candidate Selection in the Labour Party: What the Selectors Seek'. *British Journal of Political Science.* Vol. 13, no. 1, pp. 45–69.

[9] Darcy, R. and Sarah Slavin Schramm, 1977. 'When Women Run Against Men'. *Public Opinion Quarterly.* Vol. 41, pp. 1–12; and Welch, Susan and Donley T. Studlar, 1986. 'British Public Opinion Toward Women in Politics: A Comparative Perspective'. *Western Political Quarterly.* Vol. 39, pp. 138–52.

[10] For an extended discussion on the various thresholds found for preferential voting systems see Katz, Richard S., 1997. *Democracy and Elections.* Oxford: Oxford University Press.

[11] Hellevik, Ottar and Tor Bjørklund, 1995. 'Velgerne og Kvinnerepresentasjon' [Voters and women's representation], in Nina Raaum (ed.). *Kjønn og Politikk* [Gender and politics]. Oslo: Tano Press.

[12] For an extensive review of electoral systems see Reynolds, Reilly and Ellis 2005, op. cit.

[13] There is a considerable accumulation of comparative evidence that underlines the structural advantages of PR with respect to women's representation. Among countries that have Mixed Member Proportional (MMP) systems, where some portion of the electoral system is based on single-member districts while another portion is based on proportional lists either at the regional or at the national level, women's representation is consistently higher on the proportional part of the electoral systems. Furthermore, several countries have changed their electoral systems, and there is a consistent finding that when changes are made from plurality/majority to PR systems there is an increase in women's representation. Most recently these results were confirmed in a study of the changes in electoral systems in post-communist states in Central and Eastern Europe: see Matland, Richard E., 2003. 'Women's Representation in Post-Communist Europe', in Richard E. Matland and Kathleen A. Montgomery (eds). *Women's Access to Political Power in Post-Communist Europe.* Oxford: Oxford University Press.

[14] Valen, Henry, 1988. 'Norway: Decentralization and Group Representation', in Gallagher and Marsh (eds), op. cit.

[15] Matland, Richard E. and Donley T. Studlar, 1996. 'The Contagion of Women Candidates in Single-Member and Multi-Member Districts'. *Journal of Politics.* Vol. 58, no. 3, pp. 707–33.

[16] Quotas are elaborated upon in chapter 4 in this Handbook.

[17] I am fairly confident this is caused by a limited number of males who are 'local notables' and are initially placed quite low on the party list being raised above women who are initially higher than them on the party list but are relatively unknown to voters in the municipality.

[18] Schmidt, Gregory D., 2003. 'Unanticipated Successes: Lessons from Peru's Experiences with Gender Quotas in Majoritarian Closed List and Open List PR Systems', in International IDEA. *The Implementation of Quotas: Latin American Experiences.* Stockholm: International IDEA.

[19] There are, however, strong arguments both for and against open-list voting that are not tied to gender effects. Proponents emphasize that open-list voting provides the citizenry with greater input into choosing their representatives and as such it is seen as 'more

democratic'. Opponents of open-list voting argue that it reduces a party's control over its representatives and therefore threatens the 'responsible party' model of democracy many political scientists prefer.

[20] Meier, Petra, 2004. 'Gender Quotas or Electoral Reform: Why More Women Got Elected during the 2003 Belgian Elections'. Paper presented at International IDEA conference on The Implementation of Quotas: Experiences from Europe, Budapest, 22–23 October.

References and Further Reading

Bochel, John and David Denver, 1983. 'Candidate Selection in the Labour Party: What the Selectors Seek'. *British Journal of Political Science.* Vol. 13, no. 1, pp. 45–69

Dahlerup, Drude and Lenita Freidenvall, 2005. 'Quotas as a "Fast Track" to Equal Representation for Women'. *International Feminist Journal of Politics.* Vol. 7, no. 1, March, pp. 26–48

Darcy, R. and Sarah Slavin Schramm, 1977. 'When Women Run Against Men'. *Public Opinion Quarterly.* Vol. 41, pp. 1–12

Darcy, R., Susan Welch and Janet Clark, 1994. *Women, Elections, and Representation.* 2nd edn, Lincoln, Nebr.: Nebraska University Press

Fowler, Linda and Robert D. McClure, 1989. *Political Ambition: Who Decides to Run For Congress.* New Haven, Ct.: Yale University Press

Gallagher, Michael, 1988. 'Conclusions', in Michael Gallagher and Michael Marsh (eds). *Candidate Selection in Comparative Perspective: The Secret Garden of Politics.* London: Sage

Hellevik, Ottar and Tor Bjørklund, 1995. 'Velgerne og Kvinnerepresentasjon' [Voters and women's representation], in Nina Raaum (ed.). *Kjønn og Politikk* [Gender and politics]. Oslo: Tano Press

Inter-Parliamentary Union (IPU), 1995. *Women in Parliaments 1945–1995: A World Statistical Survey.* Geneva: IPU

Katz, Richard S., 1997. *Democracy and Elections.* Oxford: Oxford University Press

LeDuc, Lawrence, Richard Niemi and Pippa Norris, 1996. *Comparing Democracies: Elections and Voting in Global Perspective.* London: Sage

Matland, Richard E., 1995. 'How The Electoral System has Helped Women Close the Representation Gap in Norway', in Lauri Karvonen and Per Selle (eds). *Closing the Gap: Women in Nordic Politics.* London: Dartmouth Press

— 1998a. 'Women's Representation in National Legislatures: Developed and Developing Countries'. *Legislative Studies Quarterly.* Vol. 23, no. 1, pp. 109–25

— 2003. 'Women's Representation in Post-Communist Europe', in Richard E. Matland and Kathleen A. Montgomery (eds). *Women's Access to Political Power in Post-Communist Europe.* Oxford: Oxford University Press

— and Donley T. Studlar, 1996. 'The Contagion of Women Candidates in Single Member and Multi-Member Districts'. *Journal of Politics.* Vol. 58, no. 3, pp. 707–33

— and Michelle A. Taylor, 1997. 'Electoral System Effect on Women's Representation: Theoretical Arguments and Evidence from Costa Rica'. *Comparative Political Studies.* Vol. 30, no. 2. pp. 186–210

Meier, Petra, 2004. 'Gender Quotas or Electoral Reform: Why More Women Got Elected during the 2003 Belgian Elections'. Paper presented at the International IDEA conference on The Implementation of Quotas: Experiences from Europe. Budapest, 22–23 October

Norris, Pippa, 1996. 'Legislative Recruitment', in Lawrence LeDuc, Richard Niemi and Pippa Norris (eds). *Comparing Democracies: Elections and Voting in Global Perspective.* London: Sage

Reynolds, Andrew, Ben Reilly and Andrew Ellis, 2005. *The New International IDEA Handbook of Electoral System Design.* Stockholm: International IDEA

Schmidt, Gregory D., 2003. 'Unanticipated Successes: Lessons from Peru's Experiences with Gender Quotas in Majoritarian Closed List and Open List PR Systems', in International IDEA. *The Implementation of Quotas: Latin American Experiences.* Stockholm: International IDEA

— and Kyle L. Saunders, 2004. 'Effective Quotas, Relative Party Magnitude, and the Success of Female Candidates'. *Comparative Political Studies.* Vol. 37, no. 6, pp. 704–34

Valen, Henry, 1966. 'The Recruitment of Parliamentary Nominees in Norway'. *Scandinavian Political Studies.* Vol. 1, no. 1, pp. 121–66

— 1988. 'Norway: Decentralization and Group Representation', in Michael Gallagher and Michael Marsh (eds). *Candidate Selection in Comparative Perspective: The Secret Garden of Politics.* London: Sage

Welch, Susan and Donley T. Studlar, 1986. 'British Public Opinion Toward Women in Politics: A Comparative Perspective'. *Western Political Quarterly.* Vol. 39, pp. 138–52

Case Study: Latin America

Women, Political Parties and Electoral Systems in Latin America

Mala N. Htun

This case study analyses how political parties and electoral systems shape women's opportunities to gain access to power in Latin America. In the past 15 years, many of the region's parties have made significant efforts to promote women. Eleven countries in the region adopted quota laws for women's candidacies and a 12th, Colombia, has introduced them for senior positions in the executive branch. The influence of quotas is conditioned by electoral rules: the measure works best in countries with closed-list proportional representation (PR) electoral systems, placement mandates, and large electoral districts. Yet the weakness of the political parties and party systems in many countries, particularly in the Andean region, poses a threat to democratic consolidation and the livelihoods of women and other citizens.

As in the rest of the world, women have historically been seriously under-represented in elected office in Latin America. Their presence in political decision making has never equalled men's. Recognizing that this situation undermines democracy, political equality and justice, more and more people—including male politicians and opinion leaders—have endorsed measures to increase women's presence in power. Since 1991, 11 Latin American countries have adopted quota laws establishing minimum levels for women's participation as candidates in national elections. Although the results vary depending on the electoral rules and the enforcement of the rules, the trend towards quotas marks a watershed in public attitudes towards women in power and in official commitments to gender equality.

As a result of quotas, social and economic development, democratization and cultural changes, women's presence in power in Latin America has grown. From an average of 9 percent in 1990, by 2005 women's representation in the lower houses of the national parliaments of the region had increased to 17 percent. Women's share of seats in the senates grew from an average of 5 percent in 1990 to 13 percent in 2005. And, whereas women occupied 9 percent of ministerial posts in 1990, this had increased to an average of 14 percent by 2005. A few countries have registered dramatic increases thanks to the successful application of quota rules. Nowhere, however, have women achieved parity in presence with men.

Table 9 shows that women's share of power, while quite high in some Latin American countries (as in the congresses of Argentina and Costa Rica and the cabinet of Colombia), is low in others (e.g. in the congresses of Guatemala and Honduras and the Mexican Cabinet). On average, women's opportunities to participate in parliament have improved, but gains have not been evenly distributed.

Table 9: Women in Power in Latin America in 2005: A Snapshot

Country	% Women in the Lower House (or unicameral parliament)	% Women in the Senate	No. of Women Ministers	% of Women Ministers
Argentina	34	33	1 of 11	9
Bolivia	19	15	1 of 15	7
Brazil	9	12	2 of 23	9
Chile	13	4	3 of 17	18
Colombia	12	9	5 of 13	38
Costa Rica	35	–	3 of 16	19
Cuba	36	–	6 of 38	16
Dominican Republic	17	6	3 of 20	15
Ecuador	16	–	2 of 15	13
El Salvador	11	–	2 of 12	17
Guatemala	8	–	2 of 13	15
Honduras	6	–	3 of 23	13
Mexico	23	16	0 of 19	0
Nicaragua	21	–	1 of 13	8
Panama	17	–	2 of 12	17
Paraguay	10	9	2 of 10	20
Peru	18	–	2 of 15	13
Uruguay	12	10	0 of 14	0
Venezuela	10	–	3 of 16	19
AVERAGE	17	13		14

Sources: Data on ministerial positions are from national government web sites except for Costa Rica, the Dominican Republic, Uruguay and Venezuela, where the information was found at Georgetown University's Political Database of the Americas, available at <http://www.georgetown.edu/pdba/>. Data on national legislatures are from the Inter-Parliamentary Union, 'Women in National Parliaments: Situation as of 31 January 2005', <http://www.ipu.org/wmn-e/classif.htm>.

Public Attitudes to Women's Leadership

A survey from 2004 reveals significant differences between countries in attitudes towards men and women in power. Figure 4 shows the percentage of respondents who agreed with the statement '[M]en are better leaders than women'.

Figure 4: Public Attitudes to Women Leaders in Latin America, 2004

Percentage agreeing with the statement 'men are better leaders than women'.

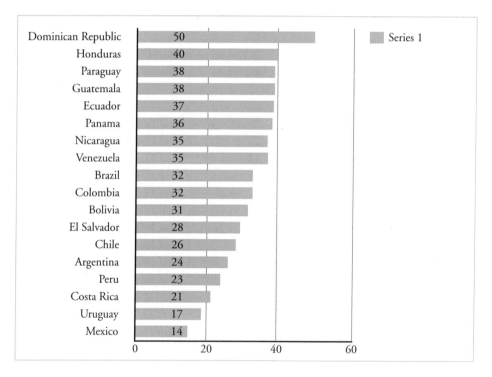

Source: Latinobarómetro, 2004. 'Una década de mediciones' [A decade of measurements]. Informe Resumen. Santiago de Chile, 13 August 2004, <http://www.latinobarometro.org>.

These findings suggest that sexist views among the electorate are not holding women back in many countries, especially Mexico, Uruguay and Costa Rica. In the Dominican Republic, however, fully half of respondents are hostile to women's leadership. Yet there is no clear correlation between the survey results and actual numbers of women in power. As this suggests, some of the clues to explaining women's opportunities lie elsewhere. We should therefore investigate the effects of political institutions—parties and electoral systems—on women's candidacies.

Political Parties

Parties are the gatekeepers to women's advancement to power. To gain positions of leadership, women must work through parties that have the unique ability to field candidates for political office. Parties, however, have historically been highly gendered institutions that incorporated women on a different basis from men and in ways that impeded their access to leadership positions. In many Latin American countries, women still make up half of party members but rarely enjoy equal status with men on party executive boards or among candidates for popular elections. Women have joined 'women's wings' of parties that mobilized voters and supported male candidates by hosting meetings and fund-raisers. Unlike the male-dominated bureaus for peasants, labourers, students and so on, these women's bureaus were not derived from a class position or occupation that women could organize around to press their collective demands. Rather, women were recruited *'as women,* whose primary association as a group was with private life'.[1] Not surprisingly, women's representation in political leadership positions is low relative to their overall participation in political parties.

Since the early 1990s, however, many women's wings have reoriented themselves to serve not as support staff but as advocates of female leaders. In Mexico's Partido de Acción Nacional (PAN, National Action Party), for example, the women's wing has been transformed from a matronly organization into an effective base for promoting women's entry into mainstream leadership positions. In elections between 1997 and 2003, the PAN's National Secretariat for the Political Promotion of Women lobbied local and national party leaders to include women as candidates. As a result of their efforts, by 2003 the PAN, despite its right-wing ideology, had more female candidates than the country's two other major parties, the Partido Revolucionario Institucional (PRI, Institutional Revolutionary Party) and the Partido Revolucionario Democrático (PRD, Party of the Democratic Revolution).[2]

Scholars (including Richard Matland, in chapter 3 of this volume) have hypothesized that women's success depends on party organization and ideology. It is argued that women will enjoy greater opportunities in rule-oriented, bureaucratic parties than in unstructured or clientelistic parties.[3] When a party has clear rules on the nomination of candidates, and these rules are respected, potential candidates can better understand the nomination process and hold party leaders accountable to the rules. Studies have also found that women tend to fare better in left parties whose ideology favours the representation of marginalized social groups and with whom feminist movements have closer ties.[4] One multi-country study found that the electoral strength of left-wing parties was a powerful predictor of women's representation in power.[5]

Yet evidence from Latin America suggests no direct correlation between women's presence and party type. Their representation in the legislature in countries with institutionalized party politics and rule-oriented parties varies dramatically, from lows of 12 and 13 percent in Uruguay and Chile, respectively, to a high of 35 percent in Costa Rica. Meanwhile, women's presence in the legislature in countries where parties are more personalistic and informal, and the party system is only weakly institutionalized, such as Bolivia and Peru (at 19 and 18 percent, respectively) is above the regional average of 17 percent.

Ironically, efforts to promote internal party democracy may thwart attempts at greater gender equity. Some parties in Latin America are adopting internal primaries to select candidates for general elections. This measure, which decentralizes power by taking the control of nominations out of the hands of party leaders, complicates efforts to enforce quota rules. Primaries also favour established candidates who have resources, most of whom tend to be men.[6]

What about the effects of party ideology? In the 1990s, it seemed that Latin America followed world trends: parties of the left, which advocated state intervention, social policy and participatory democracy, tended to get more women elected than parties of the right.[7] By 2005, however, the tendency has changed. Women do not do so badly as one might expect in parties of the right relative to the total numbers of women legislators in each country. Women's share of seats in three of the region's major right-wing parties outperforms their total presence in the respective congresses. For example, women make up 29 percent of deputies from Mexico's right-wing PAN (44 out of 151); 16 percent of the deputies elected by Chile's rightist Renovación Nacional (RN, National Renewal) party (3 of 19); and 10 percent of deputies from Brazil's right-wing Partido da Frente Liberal (PFL, Liberal Front Party) (6 of 62).

A greater concern is the weakness of parties and low citizen identification with any party. Regional public opinion surveys conducted by the Latinobarómetro organization, based in Santiago de Chile, show that on average only about 18 percent of Latin Americans have confidence in political parties (which fare worse than parliament, the judiciary, the police, television, banks, the Church and other institutions).[8] Crises in the party system go a long way towards explaining instability in Bolivia, Ecuador and Venezuela, civil violence in Colombia, and discontent with democracy in Peru. Advocates of women's representation must therefore struggle to strengthen political parties: as the main vehicle to aggregate citizen preferences and translate these into policy, as well as the single institutional route to power, parties are an indispensable component of democratic governance.

Women and Electoral Systems

Various studies have shown that electoral rules are important for women's chances of getting elected.

Countries that have PR tend to elect more women than countries with plurality/majority systems. Why? As Richard Matland argues in chapter 3, in PR systems (where seats are allocated to parties based on the percentage of the total vote they receive) parties have an incentive to 'balance' the ticket by including candidates with ties to a variety of social groups (such as women) and candidates who represent different party factions and constituencies. In majoritarian systems, by contrast, the incentives are different. Parties tend to field those candidates who have a realistic chance of winning more votes than any other candidate. In most cases, party leaders feel that their top candidates are men.

Indeed, data for the year 2000 from 182 countries show that women made up an average of 15 percent of members of Congress in PR systems, 11 percent in mixed systems (in which part of the legislature is elected using PR and part using single-member districts), and 9 percent in plurality/majority systems.[9]

All Latin American countries use some version of PR (with the exception of Cuba, which does not have competitive elections), although four countries have mixed systems combining closed-list PR and single-member districts (see table 10). Among the List PR countries, seven use closed lists and five use open lists. Uruguay has a factional list system, in which votes are pooled at the party level, distributed proportionally to the factions, and then distributed to each faction's lists of candidates. In Colombia's personal list system, the vast majority of lists contain only a single candidate. Votes are pooled across these sub-party lists, not at the party level.[10]

Table 10: Electoral Systems in Latin America (for the Lower House of the Legislature or Unicameral Parliament)

Electoral System	Country
List PR: Closed-List	Argentina, Costa Rica, El Salvador, Guatemala, Honduras, Nicaragua, Paraguay
List PR: Factional closed list	Uruguay
List PR: Personal list	Colombia
List PR: Open-List	Brazil, Chile, Dominican Republic, Ecuador*, Peru
Mixed (List PR plus single-member districts)	Bolivia, Mexico, Panama, Venezuela

* In addition, 15 percent of Ecuador's Congress is elected from a single, national closed list.

Different sets of PR rules are associated with slightly different levels of women's representation. The mean level of women's representation for the lower house was 18 percent in the closed-list systems, 17 percent in the mixed systems, and 15 percent in the open-list systems. As this suggests, women do marginally better in closed-list and mixed systems than in open-list systems. To understand why, we need to examine the interaction between electoral rules and quota laws.

Quotas for Women

Between 1991 and 2000, 11 Latin American countries adopted quota laws establishing a minimum level of 20–40 percent for women's participation as candidates in legislative elections. Venezuela, however, has since rescinded its quota law. A 12th country, Colombia, enacted a law requiring that women occupy 30 percent of appointed decision-making positions in the executive branch of government.

Have quotas actually helped more women get elected? On average, quotas boosted women's representation by ten percentage points, but the effects of quotas have varied significantly between countries (see table 11).

Table 11: The Results of Quotas in Latin America

Country	Legislative Body	% Women (before law)	% Women (after law)	Change (%)
Argentina	Chamber	6	34	+28
	Senate	3	33	+30
Bolivia	Chamber	11	19	+8
	Senate	4	15	+9
Brazil	Chamber	7	9	+2
Costa Rica	Unicameral	14	35	+21
Dominican Republic	Chamber	12	17	+5
Ecuador	Unicameral	4	16	+12
Mexico	Chamber	17	23	+6
	Senate	15	16	+1
Panama	Unicameral	8	17	+9
Paraguay	Chamber	3	10	+7
	Senate	11	9	-2
Peru	Unicameral	11	18	+7
Average		9	19	+10

The effectiveness of quotas depends largely on the nature of a country's electoral system. Quotas work best in closed-list PR systems where the law contains a placement mandate for women candidates. These mandates require parties to place women in high positions on the party list and not in ornamental slots where they stand no chance of being elected. Quotas also tend to work better in large multi-member electoral districts. In electoral districts with few members, only the party's top candidates—generally men—tend to get elected. When the district magnitude is larger, more of a party's candidates, including those in lower positions on the party list, will win seats.[11]

These factors explain the success of quotas in the Argentine Chamber and Senate and the Costa Rican Congress. They also account for growth in Mexico, where 40 percent of the Congress is elected in large closed-list PR districts. All these three countries have quota laws with rules stipulating the placement of women candidates on the list.

However, many parties have complied with quotas in the most minimal way possible without actually breaking the law. In Argentina, women must be placed in one of every three positions on the party list. Parties have tended to conform by including women in third positions, not first or second. In Costa Rica before 1999 there was no placement mandate, and parties tended to put women near the bottom of party lists. That year, however, the Supreme Court, in response to petitions from the national women's agency, issued a ruling declaring that parties must place women in positions from which they stand a realistic chance of getting elected. It reminded parties that such list spots should be easy to calculate given the average number of seats won by a party in each province in the past.[12] The ruling produced spectacular results: women's presence in Congress jumped from 14 to 35 percent after the 2002 elections.[13]

The details of the quota law are very important. Mexico's quota law, for example, technically does not apply in districts where candidates are selected through primary elections, but the Instituto Federal Electoral (IFE, Federal Electoral Institute) has offered no guidelines about what procedures count as legitimate primaries. Notwithstanding this potential loophole, women still made up more than 30 percent of candidates for the legislative elections in 2003.[14] Brazil's experiences attest to the need to draft quota laws carefully. The law states that parties must reserve 30 percent of candidate slots for women, but does not require that parties actually fill these slots. Since parties may postulate 50 percent more candidates than seats being contested in a district, a party may, in practice, field a full slate without including any women. For example, if an electoral district elects 10 members to Congress, each party is permitted to postulate 15 candidates. The quota law requires that parties reserve four of these slots for women. If a party is unwilling to recruit women, it can put forward 11 male candidates and still not violate the law.[15]

These examples suggest that for quotas to work the law must be written in such a way as to avoid loopholes that permit parties to avoid nominating women or to comply with quotas merely by placing women in supplementary or 'decorative' positions on the ballot paper. In addition, activists need to be willing and able to mobilize to monitor implementation of the quota. In Argentina, parties began to comply with quotas only after activists repeatedly challenged non-compliant lists in court.

Conclusion

Notwithstanding women's gains in the legislatures of some countries, significant challenges remain. As the Latinobarómetro poll shows, sexist attitudes persist. Women have gained formal power in several countries, and have reached a critical mass in a few, but not everywhere. They make up at least half of political party members in many places but have not achieved parity with men in the party leaderships. In most countries, men control the most important congressional committees and informal networks of power.

What is more, even when women are present, they do not always act to promote a gender equality agenda. There is a fragile link between the descriptive representation of women (evidenced by their numbers) and the substantive promotion of their gender interests through the introduction of bills and amendments, lobbying, consciousness-raising, speeches and so on. Many observers have been disappointed that women in elected office do not do more to champion gender equality issues. After centuries of state sexism, such disappointment is understandable. On the other hand, perhaps it is unreasonable to expect that a group of newcomers could so quickly modify the logic of the political marketplace. It is one thing to put women in power. It is quite another to transform the way politicians behave.

Advancing women's right to participate in power, their civil rights and their equal opportunities is linked to the consolidation of democracy, to social development and to equitable economic growth. As long as the region's income gaps widen, many women will lack basic capabilities and remain excluded from eligibility pools for leadership. As long as millions of citizens are struggling to meet their basic needs, there will be limited political space to build coalitions around a women's rights agenda. And as long as state institutions suffer from problems of corruption, inefficiency and mismanagement, it will be difficult to implement new policies such as quota laws. The embrace by so many leaders of the principle of equal opportunity for women is a cause for celebration, but Latin America requires further economic, political and social transformations to translate this principle into practice.

Notes

1 Friedman, Elisabeth, 2000. *Unfinished Transitions: Women and the Gendered Development of Democracy in Venezuela, 1936–1996.* University Park, Pa.: Pennsylvania State University Press, p. 96.

2 Baldez, Lisa, 2004a. 'Obedecieron y cumplieron? The Impact of the Gender Quota Law in Mexico'. Paper presented at the meeting of the Latin American Studies Association, Las Vegas, 7–9 October 2004. Women made up 52 percent of the PAN's PR candidates, compared to 47 percent for the PRI and 42 percent for the PRD.

3 See also Caul, Miki, 1999. 'Women's Representation in Parliament: The Role of Political Parties'. *Party Politics.* Vol. 5, no. 1; and Norris, Pippa, 'Breaking the Barriers: Positive Discrimination Policies for Women', in Jyette Klausen and Charles S. Maier (eds). *Has Liberalism Failed Women?* (forthcoming).

4 Caul 1999, op. cit., p. 81.

5 Reynolds, Andrew, 1999. 'Women in the Legislatures and Executives of the World: Knocking at the Highest Glass Ceiling'. *World Politics.* Vol. 51, no. 4 (July), p. 569.

6 Baldez, Lisa, 2004b. 'Elected Bodies: The Gender Quota Law for Legislative Candidates in Mexico'. *Legislative Studies Quarterly.* Vol. XXIX, no. 2 (May), pp. 231–58.

[7] Htun, Mala, 2001. 'Electoral Rules, Parties, and the Election of Women in Latin America'. Paper prepared for the 97th annual meeting of the American Political Science Association, San Francisco, 30 August–2 September.

[8] Latinobarómetro, 2004. 'Una década de mediciones' [A decade of measurements]. Informe Resumen. Santiago de Chile, 13 August 2004, <http://www.latinobarometro. org> (accessed 25 October 2004).

[9] Norris, Pippa, 2004. *Electoral Engineering: Voting Rules and Political Behavior.* New York: Cambridge University Press.

[10] Archer, Ronald P. and Matthew Shugart, 1997. 'The Unrealized Potential of Presidential Dominance in Colombia', in Scott Mainwaring and Matthew Shugart (eds). *Presidentialism and Democracy in Latin America.* New York: Cambridge University Press, pp. 133–4.

[11] Htun, Mala and Mark Jones, 2002. 'Engendering the Right to Participate in Decisionmaking: Electoral Quotas and Women's Leadership in Latin America', in Nikki Craske and Maxine Molyneux (eds). *Gender and the Politics of Rights and Democracy in Latin America.* London: Palgrave, pp. 39–40.

[12] García, Ana Isabel, 2003. 'Putting the Mandate into Practice: Legal Reform in Costa Rica'. Paper presented at the International IDEA Workshop, Lima, Peru, 23–24 February.

[13] Jones, Mark, 1998. 'Gender Quotas, Electoral Laws, and the Election of Women: Lessons from the Argentine Provinces', *Comparative Political Studies.* Vol. 31, no. 1 (February), pp. 3–21; and Jones, Mark, 2004. 'Quota Legislation and the Election of Women: Learning from the Costa Rican Experience'. *Journal of Politics.* Vol. 66, no. 4 (November), pp. 1203–23.

[14] Baldez 2004b, op. cit.

[15] Htun, Mala, 2001. 'Women's Leadership in Latin America: Trends and Challenges', in *Politics Matters: A Dialogue of Women Political Leaders.* Washington, DC: Inter-American Dialogue, p. 16.

Women, Political Parties and Electoral Systems in Latin America

Case Study: France

The French Experience: Institutionalizing Parity

Mariette Sineau

In Europe, French women were among the last to be granted the right to vote and to stand for election.[1] As of early 2004, the representation of women was still lagging: in the Assemblée Nationale (National Assembly) elected in June 2002, they held only 12.3 percent of the seats, making France 19th among the 25 member countries of the European Union and 66th in the world in the percentage of women parliamentarians. Imposition from above, which is traditional in France,[2] has allowed women to become ministers more easily than they become members of parliament (they make up almost one-quarter of Cabinet members). There is a striking discrepancy between the high level of economic responsibilities held by women in France and their absence in the parliament.

The 30 'glorious' years from 1945 to 1975, which brought tremendous changes in the lives of women (massive entry into the economic fields, increasing wage-labour employment, especially in the services sector, the proportion of women going on to higher education, legal emancipation, etc.) did not end women's lack of electoral legitimacy. The difficulty of electing a sizeable presence of women in the assemblies produced the radical idea of *parity*, which eventually led to major institutional reforms aimed at promoting equal access for women and men to elective office.

This case study first presents the specific historical and institutional context of France, and then elaborates on the significance of the idea of parity and the controversies it has generated. It provides an overview of the broad lines of the reforms implemented and an examination of their practical application during the 2001 municipal and Senate elections, and later the 2002 legislative elections.

Historical Context

A number of historical factors explain why women have never held more than a marginal position in the national assemblies of their respective countries. In France, first, women owe their lengthy political ostracism to the 1789 French Revolution. By positing women's political inability as an absolute principle for over 150 years, the revolution legitimized the notion that women were not competent to assume responsibility for the conduct of public affairs. More recently, further institutional constraints have impeded women's access to legislatures. Regulations and practices originating in the Fifth Republic (1958) have marginalized women, namely the uninominal (single-member) system used in legislative elections and the widespread practice of multiple terms that this system favours. This system indirectly discriminates against women since, by 'personalizing' the election, it gives the political premium to the 'notable' (usually a man): in selecting their candidates, the parties tend to choose the most well-known personality, that is someone who already holds a local mandate in the district (e.g. that of a mayor or general councillor).

The rule of incompatibility between ministerial and parliamentary functions has also been an indirect disadvantage for women since it has compelled the regime to resort to appointing high-level civil servants to executive and even legislative positions, most of whom are trained in distinguished educational institutions such as the Ecole Nationale d'Administration, all of which are male institutions par excellence.

Women have been ill-treated by both the institutions of the Fifth Republic and the political parties in charge of perpetuating them. Far from being open forums for training and selection, the French political parties, with their narrow-minded and ageing leadership, have mainly operated as nomination groups that favour the self-reproduction of male elites. The feminist movement of the 1970s must also bear a share of the responsibility for these practices, because it did not push to put women into the system of political representation: feminists expected change to come from social movements, not political parties. Consequently, for a long time women were under-represented in the leadership of the parties as well as in groups of elected representatives, and found it difficult to make their voices heard.

For many years, the Parti Communiste (PC, Communist Party) was the only party to nominate women for elected office,[3] thus implementing—without calling it this—a quota system. The Parti Socialiste (PS, Socialist Party) amended its by-laws in 1974 in order to include a quota for women in its leadership (initially 10 percent; the quota was increased to 30 percent in 1990). The PS also applied the quota system in elections for the European Parliament (under a proportional list system), and only much later, in 1996, did it vote for a 30 percent quota for female candidates in legislative elections (which came into effect in 1997). The feminist impetus came from Les Verts (the Green Party), which has male–female parity written into its by-laws. None of the right-wing parties have applied the quota system.

A final barrier to the presence of women in politics in France was judicial. On 1 November 1982, the Constitutional Council, the country's highest judicial body, struck down a provision of the law instituting a maximum of 75 percent representation for either sex on the list of candidates contesting municipal elections (in cities with a population over 3,500). By setting a precedent, this decision clouded the outlook for reforms.

To overcome all these obstacles, it was deemed necessary to reform the system from above. France and Belgium are the only European countries to have adopted a law requiring some degree of mixing of the candidates standing for election. While most of its neighbours rely on the 'wisdom' of the political parties to ensure the political representation of women, France stands as an exception by resorting to legislative directives through the law on parity.

The Concept of Parity

Parity can be defined as quantitatively guaranteed equal access to certain elective positions. The concept, which appears as a 'demand for equality' and as 'acknowledging a socially constructed otherness',[4] helps to circumvent the classic dilemma raised by the citizenship of women in democracy, that is, the choice between equality and taking into account the differences between the sexes. It has compelled a rethinking of the content of abstract universalism, and an alternative analysis of the issue of women's political representation.

Is parity equivalent to quotas? 'No' will be the answer of those who maintain that the philosophy underlying parity (perfect equality) is different from that underlying quotas (which constitute a threshold, and as such are considered discriminatory). 'Parity does not mean 50–50', says Eliane Vogel-Polsky. 'Parity is demanded in the name of equal status, and not in the name of representing a minority.'[5] Also, parity has been voted into law on a permanent basis, while the quota is, in principle, a temporary measure. Nonetheless, the French law on parity was cited in debates to defend quotas as a model for immediately increasing the number of women elected.

The concept of parity arose in the late 1980s, being put forward first by the Council of Europe.[6] It was brought to France by intellectuals and feminist movements, who put pressure on the authorities in the early 1990s. Feminists' conversion to legal reform was accelerated by the ideas of certain intellectuals. In 1992, the book *Au pouvoir citoyennes! Liberté, Egalité, Parité*[7] helped to popularize the concept. And in 1996, in her Recueil Dalloz, Francine Demichel showed that because women were legally 'not considered and invisible' they were the subsidiary sex of legal theory. She concludes from this that sex must be integrated into the theory of representation, precisely by means of parity.[8]

The call for parity was taken up by intellectuals as well as politically active women. In June 1996, ten former ministers, all women and all from the political sphere, published a manifesto in favour of parity in the magazine *L'Express*. This publication later had a major impact on the outcome of the debate.

Slowly taken up by political actors of both left and right, parity became a major issue during the 1995 presidential election and the 1997 legislative elections. In the context of the crisis of representation, it was widely held that a democracy without women was a disfigured democracy. Opinion polls also showed that people wanted to see a renewal and feminization of the elite.[9] The political change that brought the left to power in June 1997 precipitated the reforms, since one of the central issues trumpeted by Socialist leader Lionel Jospin was the renewal of the political institutions (including parity and limiting the plurality of election mandates).

The debate on parity gave rise to violent controversies over the founding principles of the republic which cut across the left–right divide and split feminists. Opposing it, orthodox republicans considered that parity would strike a blow against universalism because it groups citizens in categories. Backing parity were those who stressed the limitations of formal egalitarianism and maintained that any democracy that did not include women was not a genuine democracy. The vote for reforms brought an end to the controversy, and parity is now a matter of consensus, both in public opinion and among political actors.

The Reforms

The constitutional law of 8 July 1999 on equality between women and men authorizes legislators to take affirmative action, but remains within the bounds of constitutionality. It complements article 3 of the constitution (on the indivisibility of sovereignty) with the following item: 'The law favours equal access of women and men to electoral mandates and elective positions'. It then stipulates (in article 4) that political parties 'contribute to the implementation [of this principle] under the conditions set by the law'. The term 'equality' was preferred to 'parity', so the latter does not appear in the text. This minimalist reform merely asserts that formal equality must be implemented in practice, but it is fundamental because by redefining the sovereign people it marks a break from the symbolic order from which it arises. In place of the old order, based on 'neutral citizenship' and the 'one-ness' of a society made up of individuals, parity brings in a bi-gendered, dual order.

This new situation resulted in the adoption, on 6 June 2000, of a law on 'equal access of women and men to electoral mandates and elective positions'. This law is also known as the parity law. It requires the parties in all the elections that are run on the basis of the list system to have 50 percent of each sex (with a margin of one unit) on their lists of candidates; failing this, the list is rejected. The elections covered by this law are those to the European Parliament, regional and Senate elections (in departments with four or more seats, accounting for 50 percent of Senate seats), and municipal elections (for municipalities with at least 3,500 inhabitants).[10] For list system elections with only one round (European Parliament, Senate and regional elections), the law requires that the names on the lists alternate between men and women (or women and men) from top to bottom. For list system elections with two rounds (regional elections, and municipal elections in towns or cities with 3,500 or more inhabitants, including the Corsican Assembly), parity must be achieved per group of six candidates (men and women may be listed in any order). However, the government, which modified the electoral system in 2003 for regional elections in order to limit the extent of the proportional system, agreed to apply strict alternation on the lists in the regional elections of 2004, although these elections comprise two rounds.

For legislative elections, which use the single-member plurality/majority system, the law provides for a financial penalty for parties that fail to present 50 percent of candidates of each sex, with a margin of 2 percent. The state financing allocated to them on the basis of the number of votes obtained in the first round is reduced 'by a percentage equivalent to half the difference between the total number of candidates of each sex, out of the total number of candidates'. For instance, if one party presents 35 percent women and 65 percent men, the difference is 30 points, so its funding is reduced by 15 percent.

The departmental assemblies, which are elected by a uninominal system, are not affected by this law.

Implementation: The 2001 Municipal and Senatorial Elections and the 2002 Legislative Elections

The municipal elections of 11–18 March 2001, the first test for the new law, showed that it was capable of producing equality: some 38,000 women were elected to local councils in towns and cities with populations over 3,500, accounting for 47.5 percent of all council members. There was a significant gain (84.8 percent) compared to 1995, when 25.7 percent of council members elected were women. It would seem that the obligation to present 50 percent candidates of each sex was achieved without much difficulty: a poll of some 600 candidates heading up party lists showed that 78 percent of those interviewed deemed it 'easy' to apply the parity law in drawing up their lists.[11] The parties did not do the 'minimum service': according to a simulation carried out by the Ministry of the Interior, if, in the six candidate brackets, all parties had positioned three men on top followed by three women, the final outcome would have been 43 percent women.

The proportion of women elected varies with the size of the communities, from 47.4 percent for the smallest (population 3,500–9,000: hitherto, these municipalities had had the smallest numbers of women), to 48 percent for those with more than 30,000 inhabitants.

However, the impact of the law can also be assessed in contrary terms, since in those municipalities with less than 3,500 inhabitants (where no constraints existed previously), 30.1 percent women were elected as against 21 percent in 1995, representing a gain of more than 45 percent. There was little effect on the process of designating mayors, as they are chosen in indirect elections, about which this law is silent. Only 10.9 percent of the mayors elected were women. This percentage is an average that does not reveal the significant gap between towns and cities with more than 3,500 inhabitants (among these, only 6.9 percent were governed by women) and those with fewer than 3,500 (of which 11.2 percent were led by women). Inequality of the sexes in politics reflects inequality in the face of power.

Table 12: Women and Political Power in France

	Date	No. of Members	No. of Women	% Women	Type of Election
Government	2004 (Apr.)	42	10	23.8	
European Parliament	2004	78	34	43.5	List PR
National Assembly	2002	577	71	12.3	Majority uninominal, two rounds
Senate	2004	331	56	16.9	Parallel system: large regions: proportional list. Small regions: two-round system
Regional council	2004	1,880	895	47.6	List PR
General council (departments)	2004	3,966	411	10.4	Majority uninominal, two rounds
Local council (towns and cities with population over 3,500)	2001	8,004	38,106	47.5	Proportional list, two rounds
Local council (towns with population under 3,500)	2001	393,716	118,321	30.1	Majority list, two rounds
Mayor	2001	36,558	3,987	10.9	Majority uninominal, two rounds Indirect suffrage (by local council members)

Paradoxically, in France women figure much more prominently in the executive branch than in the legislative branch (the National Assembly and Senate).

The assemblies with the largest percentage of women are those elected by proportional list voting. The enforcement of the 6 June 2000 law, which requires male–female parity of candidates in list system elections, has accentuated the trend: after the 2001 election, women almost doubled their numbers on local councils in towns and cities with more than 3,500 inhabitants, where they now represent 47.5 percent of the council members.

Source: French Ministry of the Interior, 2004.

After the Senate elections of 23 September 2001—the second time the law was applied—10.9 percent of the seats in the upper chamber went to women (compared to 5.9 percent previously, with a gain of 84.7 percent). One-third of the seats (102 out of 321) were up for election, 74 through the list system (subject to parity) and 28 through the uninominal system (no parity requirement). Many women stood for election (42 percent of the candidates). At the end of the day, 22 out of the 102 (21.5 percent) were women. Most of the women elected (20 out of 22) won elections with proportional list voting, to which the parity constraints applied.

The number of women in the Senate was unexpected because many prominent persons (incumbent senators), particularly from the right wing, resorted to the strategy of creating multiple 'dissident' lists. Rather than run the risk of losing if placed in third position on the list, they preferred to appear in first positions on other lists. And the parties let members do as they pleased, not disavowing these 'wild card' considerations. However, far from harming the women's cause, this dispersion proved fatal to the right-wing candidates, as several left-wing women successfully challenged the right-wing candidates. For instance, four Communist women candidates, each positioned second after Socialist candidates, were elected.

Of the 22 women elected, 13 (59 percent) were from leftist parties (seven Socialists, five Communists and one Green). The Communist group has the highest proportion of women in the Senate (43.5 percent), followed by the Socialists (14.4 percent), and then by rightist groups—the Union centriste (Centrist Union) (13.2 percent), the Rassemblement Pour la République (RPR, Rally for the Republic) (4.2 percent), and the Républicains Indépendants (Independent Republicans) (2.4 percent).

Although it is effective, the new law should be improved, as it has gaps. Indeed, it has lost sight of the municipal executives, the inter-municipal structures and, above all, the departmental assemblies. As long as these remain male bastions (they have only 10.4 percent women members) they will have a negative impact on the distribution of nominations for legislative elections: the parties prefer to distribute the 'good' districts to notable party figures—those department-level elected officials who are known to voters.

Finally, and most importantly, the provisions of the law concerning legislative elections are not stringent enough, for they leave it up to the political parties: either present 50 percent candidates from each sex, or suffer financial penalties. If there is a lesson to be drawn from the legislative elections of 9 June and 16 June 2002, it is that the large parties have preferred to pay the fines rather than have more women candidates, for doing so would require 'sacrificing' the incumbents who would have to step down.

On the right, the two main parties, the Union pour la Majorité Présidentielle (UMP, Union for a Presidential Majority) and the Union pour la Démocratie Française (UDF, Union for French Democracy), have presented fewer than 20 percent women on their lists. On the left, the PS has been more respectful of the law, with 36 percent women candidates. Only the small parties, the PC and Greens, which have not had incumbents to deal with and with minorities in the legislature, have respected parity in their nominations. In the wake of the 2002 legislative elections, swept by the right, women held only 71 of 577 seats in the National Assembly as compared to 62 in 1997. This means that for the first time the parliamentarians of the right have more women than those of the left, in absolute figures: the UMP, with a majority, has 38 women out of its total 365 members, that is, 10.4 percent (the UDF has only two of 29, or 6.8 percent). The PS has no more than 23 women out of 141 deputies (16.3 percent), and the PC has four out of 21 (19 percent); and finally, the Greens have one out of three (33.3 percent).[12]

In all, the share of women in the National Assembly has increased from 11.9 percent in 1997 to 12.3 percent in 2002. These percentages summarize the failure of the law on parity in the legislative elections. Since it is not obligatory, a real concern remains that parties will continue to prefer men, who are better endowed with political resources, among their nominees.

The conclusion which can be drawn from the triple elections of 2004 is contradictory: 47.6 percent of women were elected to the regional councils (as against 27.5 percent in 1998), and 43.5 percent were elected to the European Parliament (in contrast to 40.2 percent in 1999), but only 10.9 percent of the deputies in the departmental assemblies are women (as against 8.6 percent in 1998). The law is paradoxical: it has accelerated the feminization of the assemblies elected through the proportional representation (PR) list system where women's representation was already high while not doing anything for those elected through the uninominal system. It has widened the gap between the former and the latter, which remain 'male' citadels. This is one of the negative consequences of an affirmative action law, which one would expect to have a more 'corrective' role where women are discriminated against most.

Conclusion

Despite its shortcomings, this law has resulted in a higher turnover of elected representatives, especially in PR elections. Parity, now beginning in France, has ushered in a new phase in the history of democracy.

The legislators themselves are convinced that women will bring about great changes. About 70 percent of respondents questioned in a 1999 survey thought that if one-third of the members of the National Assembly were women, politics would change in form, and 49 percent thought that it would change in substance.[13] Moreover, the concept of parity, by helping to give a new legitimacy to the debate on equality of the sexes, has spread to other sectors of society. From parity in elected assemblies, we have now shifted to parity in the civil service, in the economy, and even in the family.

Can the French law on parity be exported? Do we have to consider it as a purely French product? Born out of the deadlock of republicanism, the reform vindicates not quotas but equality, one of the terms of the republican trilogy (liberty, equality, fraternity) engraved on the frontispieces of schools and public buildings. It also emanates from a country with a Jacobin tradition, where the interventions of the central state are often codified in laws.

Technically speaking, the French legislation is easily exportable to countries that use list systems; this makes the principle of parity (such as alternating between men and women) easy to apply. Politically, however, it is hardly likely that such a law will be adopted in countries where the state is weaker or more decentralized, especially if it is not accustomed to intervening in matters specific to political parties. From the perspective of French law, the people and the representatives of the people are no longer an abstract and indivisible entity. They now have a sex, they are men and women 'who are living in this century', to use the expression of Elisabeth Guigou, then justice minister, speaking in the National Assembly.[14]

Notes

[1] They gained these rights under an ordinance of 21 April 1944.

[2] In 1936 French women did not have any political rights, yet three women became ministers.

[3] In the post-war period, the Popular Republic Movement (Catholic) also elected women, but this movement soon disappeared from the political scene.

[4] Gaspard, Françoise, 1994. 'De la parité: genèse d'un concept, naissance d'un mouvement' [On parity: the genesis of a concept, the birth of a movement]. *Nouvelles Questions Féministes*. Vol. 15, no. 4, p. 31.

[5] Vogel-Polsky, Eliane, 1994. 'Les impasses de l'égalité ou pourquoi les outils juridiques visant à l'égalité des femmes et des hommes doivent être repensés en terme de parité' [The impasse of equality, or why judicial measures for the equality of women and men have to be rethought in terms of parity]. *Parité-Infos*, special issue. No. 1, p. 9.

[6] In 1989, it organized a seminar on parity democracy.

[7] Gaspard, Françoise, Claude Servan-Schreiber and Anne Le Gall, 1992. *Au pouvoir citoyennes! Liberté, Egalité, Parité* [To power, women citizens! Liberty, equality, parity]. Paris: Seuil.

[8] Demichel, Francine, 1996. 'A parts égales: contribution au débat sur la parité' [Equal shares: Contribution to the debate on parity]. Paris: Recueil Dalloz Sirey, 21 March.

[9] According to an IPSOS poll (*Journal du Dimanche,* 22 June 1997), 80 percent of those interviewed said they approved of the idea of putting the objective of male–female parity into the constitution. See Sineau, Mariette, 1998. 'La féminisation du pouvoir vue par les Français-es et par les hommes politiques: images et représentations' [The feminization of power seen by the French and by political man: images and representations], in Jacqueline Martin (ed.). *La Parité: Enjeux et mise en oeuvre* [Parity: the stakes and the implementation]. Toulouse: Presses Universitaires du Mirail, pp. 61–81.

[10] Towns and cities with more than 3,500 inhabitants are a minority of the 36,000 municipalities, but account for two-thirds of the total number of council members elected.

[11] A CSA poll conducted from 15 to 18 February 2001.

[12] The three other women elected, who belong to small political groupings, sit (like the Green woman deputy) in the group of individuals not registered with any parliamentary group, as a minimum of 20 members of the Assembly are required to constitute such a group.

[13] Sineau, Mariette, 2001. *Profession: femme politique. Sexe et pouvoir sous la Cinquième République* [Profession: political woman. Gender and power under the Fifth Republic]. Paris: Presses de Sciences Po., p. 248.

[14] National Assembly, [official analytical report of the 3rd session], 15 December 1998.

Further Reading

Agacinski, Sylviane, 1998. *Politique des sexes* [The politics of the sexes]. Paris: Seuil 'Femmes en politique', 1997. *Pouvoirs,* No. 82

Génisson, Catherine, 2002. *La parité entre les femmes et les hommes: une avancée décisive pour la démocratie* [Parity between women and men: a decisive step forward for democracy]. Report to the Prime Minister. Observatory on parity between women and men. Paris: Documentation Française

'La Parité "pour"', 1995. *Nouvelles Questions Féministes.* Vol. 15, no. 4

'La Parité "contre"', 1995. *Nouvelles Questions Féministes.* Vol. 16, no. 2

Le piège de la parité: Arguments pour un débat [The parity trap: arguments towards a debate], 1999. Paris: Hachette-Littératures

Mossuz-Lavau, Janine, 1998. *Femmes/hommes: Pour la parité* [Women/men: for parity]. Paris: Presses de Sciences Po.

Sineau, Mariette, 2002. '*Parité* in Politics: From a Radical Idea to Consensual Reform', in Isabelle de Courtivron et al. *Beyond French Feminisms. Debates on Women, Politics and Culture in France, 1981–2001.* New York and London: Palgrave/St Martin's Press, pp. 11–126

— 2003. *Genderware: The Council of Europe and the Participation of Women in Political Life.* Strasbourg: Council of Europe Publishing

Case Study: Burkina Faso

Burkina Faso: Recruiting Women for Legislative Elections

Nestorine Compaoré

As in the other countries of francophone Africa, women are under-represented in the power structures of Burkina Faso. This case study addresses the issue of women's political participation in Burkina Faso, and in particular their access to the national legislature and the recruitment of women candidates by political parties when elections to the legislature are approaching. It emphasizes the impact of the electoral system and quotas on women's representation, the stages of the recruitment process, and the constraints women face in being elected to the legislature.

The Political Situation of Women

The available information indicates that women have unequal access to parliamentary representation compared with men. From 1946 to 2002, according to the cumulative data, a total of 750 men and 23 women (3 percent) served as members of the legislature, varying with successive political systems. The May 2002 elections saw only a modest rise, as the number of women legislators went from ten to 13. The statistics highlight the fact that women remain a silent majority in Burkina Faso; more than half the population (52 percent) continues to be marginalized and excluded from decision-making positions. It is men who hold a monopoly on power, who decide on the major plans for society, and who determine the current course of the nation. Several factors explain this state of affairs.

Influence of the Electoral System on Women

During the 1992 legislative elections, Burkina Faso used the proportional system with closed lists based on the highest average. Those elections followed a long period of rule under a state of emergency marked by numerous outbreaks of political violence.

In such a context, women and men were afraid and reluctant to play an active role in the political life of the country. These elections offered a sort of apprenticeship in democracy to the citizens of Burkina Faso, who were hesitant to become involved. Few women stood as candidates in those elections, and as a result few were elected.

During the 1997 legislative elections, using the same electoral arrangements, women's organizations took action and pleaded their cause vis-à-vis the political decision makers and the party leaderships, calling for more women candidates and for the use of quotas. Most of the leading parties promised different quotas for women on their lists. This was the case of the majority party, the Congrès pour la Démocratie et le Progrès (CPD, Congress for Democracy and Progress) which pledged a 30 percent quota for women. Although this promise was informal and was not carried out to the letter, women fared better in the elections and a change had taken place.

In the context of the 2002 legislative elections, the proportional system remained in place, but this time based on the largest remainder. This system accords priority to closed lists, with two different lists per party, one regional and one national. However, the lobbying efforts by the women's organizations did not have the anticipated effects because of an ill-defined strategy. They demanded that all parties' lists include at least 25 percent women candidates. When the lists were published, however, women accounted for only 16 percent of the names on the national lists and less than 10 percent of the total on the national and regional lists, and there were major disparities between the different parties. As Yacouba Ouedraogo noted, 'With 39 candidates of a total of 222 hopefuls (i.e. 17.5 percent) in the 13 electoral regions, the Alliance pour la Démocratie et la Fédération/ Rassemblement des Démocrates Africains [ADF/RDA: Alliance for Democracy and Federation/African Democrats Coalition] went furthest in seeking to strike a gender balance'.[1] In the Front des Forces Sociales (FFS, Front of Social Forces) and the Coalition des Forces Démocratiques (CFD, Coalition of Democratic Forces), the ratio was 13 men to one woman, that is, women made up just over 7 percent of the candidates.

While the proportional list system may facilitate the promotion of women, its effects are not really felt unless the political parties have made the decision to promote women and place them on their lists in positions such that they have a chance of getting elected. Few parties nominate women, and they are generally placed at the bottom of the lists. An analysis of nominations of the five leading parties for the 2002 elections shows a very marked imbalance between the sexes. Women were largely relegated to the lists of alternate candidates; neither their number nor their positions on the lists yielded good results.

This situation is explained in part by the way the candidates were recruited to make up the parties' lists.

The Recruitment of Women for the Political Parties' Lists

Some 20 people (political leaders and candidates of both sexes) were interviewed during the legislative elections in 2002 for this case study. The interviews reveal that the selection of women was a function of five main criteria: the payment of a deposit; personal ties with a political leader; the need to attract female voters; the place of origin of the candidates; and finally their abilities.

The payment of a deposit. In order to register on a list of candidates, some contending parties required that nominees pay a deposit of more than 3,500,000 CFA francs. Such a sum is not possible for the vast majority of women who would be willing to run for office. Very often, women whose experience and skills would qualify them to run are ruled out because they lack the financial means to meet this requirement. The financial problem is thus the first barrier women candidates face, because many political parties do not pay the deposit required of candidates.

Personal ties to a party leader. Frequently, family or friendship ties with certain party leaders have been the catalyst for women's being recruited to political groupings. Certain parties whose recruitment is based on ethnicity or region, or those whose financial base is limited, go to their women friends or allies to draw up their lists of candidates. In such cases, women join political parties without the proper preparation and without any experience.

Often they are used to replace elected women who have started to become autonomous and independent of their male supporters in the political sphere. Thus, some women who are totally unknown in the public sphere are selected to run for seats without any previous experience, rather than more experienced women who have held elective office. Some women who had been elected in the past stated that this was the reason why they were not nominated to run for the 2002 legislative elections. This kind of selection criterion is unclear, changeable and a deterrent for those women who are interested in seeking a party nomination.

Yet, while this kind of recruitment can give politically inexperienced women a chance, it can also make these same women victims, that is, they are subject to the changing motivations of their backer. Many women who were elected in the past state that they have been cast aside after changes in the ties with their supporters or because of the power or leadership struggle between male party leaders. With this form of recruitment, the placement of women in the parties, and their tenure, are all subjected to the personal ties and interests of certain political leaders. The latter's personal preferences replace objective criteria.

This practice on the part of political leaders raises some questions about their perception of the citizenship of women in the country and the meaning of democracy. As Naila Kabeer points out, Burkina Faso was colonized and the idea of citizenship which means that individuals are the bearers of rights has not yet taken root in society.[2] The notion of equality which is central to the idea of citizenship and democracy is still a vague word, because men and women are not considered equal in rights when it comes to competition for elective office.

The need to attract the female electorate. The percentage of females in the population of Burkina Faso (52 percent) is reason enough for the parties to try to attract the women's vote during elections. Thanks to the network of women's organizations, women are easier to mobilize for campaign rallies and balloting, and go to the polling places in larger numbers. Women are often labelled 'electoral cattle'. Mindful of the weight of the women's vote in election results, the political parties have included some women candidates to lure this female electorate. Unfortunately, too many women have yet to become conscious of their electoral potential.

Candidates' place of origin. The division of the national territory into 13 electoral regions for the 2002 legislative elections forced the political parties to recruit candidates from these different regions in order to attract the local electorate. This approach meant that some women, who enjoy a certain level of socio-economic power, registered in regions for which there were few male candidates. In such cases, parties did not seek candidates because of their competence, but instead nominated women who had leverage, either regionally or nationally.

The candidates' qualifications. In Burkina Faso, several women intellectuals have emerged as a group; they have been inspired by the political context to master the art of participation in politics. These women joined different parties depending on their personal political convictions in some cases, or were sought out by the leadership of the major parties because of their qualifications in other cases. Women leading national women's organizations were encouraged to participate because of their ability to mobilize the female electorate. This trend is embryonic, and involves only a minority of well-to-do women intellectuals. The party leaders who really make qualifications a criterion in choosing women candidates for their lists are still few and far between. Accordingly, even though the change that has begun may have an impact on the quality of women's representation in future, it still needs to be consolidated.

Other information suggests that subjective criteria often prevail when it comes to recruiting women to the political parties' electoral lists. In his article, Yacouba Ouedraogo further notes that one woman candidate has denounced 'the senseless reasons given for excluding women from public office'. The candidate added that often the only reason invoked for not giving a woman a place on a list is the fact that she is not a man.

In general, the selection of candidates for the parties' lists has been disputed by several contenders (men and women), as testified to by the highly-publicized conflicts provoked by this procedure. The political weight of the candidates within the parties is determined by their placement on the party lists. In this context, the promoters of women candidates have limited room for manoeuvre to defend their own position and those of their 'protégées' vis-à-vis dissatisfied male colleagues. The problems related to candidate selection are among the causes of women's weak representation on the party lists.

Lessons Learned

The influence of the electoral system on the recruitment of women cannot yet be discerned in the context of Burkina Faso. Several other factors appear to be more important, such as the selection and positioning of candidates on the electoral lists. This is influenced by clientelism, allegiance to the parties, and power struggles between political leaders, creating unstable alliances.

Without a solid network of women's groups there can be little influence on the nomination and selection criteria and the political parties' procedures to press for increased female representation and participation. Advocacy and lobbying activities conducted to promote a higher proportion of women in winnable positions on party lists have had only limited impact because of inadequate advocacy and lobbying strategies.

The political culture of Burkina Faso does not as yet allow for the selection of candidates in a democratic manner. Political immaturity is expressed in the lack of clear criteria for choosing candidates to elected office. The rules of conduct are not sufficiently clear or respected by the political leadership.

The political parties do not respect their pledges to implement quotas for women's participation. There is no pressure on them to do so insofar as women's groups are not well organized in their advocacy activities.

In general, young women (with or without schooling) are not socialized to participate equally in politics. In many cases they do not have the experience needed to be able to claim leadership. They still need much more support from male political leaders in order to gain access to and influence in the political arena.

The place and the role of women in the political parties affect their access to government posts. Only one of the 48 official recognized political parties is led by a woman, and the leadership of the major parties is still the exclusive domain of men. Women are rarely active members of the parties, which makes it difficult for them to reach leadership positions. In general, their membership is controlled by men (relatives or friends) who choose them and back them in line with their own interests. In these conditions, the risk is that the commitment of some women who are politically active may not be the result of their own individual decisions and motivations.

The way women are recruited in many instances deprives them of autonomy. The alliances and allegiance to their backers have resulted in tokenism rather than activism. Many women feel insecure, which hinders them from defending their ideals and political programmes as representatives of a particular social group with specific interests.

Challenges

The contemporary challenges women face in increasing their representation in the National Assembly include:

- gaining political knowledge and experience;
- building a solid network of women's groups and creating strategic alliances;
- mobilizing and involving large numbers of qualified women of all ages in active politics;
- enabling women to exercise full citizenship equal to that of men;
- changing the role and enhancing the position of women within the leadership bodies of the political parties;
- influencing the nomination and selection of candidates (men and women) on electoral lists; and
- mobilizing or gaining access to financial resources (especially state allocation to parties) to fund their electoral activities.

Strategies

On the basis of the above, several strategies are recommended to increase women's representation.

Building a solid and inclusive network to promote women's political participation. Without an active and sustained pressure group, there is no doubt that women's political participation will not increase as quickly as desired. However, divisions and conflicts between women's groups result in a lack of solidarity regarding this goal. Women have to find a way to build a solid and inclusive network to support women's candidacies and develop a common voice with specific interests and political agendas. Being supported by grass-roots associations and collectives is a means to help women candidates overcome their sense of insecurity and become politically empowered.

Lobbying for formal quotas and control. For many years, political parties have lured women with promises regarding the implementation of informal quotas. However, in practice they were not implemented, and the introduction of formal legal quotas, with a placement mandate for women to be placed in winnable positions, should be considered.

Increasing knowledge about politics. For more effective political participation, women must have their own political opinions; they need to be able to express them clearly and in a relevant manner, and they must be able to discern the differences between the orientations and programmes of the political parties. They should be able to grasp the stakes and the rules of the political game, and master the abstract and specialized language used in political debate. Thus training is needed to meet the immense needs of women at these different levels.

The civic education of female students in primary and secondary schools is also useful for forming a contingent of women who are well versed in political issues. Education and learning through political action from a young age should help raise the civic consciousness of girls and encourage them to participate in the political parties at the grass-roots level so as to gain access to positions of authority in leadership structures later.

Mobilizing and involving large numbers of women in active politics. Women need to be mobilized to articulate their specific needs, insights and motivations in order to allow for the emergence of leaders who are capable of expressing the points of view of the hitherto-silent half of society. Supported from grass-roots associations and collectives is a means to help women candidates overcome their sense of insecurity and become politically empowered.

Setting up a fund to support women's political participation. If the most qualified women are excluded from becoming candidates because of their poverty, creating a fund to support women's political participation is one of the strategies needed if the best-qualified women are to emerge in national politics.

This case study has shown that a variety of factors influence the recruitment of women as candidates for election. The electoral system therefore has less influence than in other established democracies which use proportional representation. To be better represented in the legislature, women must mobilize, gain the skills needed, and receive financial support from, if possible, a special support fund. Finally, a law imposing a minimum quota of women candidates is also proposed to overcome the challenges of candidate selection by the political parties.

Notes

[1] Ouedraogo, Yacouba, 2002. 'La palme de la misogynie au FFS et à la CFD' [The prize for misogyny goes to the FFS and the CFD]. *Journal Le Pays.* No. 2604, p. 3.

[2] Kabeer, Naila, 2002. 'Citizenship, Affiliation and Exclusion: Perspective from the South'. *IDS Bulletin.* Vol. 33, no. 2.

Chapter 4

Chapter 4

Drude Dahlerup

Increasing Women's Political Representation: New Trends in Gender Quotas

Given the slow speed at which the number of women in politics is growing, different policy measures are being introduced to reach gender balance in political institutions. Quotas present one such mechanism to increase, and safeguard, women's presence in parliaments and are now being introduced all over the world. What are the arguments for and against the use of quotas? What types of quota have led to substantial increase in women's political representation in practice? Which quotas work best in different electoral systems and how can they be effectively enforced? This chapter examines the world of electoral quotas and the ways in which quotas can lead, and have led, to historic leaps in women's political representation.

1. What are Quotas?

Quotas for women entail that women must constitute a certain number or percentage of the members of a body, whether it is a candidate list, a parliamentary assembly, a committee or a government. Quotas aim at increasing women's representation in publicly elected or appointed institutions such as governments, parliaments and local councils. Gender quotas draw legitimacy from the discourse of exclusion, according to which the main reasons for women's under-representation are the exclusionary practices of the political parties and the political institutions at large. Quotas place the burden of candidate recruitment not on the individual woman, but on those who control the recruitment process, first and foremost the political parties.[1] Quotas force those who nominate and select to start recruiting women and give women a chance which they do not have today in most parts of the world.

141

The two most common types of electoral gender quotas are candidate quotas and reserved seats.

Candidate quotas specify the minimum percentage of candidates for election that must be women, and apply to political parties' lists of candidates for election. *Legal candidate quotas* are laid down in the constitution, in electoral laws or in political party laws. Such quotas as are enacted in legislation force all political parties to recruit the required percentage of women. *Voluntary party quotas* are adopted voluntarily by political parties, and are most common in centre–left-leaning parties, while liberal and conservative parties generally tend to be reluctant about or strongly opposed to adopting quotas.

Reserved seats set aside a certain number of seats for women among representatives in a legislature, specified either in the constitution or by legislation. One might argue that reserved seats should not be counted among electoral quotas. However, reserved seats today come in many different types, some excluding, others including, the election of women, rather than appointment, to fill these seats. In Uganda 56 seats, one elected in each district by a special electorate, are reserved for women. In Rwanda, 30 percent of the seats, elected by a special procedure, are reserved for women according to the constitution. In Tanzania 20 percent of the seats are reserved for women and allocated to the political parties in proportion to the number of parliamentary seats won in an election. Reserved seats can also be filled by appointment, as in Kenya and some Arab states.

Previous notions of having reserved seats for only one or for very few women, representing a vague and all-embracing category of 'women', are no longer considered sufficient. Today, quota systems aim at ensuring that women constitute at least a 'critical minority' of 30 or 40 percent or aim for 'gender balance' as demanded in various international treaties and conventions. Quotas may be seen as a temporary measure, that is to say, until the barriers for women's entry into politics are removed.

Most quotas aim at increasing women's representation because the problem to be addressed is usually the under-representation of women. This is particularly relevant since women constitute more than 50 percent of the population in most countries, but worldwide they hold less than 16 percent of the parliamentary seats.

Gender-neutral quotas. Quota systems may, however, be constructed as gender-neutral. In this case, the requirement may be, for example, that neither gender should occupy more than 60 percent or less that 40 percent of the positions on a party list or in a decision-making body. While quotas for women set a maximum for men's representation, gender-neutral quotas construct a maximum limit for both sexes. Gender-neutral quota rules are sometimes used as a strategic choice in order to refute the arguments of opponents of quotas that they are discriminatory against men.

Quotas as a 'fast track'. Today we see quotas being introduced where women historically have been almost totally excluded from politics, as in Jordan or Afghanistan. In such cases, gender quotas represent a kick-start for women to gain entry to politics. In other cases, quotas are introduced to consolidate and further strengthen the gains women have made in accessing decision-making positions—or to prevent a backlash. While the Scandinavian countries represent a model of gradual increase in women's representation (see the Dahl quotation below), countries like Argentina, Costa Rica, South Africa and Rwanda represent a new 'fast track model'.[2]

'One cannot deal with the problem of female representation by a quota system alone. Political parties, the educational system, NGOs, trade unions, churches—all must take responsibility within their own organizations to systematically promote women's participation, from the bottom up. This will take time. It will not happen overnight, or in one year or five years; it will take one or two generations to realize significant change. This is what we are working on in Sweden. We did not start with a quota system. First we laid the groundwork to facilitate women's entry into politics. We prepared the women to ensure they were competent to enter the field; and we prepared the system, which made it a little less shameful for men to step aside. Then we used quotas as an instrument in segments and institutions where we needed a breakthrough.'

Birgitta Dahl, former Speaker of Parliament, Sweden

2. Quotas: Pros and Cons

Various arguments have been put forward for and against the introduction of quotas as a means to increase the political presence of women. The pros and cons are listed below.

2.1. Cons

- Quotas are against the principle of equal opportunity for all, since women are given preference.
- Political representation should be a choice between ideas and party platforms, not between social categories.
- Quotas are undemocratic, because voters should be able to decide who is elected.
- Quotas imply that politicians are elected because of their gender, not because of their qualifications, and that better-qualified candidates are pushed aside.
- Many women do not want to get elected just because they are women.
- Introducing quotas creates significant conflicts within the party organization.
- Quotas for women will be followed by demands for quotas for other groups, which will result in a politics of sheer group-interest representation.

2.2. Pros

- Quotas for women do not discriminate, but compensate for actual barriers that prevent women from their fair share of the political seats.
- Quotas imply that there are several women together in a committee or assembly, thus minimizing the stress often experienced by the token women.
- Women have the right as citizens to equal representation.
- Women's experience is needed in political life.
- Men cannot represent the interest of women. Only many women can represent the diversity of women.
- Election is about representation, not educational qualifications.
- Women are just as qualified as men, but women's qualifications are downgraded and minimized in a male-dominated political system.
- Quotas do not discriminate against individual men. Rather quota rules limit the tendency of political parties to nominate only men. For the voters, the opportunities are expanded, since it now becomes possible to vote for women candidates.
- Introducing quotas may cause conflicts, but only temporarily.
- Several internationally recognized conventions on gender equality have set targets for women's political representation, including the Convention on the Elimination of All Forms of Discrimination Against Women (CEDAW) which 179 countries are now party to, as well as the 1995 Beijing Platform for Action.
- How can it be justified that men occupy more than 80 percent of the parliamentary seats in the world?

The ways in which the problems of women's under-representation are framed have important consequences for what strategies are considered to be relevant. If the problem is discursively constructed as women's limited knowledge or experience, then educating women is seen as the right remedy. If, on the other hand, institutional mechanisms of exclusion are considered to be the main problem, then the burden of change is placed on the institutions and political parties, which are seen as responsible for the discriminatory practices.

2.3. Two Concepts of Equality

In general, quotas for women represent a shift from one concept of equality to another. The classic liberal notion of equality was a notion of 'equal opportunity' or 'competitive equality'. Removing the formal barriers, for example, giving women voting rights, was considered sufficient. The rest was up to the individual women.

Following strong feminist pressure in the last few decades, a second concept of equality is gaining increasing relevance and support—the notion of 'equality of result'. The argument is that just removing formal barriers does not produce real equal opportunity. Direct discrimination, as well as a complex pattern of hidden barriers, prevents women from getting their share of political influence. Quotas and other forms of active equality measures are thus a means towards equality of result. The argument is based on the experience that equality as a goal cannot be reached by formal equal treatment as a means. If barriers exist, it is argued, compensatory measures must be introduced as a means to reach equality of result.

3. The World of Quotas

In 2005, more than 40 countries have introduced electoral quotas by amending the constitution or introducing different types of legislation. In more than 50 other countries, major political parties have voluntarily introduced quotas requiring women to comprise a certain percentage of the candidates they nominate for election. Because of quotas, countries like Argentina, Costa Rica, Mozambique, Rwanda and South Africa are now contending with the Nordic countries as world leaders, countries which for many decades have topped the ranking in terms of women's parliamentary representation.

An overview over the use of legal electoral quotas is given in table 13. As the table shows, most legal gender quota systems in politics were introduced only during the last decade.

Different types of quota are prominent in the world's regions.[3] In Latin America, the leading region in terms of quotas, constitutional or legal changes have opened up the way for gender quotas in politics. In the regions of Africa, the Balkans and South Asia many different types of quotas regimes have been introduced recently. In Western Europe quotas mainly come in the form of voluntary party quotas, but with France and Belgium as exceptions. In Eastern and Central Europe very few parties have passed quota regulations and no legal gender quota regulations for parliament are in place. The legacy of quotas as 'forced emancipation' under communism strengthens the opponents of quotas in this region, even if this legacy partly rests on a myth. In the Arab world, quotas as reserved seats for various groups (religious, ethnic and clan) are well known, and very recently a number of countries have included 'women' as a group for whom certain seats should also be reserved.

As a consequence of gender quotas, a dramatic change has taken place recently in the global ranking order of countries based on their level of female political representation. As a result of quota provisions, Rwanda, Costa Rica, Argentina, Mozambique and South Africa are now placed very high in the world league of the Inter-Parliamentary Union. The five Nordic states, Denmark, Finland, Iceland, Norway and Sweden, which for a long time were virtually alone at the top of the ranking table, are now being challenged.

Table 13: Countries with Constitutional Quota and/or Election Law Quota Regulation for the National Parliament*

	Quota Type (in Constitution and/or in Law)**	Year Introduced	Present Quota System (Percentage)	Percentage of Women in Parliament (Most Recent Election)	
Americas					
Argentina	C, L	1991, 1991	30	34.1	(2003)
Bolivia	L	1997	30	18.5	(2002)
Brazil	L	1997	30	8.2	(2002)
Costa Rica	L	1996	40	35.1	(2002)
Dominican Republic	L	1997	25	17.3	(2002)
Ecuador	L	1997	20	16.0	(2002)
Guyana	C	N/A	33	20.0	(2001)
Honduras	L	2000	30	5.5	(2001)
Mexico	L	2002	30	22.6	(2003)
Panama	L	1997	30	9.9	(1999)
Paraguay	L	1996	20	10.0	(2003)
Peru	L	1997	30	17.5	(2001)
Europe					
Belgium	L	1994	33	35.3	(2003)
Bosnia and Herzegovina	L	2001	33	16.7	(2002)
France	C, L	1999, 2000	50	12.1	(2002)
Macedonia	L	2002	30	17.5	(2002)
Serbia and Montenegro	L	2002	30	7.9	(2003)
Africa and the Middle East					
Djibouti	L	2002	10	10.8	(2003)
Eritrea	C	N/A	30	N/A	(2001)
Jordan	L	2003	6 seats	5.5	(2003)
Kenya	C	1997	6 seats	6.7	(2002)
Morocco	L	2002	30 seats	10.8	(2002)
Rwanda	C, L	2003	30	48.8	(2003)
Sudan	L	N/A	10	9.7	(2000)
Tanzania	C, L	2000	20–30	22.3	(2000)
Uganda	C, L	1995, 1989	56 seats	24.7	(2001)
Asia					
Afghanistan	C	2004	25	25.0	(2004)
Armenia	L	1999	5	4.6	(2003)
Bangladesh	C	2004	45 seats	2.0	(2001)
Indonesia	L	2003	30	11,0	(2004)
Korea, Democratic Rep.	L	N/A	20	N/A	(2003)
Nepal	C, L	1990, 1990	5	5.9	(1999)
Pakistan	L	2002	60 seats	21.6	(2002)
Philippines	C, L	1995, 1995	20	17.8	(2001)
Taiwan	C	1997	10–25	22.2	(2001)

* Lower house or single house in a unicameral legislature. Bolivia, Brazil, Peru, Greece, Serbia and Montenegro, Namibia, South Africa, Tanzania, Bangladesh, China, India, Nepal, Pakistan, the Philippines and Taiwan also have *constitutional* quotas for local and/or regional parliaments. See <http://www.quotaproject.org>.
** C refers to quota provisions stipulated in the constitution, and L refers to quota provisions stipulated in law.
Source: Dahlerup, Drude and Lenita Freidenvall, 2005. 'Quotas as a "Fast Track" to Equal Representation for *Women*'. *International Feminist Journal of Politics.* Vol. 7, no. 1, March; and <http://www.quotaproject.org>.

3.1. The Nordic Countries

The Nordic countries have for decades had the highest political representation of women in the world. This increase took place largely during the last 30 years. In 2005, women constituted over 45 percent of the members of parliament in Sweden, 38 percent in Finland, 37 percent in Denmark, 36 percent in Norway and 30 percent in Iceland following elections held between 2001 and 2005.

Contrary to common perceptions, no constitutional clause or law demands a high representation of women in Scandinavia. For the most part the increase can be attributed to sustained pressure by women's groups within parties as well as the women's movement in general. Women mobilized and organized to ensure that the political parties increased their number of women candidates, that is to say, women candidates who had a fair chance of winning. The real take-off of the increase in women's representation in the Nordic countries happened in the 1970s before any party-installed candidate quotas.

The pressure to increase women's representation was applied to all political parties in Scandinavia. Some parties, especially centre–left parties, responded by applying voluntary party quotas. In three Scandinavian countries, quotas were introduced based on decisions made by the political parties themselves, first in parties to the left and in the social democratic parties during the 1970s, 1980s and 1990s. Most centre and right-wing parties, however, have considered quotas 'un-liberal'. It was not until 1993 that the Swedish Social Democratic Party introduced the principle of 'every second on the list a woman'. In a 50 : 50 percent quota system like this, the women are no more 'quota women' than the men are 'quota men'.

3.2. Political Parties and Quotas

At elections, the quota system touches the very foundation of the democratic process, and according to opponents it may clash with the principle of the voters' right to choose the representatives they want. However, as chapter 3 has indicated, nominations are the crucial stage and the power of the nominations rests with the political parties, not with the voters. Since the political parties in most countries are the real gatekeepers to political office, quotas may lead to a dispute between the central and regional/local branches of the political parties. The local branches often fight for their right to choose their own candidates without the interference of the central party organization.

Undoubtedly, it is easier to introduce quotas for women when other forms of quota are also formally introduced, for example, quotas based on occupational or ethnic criteria. Regional 'quotas' which distribute the parliamentary seats to various parts of the country, not just according to their share of the population, but giving non-proportional shares of the seats to certain regions over others, are in fact used in most countries. However, such arrangements are seldom called quotas.

3.3. Transitional States and Parliamentary Turnover

> The implementation of a quota system is easier in a new political system than in an older one, where most seats might be 'occupied'.

History seems to prove that the implementation of a quota system is made easier in a new political system than in an older one, where most seats might be 'occupied', and consequently a conflict may arise between the interests of new groups and those of the incumbents. In general, it is less complicated to implement quotas for an appointed post than for an elected one. Also, gender quotas are easier to implement in proportional list systems than in plurality–majority systems, where each party only presents one candidate in each constituency. In post-conflict societies, the international community today is putting strong pressure on the actors of reconstruction to take effective measures to include women. Thus we see gender quotas of 25–35 percent being introduced in strongly patriarchal cultures where very few women were represented earlier, for example, in the post-conflict societies of Afghanistan and Iraq. Quota provisions have also been introduced in the Balkans following strong pressure from the local women's movements in alliance with the international community.

3.4. Token Women?

In India, the 74th constitutional amendment requires that 33 percent of the seats in local elected bodies in the towns and in the countryside (the *panchayats*) are reserved for women. The policy of reservation, as well as of quotas, is a well known, and much disputed, measure in Indian politics. Gender quotas are thus combined with reserved seats for scheduled castes as part of a rotation system, according to which it is decided in advance which category will be allowed to contest for the seat of every ward. This system has resulted in the election of several million Indian women to local councils. The Indian women's movement has mobilized and educated women candidates. Quotas for women in the Lok Sabha (the lower house of the national parliament) have been proposed but rejected again and again by the parliament. Bangladesh and

Pakistan have also introduced gender quotas for local councils, as have Namibia, Eritrea, Tanzania and Uganda.

> 'We have tried reserved parliamentary seats for village panchayats, and from my experience, this is a very effective measure. We have reserved 33 percent of the seats in panchayats for women. Before this policy, we did not have women prepared for leadership positions; but as a result of the policy, political parties have to search for women. We got a mixed response. Some men did not want women to come forward, so they put forward their wives, sisters-in-law and mothers. But talented, educated women also came forward. Now the old argument that there are no able women to become candidates for legislative assemblies no longer holds. Because now the women serving as mayors and as chairmen of the municipal committees will be groomed as prospective candidates for parliament. More and more women have been elected to panchayats—and this is a valuable pool of women for legislative assemblies. Thus the reservation of seats is a very effective measure, especially in countries such as India where there is such meager representation of women in parliament. In India, only 6.5 percent of parliamentarians, 39 members of a house of 543, are women. A bill for reservation of seats for women in parliament is also pending; discussions are ongoing. It has not yet passed, but I think it will see the light of day.'
>
> *Sushma Swaraj, MP, India*

In India, women elected on the basis of quotas have been labelled 'proxy women', because they could be placed in the local council as stand-ins for their husbands, who might even participate in the meetings in their place. In other parts of the world as well, women in politics, especially those elected through quotas, might be seen as 'token women'. Research on 'quota' women has revealed many cases of purely symbolic representation of women, especially if the women elected have no power base in a constituency of their own, or in the parties or in strong movements outside the political institutions. However, there are also many success stories of women who felt totally isolated and powerless in the beginning but eventually gained confidence and influence. It seems to be crucial for the effectiveness of women politicians that capacity-building programmes are offered by women's movements or by international organizations.[4]

> 'Quotas are a double-edged sword. On the one hand, they oblige men to think about including women in decision-making, since men must create spaces for women. On the other hand, since it is men who are opening up these spaces, they will seek out women who they will be able to manage—women who will more easily accept the hegemony of men.'
>
> *Anna Balletbo, former MP, Spain*

Double standards are at play, however, when women politicians are accused of being too dependent on their parties to which they owe their seat, as if this were not the case for most male politicians as well. Women politicians are also accused of being in politics just because of their family connections—as if this is not the case for male politicians, too, especially in clientelist systems. Even if creating loyal women politicians was no doubt the motive behind some quota reforms, as it was for instance in Pakistan and Peru, token women may not necessarily be the result provided capacity-building and critical support by women's organizations are available for the women elected.

4. The Implementation of Quotas

Quotas rules are not enough. Whether a quota system meets its objective depends largely on the process and method of implementation and enforcement. While reserved seats are by their nature enforceable, candidate quotas are often not enforced. If the method of implementation is not clearly defined and enforceable, a candidate quota requirement of 30, 40 or 50 percent is not likely to be met. The quota must be embedded in the selection and the nomination processes of political parties from the very beginning.

From single-country studies we know, for instance, that the introduction of quotas requiring a minimum of 30 percent of each gender on an electoral list does not automatically result in women winning 30 percent of seats. Political parties may meet requirement that 30 percent of their candidates must be women but place them at the bottom of the lists, in largely unwinnable positions. Additionally, if the number of seats to be filled in a constituency is small and many parties stand for election, by and large men will be elected as they usually hold the top positions on a party list. In some countries using a proportional representation (PR) electoral system with open lists, voters may demote women candidates (or promote male candidates), thereby negating women's chances of election. In other recent cases, however, voters do seem to prefer women candidates, especially on the lists of left-leaning candidates, in which cases open lists with preferential voting possibilities will benefit women candidates.

> Rules are not enough. Whether a quota system reaches its objective depends largely on the process of implementation.

For these reasons it is crucial that quota systems and their rules for enforcement are introduced that work with the electoral system. Several quota laws have been amended, or today are drafted, with **placement mandates** specifying which positions women are to hold on electoral lists. The following are examples of quotas that are enforceable in practice.

Iraq. According to section 4(3) of the 2004 electoral law, political parties must place women in every third position on political party lists—'no fewer than 1 out of the first 3 candidates on the list must be a woman, no fewer than 2 out of the first 6 candidates' until the end of the list. As a result, 31 percent of representatives elected in 2005 were women.

Argentina. The 1991 law on quotas requires party lists to have a minimum of 30 percent women among their candidates. Subsequent revisions of the law fixed a minimum number of positions that would have to be accorded to women: one woman where between two and four positions are available; at least two women where between five and eight positions are available; at least three women where between nine and 11 positions are available; and at least four women where 12–14 positions are available. As a result, 34 percent of the representatives elected in 2003 were women.

Sweden. Several political parties, including the Social Democrats, the Left Party and the Green Party, have adopted 'zipper' lists where a list of male candidates is 'zipped' or alternated with a list of female candidates, resulting in women in every 'other' position on the party list.

However, too often scant attention is paid to enforcement of the quota system. This may be because of an underlying perception that quotas are supposed to be purely symbolic, or because the connection between the goals of a policy and the measures needed to implement it has been overlooked. Some general rules can be considered.

1. The type of quota system needs to be compatible with the electoral system in use.

2. Rules about the ranking order of the candidates, or placement mandates, are essential for the implementation of candidate quotas.

3. Sanctions for non-compliance are very important. Appropriate authority must be given to the implementation agency, such as the electoral management body, to reject candidate lists that do not comply with the requirements. In the case of voluntary party quotas, a high-level organ within political parties should be tasked with ensuring compliance.

Without specifications regarding the ranking of candidates on party lists, as well as sanctions for non-compliance, quota provisions may be merely symbolic. On the other hand, where electoral gender quotas have fulfilled these qualifications, they have proved extremely effective in increasing the political representation of women the world over.

5. In Summary

1. The aim of quota systems is to increase considerably the political representation of women.

2. Successful quota systems lead to:
- the active recruitment of women by political parties in order to have a sufficient number of qualified candidates to fulfil the quota;
- a larger minority of women, rather than a token few, who will be able to influence political norms and culture; and
- women having the possibility to influence the decision-making process as individuals or with specific points of view and concerns.

3. It is not sufficient to pass rules that ensure women 30 percent of the seats. The next step of implementing quotas is critical. With respect to implementation, the following should be kept in mind.
- The more vague the regulations, the higher the risk that the quota regulations will not be properly implemented. Quotas for candidates do not automatically lead to the election of more women.
- Pressure from women's organizations and other groups is necessary for the successful implementation of quotas.
- There must be sanctions for non-compliance with the quota requirement.

4. Contrary to what many supporters of quotas believed or hoped for, in quite a lot of countries conflicts over quotas for women seem to return again and again with each electoral cycle. In other countries where there had been vehement discussions about the introduction of quotas, the conflicts died down once the quota system was in place. But in still other parts of the world, gender quotas have been introduced after almost no controversy at all.

5. It is important to remember that quotas for women do not remove all barriers for women in politics. Stigmatization of women politicians may even increase in quota systems. Difficulties combining family life, work life and politics still remain a severe obstacle to women's full citizenship. Further, political representation cannot stand alone, but must be complemented with necessary socio-economic changes in society at large.

Although there is no single remedy for increasing women's presence in parliament, the discussions on quotas and electoral systems point to some important options. Some countries have refined certain approaches as a result of trial and error and long years of experimentation. By making these experiences available to women around the world, we hope to provide some guidelines and directions for future trials in this field. In the next chapter, we look at the women already in parliament and discuss what they can do to enhance their effectiveness.

Notes

[1] Dahlerup, Drude and Lenita Freidenvall, 2005. 'Quotas as a "Fast Track" to Equal Representation for Women'. *International Feminist Journal of Politics*. Vol. 7, no. 1, pp. 26–48.

[2] Dahlerup and Freidenwall 2005, op. cit.

[3] Electoral gender quotas in all major regions of the world are compared in Dahlerup, Drude (ed.), forthcoming 2006. *Women, Quotas and Politics*. London: Routledge.

[4] The 'effectiveness' of women politicians is discussed further in Dahlerup, forthcoming 2006 (op. cit.), and in Hassim, Shireen, 2003. 'Representation, Participation and Democratic Effectiveness: Feminist Challenges to Representative Democracy in South Africa', in A. M. Goetz and S. Hassim (eds). *No Shortcuts to Power: African Women in Politics and Policy Making*. London: Zed Books, pp. 81–109.

References and Further Reading

Ballington, Julie (ed.), 2004. *The Implementation of Quotas: African Experiences*. Stockholm: International IDEA

Dahlerup, Drude, 1988. 'From a Small to a Large Minority: Women in Scandinavian Politics'. *Scandinavian Political Studies*. Vol. 11, no. 4, pp. 275–98

— (ed.), forthcoming 2006. *Women, Quotas and Politics*. London: Routledge

— and Lenita Freidenvall, 2005. 'Quotas as a "Fast Track" to Equal Representation for Women'. *International Feminist Journal of Politics*. Vol. 7, no. 1, March, pp. 26–48

Hassim, Shireen, 2003. 'Representation, Participation and Democratic Effectiveness: Feminist Challenges to Representative Democracy in South Africa', in A. M. Goetz and S. Hassim (eds). *No Shortcuts to Power: African Women in Politics and Policy Making*. London: Zed Books, pp. 81–109

International IDEA, 2003. *The Implementation of Quotas: Asian Experiences*. Stockholm: International IDEA

— 2003. *The Implementation of Quotas: Latin American Experiences*. Stockholm: International IDEA

— and Stockholm University, Global Database of Electoral Quotas for Women, available at <http://www.quotaproject.org>

Inter-Parliamentary Union (IPU), 'Women in National Parliaments', available at <http://www.ipu.org>

A series of country case studies on electoral quotas collected by International IDEA is available at International IDEA and Stockholm University, Global Database of Electoral Quotas for Women, available at <http://www.quotaproject.org/case_studies.cfm>

A series of working papers on quotas produced by Stockholm University is available at <http://www.statsvet.su.se/quotas>

Case Study: Rwanda

Rwanda:
Women Hold Up Half
the Parliament

Elizabeth Powley[1]

In October 2003, women won 48.8 percent of seats in Rwanda's lower house of Parliament.[2] Having achieved near-parity in the representation of men and women its legislature, this small African country now ranks first among all countries of the world in terms of the number of women elected to parliament.

The percentage of women's participation is all the more noteworthy in the context of Rwanda's recent history. Rwandan women were fully enfranchised and granted the right to stand for election in 1961, with independence from Belgium. The first female parliamentarian began serving in 1965.[3] However, before its civil war in the early 1990s and the genocide in 1994, Rwandan women never held more than 18 percent of seats in the country's Parliament.[4]

The 1994 genocide in Rwanda, perpetrated by Hutu extremists against the Tutsi minority and Hutu moderates, killed an estimated 800,000 people (one-tenth of the population), traumatized survivors, and destroyed the country's infrastructure, including the Parliament building. Lasting approximately 100 days, the slaughter ended in July 1994 when the Tutsi-dominated Rwandan Patriotic Front (RPF), which had been engaged in a four-year civil war with the Hutu-dominated regime of President Juvenal Habyarimana, secured military victory. Once an opposition movement and guerilla army, the RPF is now a predominately (but not exclusively) Tutsi political party. It is in power in Rwanda today.

During the nine-year period of post-genocide transitional government, from 1994 to 2003, women's representation in Parliament (by appointment) reached 25.7 percent and a new gender-sensitive constitution was adopted. But it was the first post-genocide parliamentary elections of October 2003 that saw women achieve nearly 50 percent representation.

The dramatic gains for women are a result of specific mechanisms used to increase women's political participation, among them a constitutional guarantee, a quota system, and innovative electoral structures. This case study will describe those mechanisms and attempt to explain their origins, focusing in particular on the relationship between women's political representation and the organized women's movement, significant changes in gender roles in post-genocide Rwanda, and the commitment of Rwanda's ruling party, the RPF, to gender issues. It will also briefly introduce some of the achievements and challenges ahead for women in Rwanda's Parliament.

The Constitutional Framework

In 2000, nearing the end of its post-genocide transitional period, Rwanda undertook the drafting of a new constitution and established a 12-member Constitutional Commission. Three members of the commission were women, including one, Judith Kanakuze, who was also the only representative of civil society on the commission. She played an important role both as a 'gender expert' within the commission ranks and as a liaison to her primary constituency, the women's movement in Rwanda.[5]

The commission was charged with drafting the constitution and with taking the draft to the population in a series of consultations designed to both solicit input and sensitize the population as to the significance and principal ideas of the document.[6] Although political elites controlled both the content and the process of the consultations with Rwanda's largely illiterate population, it was—at least on the face of it—a participatory process, and its participatory nature allowed for significant input by women and women's organizations.[7]

The women's movement mobilized actively around the drafting of the constitution to ensure that equality became a cornerstone of the new document. The umbrella organization, Collectifs Pro-Femmes/Twese Hamwe (Pro-Femmes) and its member NGOs brought pressure to bear on the process and carefully coordinated efforts with women parliamentarians and the Ministry of Gender and Women in Development.

Rwanda's new constitution was formally adopted in May 2003.[8] It enshrines a commitment to gender equality. The preamble, for instance, cites various international human rights instruments and conventions to which Rwanda is a signatory, including specific reference to the 1979 Convention on the Elimination of All Forms of Discrimination Against Women (CEDAW). It also states a commitment to 'ensuring equal rights between Rwandans and between women and men without prejudice to the principles of gender equality and complementarity in national development'. Title One of the constitution also establishes, as one of its 'fundamental principles', the equality of Rwandans. This respect for equality is to be ensured in part by granting women 'at least' 30 percent of posts 'in all decision-making organs'.

It is important to note, however, that, although Rwanda's constitution is progressive in terms of equal rights, gender equality and women's representation, it is limiting in other important ways; specific concerns have been raised about restrictions on freedom of speech around issues of ethnicity.

The Quota System and Innovative Electoral Structures

Since the genocide, several innovative electoral structures have been introduced to increase the numbers of women in elected office.[9] Towards the end of its transition period, Rwanda experimented with the representation of women in the Parliament. Two women were elected to the then unicameral legislature on the basis of descriptive representation, with a mandate to act on behalf of women's concerns. Those two women came not from political parties but from a parallel system of women's councils (described in more detail below) that had been established at the grass-roots level throughout the country.

The 2003 constitution increased exponentially the number of seats to be held by women in all structures of government.

The Senate

In the upper house of Rwanda's (now) bicameral legislature, the Senate, 26 members are elected or appointed for eight-year terms. Some members of the Senate are elected by provincial and sectoral councils, others are appointed by the president and other organs (e.g. the national university). Women, as mandated in the constitution, hold 30 percent of seats in the Senate.

The Chamber of Deputies

The lower house of the Rwandan Parliament is the Chambre des Députés (Chamber of Deputies). There are 80 members serving five-year terms, 53 of whom are directly elected by a proportional representation (PR) system. The additional seats are contested as follows: 24 deputies (30 percent) are elected by women from each province and the capital city, Kigali; two are elected by the National Youth Council; and one is elected by the Federation of the Associations of the Disabled.

The 24 seats that are reserved for women are contested in women-only elections, that is, only women can stand for election and only women can vote. The election for the women's seats was coordinated by the national system of women's councils and took place in the same week as the general election in September 2003. Notably, in addition to the 24 reserved seats in the Chamber of Deputies, the elections saw an additional 15 women elected in openly competed seats. Women thus had in total 39 out of 80 seats, or 48.8 percent.

The Women's Councils

The Ministry of Gender and Women in Development first established a national system of women's councils shortly after the genocide, and their role has since been expanded. The women's councils are grass-roots structures elected at the cell level (the smallest administrative unit) by women only, and then through indirect election at each successive administrative levels (sector, district, province). They operate in parallel to general local councils and represent women's concerns. The ten-member councils are involved in skills training at the local level and in awareness-raising about women's rights. The head of the women's council holds a reserved seat on the general local council, ensuring official representation of women's concerns and providing links between the two systems.

Berthe Mukamusoni, a parliamentarian elected through the women's councils, explains the importance of this system as follows:

> In the history of our country and society, women could not go in public with men. Where men were, women were not supposed to talk, to show their needs. Men were to talk and think for them. So with [the women's councils], it has been a mobilization tool, it has mobilized them, it has educated [women] . . . It has brought them to some [level of] self-confidence, such that when the general elections are approaching, it becomes a topic in the women's [councils]. 'Women as citizens, you are supposed to stand, to campaign, give candidates, support other women'. They have acquired a confidence of leadership.[10]

While the women's councils are important in terms of decentralization and grass-roots engagement, lack of resources prevents them from maximizing their impact and they are not consistently active throughout the country. Members of local women's councils are not paid, and because they have to volunteer in addition to performing their paid work and family responsibilities the councils are less effective than they could be. Nevertheless, women in these grass-roots councils have been successful in carving out new political space. And the 2003 constitution increased their importance by drawing on these structures to fill reserved seats for women in the Chamber of Deputies.

The Factors Giving Rise to Women's Increased Parliamentary Presence

The Women's Movement and Civil Society Mobilization
Immediately after the genocide, while society and government were in disarray, women's NGOs stepped in to fill the vacuum, providing a variety of much-needed services to the traumatized population. Women came together on a multi-ethnic basis to reconstitute the umbrella organization Pro-Femmes, which had been established in 1992. Pro-Femmes, which coordinated the activities of 13 women's NGOs in 1992, now coordinates more than 40 such organizations.[11] It has been particularly effective in organizing the activities of women, advising the government on issues of women's political participation, and promoting reconciliation.

Women in Rwanda's civil society have developed a three-pronged mechanism for coordinating their advocacy among civil society (represented by Pro-Femmes), the executive branch (Ministry of Gender and Women in Development), and the legislative branch (Forum of Women Parliamentarians).

An example of the effectiveness of this mechanism is the process the Rwandan women's movement initiated around the ratification of the new constitution. To elicit concerns, interests and suggestions regarding a new constitution, Pro-Femmes held consultations with its member NGOs and women at the grass-roots level. They then met with representatives of the Ministry of Gender and Women in Development and the Forum of Women Parliamentarians to report members' concerns. Together the three sectors contributed to a policy paper that recommended specific actions to make the constitution gender-sensitive and increase women's representation in government, which was submitted to the Constitutional Commission. Once the draft constitution sufficiently reflected their interests, Pro-Femmes engaged in a mobilization campaign encouraging women to support the adoption of the document in the countrywide referendum.

Through the coordination mechanism that Pro-Femmes has forged with women in the executive and legislative branches of government, the women's movement has an increasingly powerful voice. A 2002 report commissioned by the US Agency for International Development (USAID) recognized the significant challenges faced by Rwandan civil society, including limited capacity, problems of coordination, and excessive control by the government,[12] but commended the significant role Pro-Femmes plays in shaping public policy. The study concluded that women's NGOs are the 'most vibrant sector' of civil society in Rwanda and that 'Pro-Femmes is one of the few organizations in Rwandan civil society that has taken an effective public advocacy role'.[13] Its effectiveness is a result of a highly cooperative and collaborative relationship forged with women in government. Unfortunately, the close relationship has also compromised Pro-Femmes' independence and ability to criticize the government.

Changing Gender Roles

In addition to an effective women's movement, the dramatic gains for women in Parliament can also be traced to the significant changes in gender roles in post-genocide Rwanda. Women were targeted during the genocide on the basis not only of their ethnicity, but also of their gender: they were subjected to sexual assault and torture, including rape, forced incest and breast oblation. Women who survived the genocide witnessed unspeakable cruelty and lost husbands, children, relatives and communities. In addition to this violence, women lost their livelihoods and property, were displaced from their homes, and saw their families separated. In the immediate aftermath, the population was 70 percent female (women and girls).[14] Given this demographic imbalance, women immediately assumed roles as heads of household, community leaders and financial providers, meeting the needs of devastated families and communities. The genocide forced women to think of themselves differently and in many cases develop skills they would not otherwise have acquired. Today, women remain a demographic majority in Rwanda, comprising 54 percent of the population and contributing significantly to the productive capacity of the nation.

The overwhelming burdens on women and their extraordinary contributions are very much part of the public discourse in Rwanda. In April 2003, speaking about the parliamentary elections, President Paul Kagame said, 'We shall continue to appeal to women to offer themselves as candidates and also to vote for gender sensitive men who will defend and protect their interests'. He continued, 'Women's under-representation distances elected representatives from a part of their constituency and, as such, affects the legitimacy of political decisions . . . Increased participation of women in politics is, therefore, necessary for improved social, economic and political conditions of their families and the entire country'.[15]

The Commitment of the Rwandan Patriotic Front

The Rwandan Government, specifically the ruling RPF, has made women's inclusion a hallmark of its programme for post-genocide recovery and reconstruction.[16] This approach is novel in both intent and scope; it deserves further study in part because it contradicts the notion that the inclusion of women is solely a 'Western' value imposed upon developing countries.

The government's decision to include women in the governance of the country is based on a number of factors. The policy of inclusion owes much to the RPF's exposure to gender equality issues in Uganda, where many of its members spent years in exile. Uganda uses a system of reserved seats to guarantee women 20 percent of the seats in Parliament: one seat from each of the 56 electoral districts is reserved for a woman. Men and women in the RPF were familiar with this system, as they were with the contributions and successes of women in South Africa's African National Congress (ANC). Within its own ranks, too, women played a significant role in the success of the movement. They played critical roles from the RPF's early days as an exile movement through the years of armed struggle. Such involvement provided them with a platform from which to advocate for women's inclusion during the transitional phase and consolidate their gains in the new constitution.

The RPF's liberation rhetoric was embraced by its own members and was applied to the historic exclusion of women as well as the Tutsi minority; this gender-sensitivity is now government policy. As John Mutamba, an official at the Ministry of Gender and Women in Development explains, 'Men who grew up in exile know the experience of discrimination . . . Gender is now part of our political thinking. We appreciate all components of our population across all the social divides, because our country . . . [has] seen what it means to exclude a group'.[17] RPF members who embraced notions of gender equality have informed the development of gender-sensitive governance structures in post-genocide Rwanda.

During the transitional period, before quotas were established in Rwanda, the RPF consistently appointed women to nearly 50 percent of the seats it controlled in Parliament. Other political parties lagged behind in their appointment of women, and therefore women never made up more than 25.7 percent of the Parliament during the transitional period.[18]

The RPF dominated the transitional government and consolidated its grip on power in the August 2003 post-transition election of President Paul Kagame and the installation of a new Parliament in October 2003. The RPF, together with its coalition, controls 73.8 percent of the openly contested seats in the Chamber of Deputies. The women's seats were not contested by political parties, but observers charge that a majority of the women in the reserved seats are also sympathetic to the RPF. Freedom House, in its most recent survey of nations, ranked Rwanda as 'not free', with concern about political rights and civil liberties.[19] This puts Rwandan women and the women's movement in a precarious position, as they owe their ability to participate in democratic institutions to a political party that is less than fully democratic, and cannot be truly independent of the state.

Achievements and Challenges Ahead

In addition to performing all the functions their male counterparts do, women in Rwanda's Parliament have formed a caucus, the Forum of Women Parliamentarians, with international funding and support. This is the first such caucus in Rwanda, where members work together on a set of issues across party lines. Member of Parliament (MP) Connie Bwiza Sekamana explains, 'When it comes to the Forum, we [unite] as women, irrespective of political parties. So we don't think of our parties, [we think of] the challenges that surround us as women'.[20] The Forum has several roles: it reviews existing laws and introduces amendments to discriminatory legislation, examines proposed laws with an eye to gender sensitivity, liaises with the women's movement, and conducts meetings and training with women's organizations to sensitize the population to and advise about legal issues.

A key legislative achievement was the revoking of laws that prohibited women from inheriting land in 1999. Rwandan women parliamentarians, particularly the 24 who specifically represent the women's movement but also those who contested open seats and represent political parties, feel that it is their responsibility to bring a gender-sensitive perspective to legislating.

As elsewhere in the world, there are challenges related to descriptive representation. Many of the new parliamentarians are inexperienced legislators and have to overcome stereotypes about their (lack of) competence as leaders and their supposed naiveté, as well as some resistance to the fact that they owe their positions to the new quotas. There is an obvious status difference between those seats that are reserved for women and those that are gained in open competition with men, at both the local and the national levels.

It is also problematic, in the long term, to consider all Rwandan women a single constituency. Currently, the women's movement is represented most effectively by one organization, Pro-Femmes, and there is a great deal of consensus among women parliamentarians about the needs and priorities of women. In a mature democracy, however, women disagree on policies and desired political outcomes, even those, such as the usc of quotas, which directly affect women's access to power. Perhaps because the quotas are so new and because the dominant voices in the women's movement supported their introduction so vigorously, there has not been public dissent within the movement about their utility.

There is, however, a sense, as in many other parts of the world, that quotas, reserved seats and descriptive representation are only a first step. Aloisea Inyumba, former women's minister, explains that at this point in Rwanda's development the new electoral mechanisms in Rwanda are needed to compensate for women's historic exclusion: 'If you have a child who has been malnourished, you can't compare her to your other children. You have to give her a special feeding'.[21]

It also remains to be seen what impact women will have, particularly on those issues that are not traditionally 'women's issues'. These women carry a double burden, as they must find ways to insert a gender perspective into a new range of issues—foreign affairs, for example—and yet remain loyal to their constituency of women in a country where the basic development needs are so great and women still lag behind men in terms of rights, status, and access to resources and education.

Conclusion

The representation of women in Rwanda's Parliament can be seen in the larger context of two trends: the use of quotas in Africa; and the post-conflict situation. The rate of increase of numbers of women in Parliament has been faster in sub-Saharan Africa in the last 40 years than in any other region of the world, primarily through the use of quotas.[22] And, according to the Inter-Parliamentary Union (IPU), in the last five years post-conflict countries have 'featured prominently in the top 30 of the IPU's world ranking of women in national parliaments', and these countries have been effective at using quotas and reserved seats to 'ensure the presence and participation of women in [their] newly-created institutions'.[23]

The ten years since the Rwandan genocide have been ones of enormous change for all Rwandans, but most dramatically for women. Rwanda is still vastly underdeveloped and the great majority of Rwandan women are disadvantaged vis-à-vis men with regard to education, legal rights, health and access to resources. Furthermore, the nearly equal representation of men and women in Rwanda's Parliament has been achieved in a country that is less than democratic and where a single political party dominates the political landscape.

Despite these challenges, women are beginning to consolidate their dramatic gains, with the new gender-sensitive constitution of 2003 and parliamentary elections that saw them earn 48.8 percent of seats in the Chamber of Deputies. These successes were the result of the specific circumstances of Rwanda's genocide, the quota system, and a sustained campaign by the women's movement in Rwanda, in collaboration with women in government and with the explicit support of the Rwandan Patriotic Front. The Rwandan case provides us with examples of gender-sensitive policy making and innovative electoral mechanisms that could be models for other parts of the world.

Notes

1   This case study draws on and excerpts previously published material by the same author. Powley, Elizabeth, 2003. *Strengthening Governance: The Role of Women in Rwanda's Transition.* Washington, DC: Women Waging Peace; and Powley, Elizabeth, 2005. 'Rwanda: La moitié des sièges pour les femmes au Parlement' [Rwanda: half the seats for women in Parliament], in Manon Tremblay (ed.). *Femmes et parlements: un regard international* [Women and parliaments: an international view]. Montreal: Remue-ménage.

2   Inter-Parliamentary Union (IPU), 2003. 'Rwanda Leads World Ranking of Women in Parliament', 23 October. See <http://www.ipu.org/press-e/gen176.htm>.

3   'Africa: Rwanda: Government'. Nationmaster, <http://www.nationmaster.com/country/ rw/Government>.

4   Inter-Parliamentary Union (IPU), 1995. *Women in Parliaments 1945–1995: A World Statistical Survey.* Geneva: IPU.

5   Judith Kanakuze, personal interview, July 2003.

6   'Legal and Constitutional Commission', <http://www.cjcr.gov.rw/eng/index.htm>.

7   Hart, Vivien, 2003. 'Democratic Constitution Making'. United States Institute of Peace, Special Report 107, <http://www.usip.org/pubs/specialreports/sr107.html>.

8   Constitution of the Republic of Rwanda, <http://www.cjcr.gov.rw/eng/constitution_eng. doc>.

9   For a more complete description of electoral mechanisms designed to increase women's participation, including triple balloting in the 2001 district-level elections, see Powley 2003, op. cit.

10 Berte Mukamusoni, personal interview, translated in part by Connie Bwiza Sekamana, July 2002.

11 For more information on women's NGOs in Rwanda, see Newbury, Catharine, and Hannah Baldwin, 2001. 'Confronting the Aftermath of Conflict: Women's Organizations in Postgenocide Rwanda', in Krishna Kumar (ed.). *Women and Civil War: Impact, Organizations, and Action.* Boulder, Colo.: Lynne Rienner Publishers, pp. 97–128.

12 'Rwanda Democracy and Governance Assessment', produced for USAID by Management Systems International, November 2002, p. 35.

13 'Rwanda Democracy and Governance Assessment', op. cit., p. 37.

14 Women's Commission for Refugee Women and Children, 1997. *Rwanda's Women and Children: The Long Road to Reconciliation.* New York: Women's Commission, p. 6.

15 'Rwandan President Urges Women to Stand for Public Office'. Xinhua News Agency, 23 April 2003, <http://www.xinhua.org/english/>.

16 Rwandan Government, 'Good Governance Strategy Paper (2001)', <http://www. rwanda1.com/government/president/speeches/2001/strategygov.htm>.

17 John Mutamba, personal interview, July 2003.

18 Powley 2003, op. cit.

19 Freedom House, *Freedom in the World 2004*, <http://www.freedomhouse.org/research/freeworld/2004/table2004.pdf>.

20 Connie Bwiza Sekamana, personal interview, July 2002.

21 Aloisea Inyumba, personal interview, July 2002.

22 Tripp, Aili Mari, 2004. 'Quotas in Africa', in Julia Ballington (ed.). *The Implementation of Quotas: Africa Experiences,* Stockholm: International IDEA.

23 Inter-Parliamentary Union (IPU), 2004. 'Women in Parliaments 2003: Nordic and Post-Conflict Countries in the Lead', <http://www.ipu.org/press-e/gen183.htm> (accessed 8 September 2004).

Case Study: Argentina

Argentina: A New Look at the Challenges of Women's Participation in the Legislature

Elisa María Carrio

In Argentina, mass-based political parties have had a certain degree of women's participation since their early days, from the late 19th century to the mid-20th century, but it was only in the 1980s that women increasingly emerged in party politics. This led to changes in attitude in the search for points of agreement and common objectives. Many women understood that the struggle against women's oppression should not be subordinated to other struggles, as it was actually compatible with them, and should be waged simultaneously. It was an historic opportunity, as Argentina was emerging from a lengthy dictatorship in which women had the precedent of the mobilization of the grandmothers and mothers of the Plaza de Mayo, in their white scarves.

While women in Argentina have had the right to vote and to stand for election since 1947, women's systematic exclusion from the real spheres of public power posed one of the most crucial challenges to, and criticisms of, Argentina's democracy. The political system and the legal order have not taken into account the diverse situations of women or their demands. Both have incorporated a formalist and 'neutral' point of view, which made it impossible for the system to be capable of identifying and responding to women's concerns and needs.

During the democratic transition of the 1980s, the organized groups of activists understood the importance of undertaking the struggle against gender discrimination in the context of rebuilding democracy. Women thus began their endeavour for 'parity democracy', developing practices and strategies that would reach out to women as a whole and foster greater gender awareness, with feminist demands and new analyses of power.

Argentina was the first country in Latin America to adopt a quota for women's participation in Congress. In 2005, Argentina is among the top 15 ranked countries in the world after Rwanda, Sweden, Norway, Denmark, Finland, the Netherlands, Cuba, Spain, Costa Rica, Mozambique, Belgium and Austria in terms of the representation of women in the national legislature.

Despite the evident accomplishments, and given that the realm of politics has evolved historically based on a male model, the political culture today is profoundly gender-biased. Values and practices in the world of public affairs are particular to the male world. The dynamics of political activity, the practices and functioning of the parties, and the very way of doing politics, its language and its recognized values have been cast in the image of male models. In this context the challenges Argentine women face are still huge, although their numbers and active participation in politics have expanded.

This case study analyses women's path to power, illustrating the different legal and social mechanisms that have been used to increase the number of women legislators, and examines the role of Argentina's political parties in promoting women's participation.

The Struggle for 'Parity Democracy' in Argentina

In the late 1980s, women began to occupy positions of authority in government. One of the mechanisms used to achieve this objective was the quota system.[1] At present, Argentina has several constitutional and statutory provisions to ensure the necessary participation of women in politics, and, in particular, in the legislature.

Article 37 of the national constitution provides that real equality of opportunity as between men and women to gain access to elective and political party posts shall be guaranteed by affirmative action in regulating the political parties and in the electoral regime.

The 'women's share', or quota system, was incorporated into Argentine law by Law No. 24,012. The history of this legislation goes back to November 1989, when Margarita Malharro de Torres, national legislator for the Unión Cívica Radical (UCR, Radical Civic Union) from Mendoza, introduced legislation to amend the National Electoral Code to require that there be women members of Congress. Days later, a group of women legislators from different parties (the UCR, the Partido Justicialista, Democracia Popular, and the Partido Federal) introduced a bill using similar language in the Chamber of Deputies. That bill was debated in September 1990 and adopted by the Chamber by an overwhelming majority on 6 November 1991, with the consensus of all the political groupings except the Unión de Centro Democrático (Union of the Democratic Centre) and the Movimiento al Socialismo (MAS, Movement for Socialism) and became law (it was known at the time as the Malharro Act). It amended article 60 of the National Electoral Code by providing that at least 30 percent of the candidates on the lists proposed by the political parties must be women, and in such positions that they have a chance of getting elected. In addition, it provided that no party list would be registered that did not meet those requirements.

An analysis of the historical reasons that led to the adoption of the Quota Law could well be the subject of an extensive research project. Suffice it here to mention just some of the decisive factors. These include the evolution of women political figures and their relationship with the women's movement, the coming together of women from the different political parties, their knowledge and analysis of comparative experiences and legislation, their grasp of the problem and visions of the future, and the massive mobilization of women, especially through the Encuentros Feministas, or Feminist Gatherings, and the National Women's Meetings.

Later, the 1994 constitutional reform (adopted by a constitutional convention whose delegates were elected under the Quota Law) cleared up any lingering doubts about the law's constitutionality, as it expressly incorporated the principles underlying such measures.

Article 37 of the national constitution provides that real equality of opportunity between men and women, to gain access to elective and political party posts, shall be guaranteed by affirmative action in regulating the political parties and in the electoral regime. In addition, Article 75 gives Congress powers to adopt and promote affirmative action measures that guarantee real equality of opportunity and equal treatment. The article also guarantees the full enjoyment and exercise of the rights recognized by this constitution and the international human rights treaties in force, in particular with respect to women (section 23), according constitutional status to the 1979 Convention on the Elimination of All Forms of Discrimination Against Women (section 22).

Finally, the second clause provides that the affirmative action alluded to in article 37 may not amount to less than the provisions in force at the time the constitution was adopted, and shall last as long as the law provides, thereby thwarting any effort to roll back the rights recognized by Law No. 24,012. This constitutionally guaranteed minimum of women's participation in politics resulted in a notable increase in the number of women in the Argentine Congress, significantly strengthening the quality of democracy.

The inclusion of women in the Chamber of Deputies, 30 percent of whose members are women at the time of writing, began in 1983. In the Senate, although the first woman was also elected in 1983, women's participation was not truly effective until 2001, when it passed 35 percent. From this time, senators were elected directly, and the full Senate was up for election, with application of the 1994 constitutional reform.

The slow implementation of the quota for the Chamber of Deputies, only half of whose members are elected at any one time, contrasts with the situation in the Senate. There, the 1994 constitutional reform mandated that all the seats be up for re-election, as noted earlier, prompting an increase in women's participation to more than 30 percent in just one year.

Figure 5: The Argentine Congress, Chamber of Deputies, 1983–2001: Numbers of Women Members and Women as a Percentage of All Members

Year	Total Members	No. of Women Candidates	Percentage of Total
1983	254	11	4.3
1984	254	13	5.1
1985	254	11	4.3
1986	254	12	4.7
1987	254	12	4.7
1988	254	12	4.7
1989	254	14	5.5
1990	254	16	6.3
1991	257*	15	5.9
1992	257	15	5.9
1993**	257	36	14.0
1994	257	38	14.8
1995	257	62	24.5
1997	257	71	27.6
1999	257	72	28.0
2001	257	77	30.0
2005	255	86	33.7

Sources: Botte, Susana and Evangelina Dorola, 1996. 'La representación femenina en el Congreso de la Nación' [Women's representation in the Argentine Congress]. HCND, Sec. Parlamentaria, DIP. Estudios e investigaciones 9, Mujer; Consejo Nacional de la Mujer, October 2001; Argentine Chamber of Deputies, February 2002; and Inter-Parliamentary Union (IPU), January 2005.

* The representatives from the Province of Tierra del Fuego, Antártida, and the Islas del Atlántico Sur were included.

** The National Quota Law entered into force.

Decree No. 1,246, signed in December 2000, paved the way for this. This law addressed several long-standing grievances of women in politics and civil society as expressed through the non-governmental organizations by instituting the effective placement of women candidates on the party lists for elections to the Senate, thereby expanding the scope of the Quota Law. The decree also specified that the required 30 percent is a minimum, since it provides expressly that this percentage must be applied to all candidates of the respective lists of each political party, coalition or transitory alliance. For this rule to be implemented, it must be applied to the posts up for re-election, and from the first position on the list.

Figure 6: The Argentine Congress, Senate, 1983–2001, Number of Women Members and Women as a Percentage of Total Senators

Year	Total Members	No. of Women Candidates	Percentage of Total
1983	46	3	6.5
1984	46	3	6.5
1985	46	3	6.5
1986	46	3	6.5
1987	46	3	6.5
1988	46	4	8.7
1989	46	4	8.7
1990	46	4	8.7
1991	46	4	8.7
1992	48 *	4	8.7
1993	48	2	4.2
1994	48	2	4.2
1995	65**	4	6.1
1996	65	4	6.1
1997	65	4	6.1
1999	66	2	3.0
2001***	71	25	35.2
2005	72	24	33.3

Sources: Botte, Susana and Evangelina Dorola, 1996. 'La representación femenina en el Congreso de la Nación' [Women's representation in the Argentine Congress]. HCND, Sec. Parlamentaria, DIP. Estudios e investigaciones 9, Mujer; Consejo Nacional de la Mujer, October 2001; and Argentine Chamber of Deputies, February 2002.

* The representatives of the Province of Tierra del Fuego, Antártida, and the Islas del Atlántico Sur were included.

** The composition of the Chamber was modified by the incorporation of the third senator per electoral district. Entry into force of the Quota Law as it was the first time it was applied.

*** Direct election of representatives from the provinces.

Furthermore, a uniform criterion was used in applying the 30 percent: if 30 percent resulted in a fractional number, that number would have to be rounded up to obtain the applicable figure, and a table was included in the decree to make this requirement clear. The lack of such a criterion in the 1990s led to the unjust exclusion of many women candidates throughout the country.

Finally, it is worth noting that practically all the provinces of Argentina currently have a quota law regulating the elections of their respective legislatures, and that these laws also govern local councils.

Political Parties and their Role in Promoting Women's Political Participation

Political parties play a key role in determining women's political participation. However, many of the parties do not yet have their own rules on quotas. The absence of compulsory regulation within political parties is a challenge and is undoubtedly one of the issues pending in the struggle for equal opportunity for women political activists. Nonetheless, most of the parties are gradually amending their charters or by-laws. The new progressive movements, such as Alternativa para una República de Iguales (ARI, Alternative for a Republic of Equals), have been formed without any 'glass ceiling'.[2]

Factors Affecting Women's Participation in Political Parties

In favour:

The proportional representation (PR) system with closed and blocked lists. In the Argentine case, the *lista sábana,* as it is called (closed and blocked lists) has been a positive factor in determining the proportion of women to be included in the lists. Its effectiveness can be verified by observing the smaller number of women elected in some of the provinces that have other electoral regimes.

Women's activism. The women who are able to surmount existing barriers and become included in the lists are generally activists with varying backgrounds— teachers, professionals, academics, artists, social workers and human rights activists. They are the same women who are on the lists of the new movements and alliances of the progressive sector—women who can hold their own and for whom experience in Congress is marked by both adversity and success. They are key legislators, and ardent defenders of the constitution and of strict compliance with its terms; they are the authors of most of the bills aimed at addressing women's concerns, and are responsible for significant gains in women's human rights.

Parties are required to comply with the law. Compliance with the quota resulted from the political will and organization of the majority of women activists who, even while participating actively in the political party structures, were not able to accede to decision-making positions. Women have been zealous guardians of the law, and of compliance with the sanctions provided for by law.

Sanctions. In the National Electoral Code, Law No. 24,012 provides that no party list will be registered that does not have at least 30 percent women, and in electable positions.

Against:

The mechanisms for choosing candidates. Since the Quota Law was adopted, traditional political parties have turned to various unconventional mechanisms for selecting candidates; these merit a close look. The terms for gaining access to Congress

169

are quite unequal. While for men the traditional 'old boys' network' of the political parties continues to function, the macho leadership appears to have decided that it is another matter for women. Based on the conception that a woman's role is an asset that is part of the community property (by virtue of marriage), wives are placed in the positions their husbands by law cannot occupy. Indeed, legislative seats likely to be occupied by women elected under the quota system are even considered family property, and daughters, sisters, friends and so on are nominated for a seat that male politicians consider they deserve. Even today, the macho leadership keeps talking about 'paying the quota' and trying, if they can, to get docile and obedient women elected to those posts.

Lessons Learned

Argentina's experience yields a series of lessons that are worth highlighting. In addition, several challenges need to be addressed to attain equality.

Among the most important lessons learned are the following.

- The quota law is a means to an end. Its proponents always considered it a means to make it possible to attain gender equality and never as an end in itself.
- The quota law sets a minimum, not a ceiling. In addition, 30 percent women's representation was considered merely the basis; it was necessary to deal with a long list of issues and questions that came up in the political parties. In many cases, even today they have not been fully addressed.
- Opening up what had been exclusive spaces is not a gratuitous concession for some women activists to gain access to candidacies from which they have hitherto been barred.
- Despite the criticisms, the implementation of the new system has led to an effective increase in the presence of women in Congress, which otherwise might well not have been attained. Therefore, beyond the polemics stirred by the measure, it has been effective in attaining the proposed objective.
- Considerable solidarity was mustered around the Quota Law among the women of different political forces, especially in cases in which the legal minimum of 30 percent was not being respected. Solidarity among women was more important than party allegiance.
- The mere fact of belonging to the female sex does not per se guarantee a gender commitment or solidarity in this effort. Some women seem to forget their own gender grievances the more quickly the closer they get to power.
- A warning is also in order regarding the attitude of women who expressly opposed quotas and showed a clear lack of solidarity, but do not hesitate to stand as candidates to fill the quota, thereby benefiting from what they opposed. This attitude is a fault which should be characterized at least as 'ethical surrender'.

Challenges

- Now that there are more women in Congress, the agenda is focused on the work that must be done to effectively promote laws and regulations to correct the socio-cultural and economic inequalities that hold back women as a whole, in order to bring about a society with more solidarity, equality and justice.

- In the legislative area, recent years have witnessed some gains and some setbacks. In several provinces laws have been adopted on family violence. Nonetheless, effective and sufficient procedures capable of guaranteeing the exercise and enjoyment of these rights have yet to be devised. In effect, such advances in the legislative sphere do not reflect the general conditions in the country, nor have they been accompanied by the support of a strong judiciary ready to ensure the implementation of and respect for such laws. On the contrary, Argentina has a justice system that is on the verge of collapse, and therefore incapable of enforcing the laws.

- Still awaiting adoption are a National Law on Reproductive Health and a Sexual Harassment in the Workplace Law that covers the cases that arise in private business: such laws as already exist only cover the federal public administration, the government of the city of Buenos Aires, and the province of Buenos Aires.

- It is also worth highlighting the need to allocate sufficient funding to support programmes that promote genuine equality of opportunity, to bolster the effectiveness of the judicial organs and to create the necessary number of shelters for abused women, and there is a need to develop efficient legislation to prevent, sanction and eradicate violence against women, which provides the necessary public policies to ensure that the commitments undertaken by the Argentine state are carried out in keeping with Inter-American Convention on the Prevention, Punishment and Eradication of Violence Against Women (Convention of Belem do para).

Conclusion

As Marcela Rodríguez states,[3] the representation of women's voices, interests, perspectives and values in decision making is a necessary condition for the effective observance of women's human rights. The Argentine case bears this out. In effect, the history of democracy and human rights is the history of the successive expansion of citizenship, of including those who are marginalized by the system, of amplifying the voices and interests of those who participate in the public debate. Guaranteeing the presence of all voices in the public debate and in political processes and practices implies not only more genuine representation but a more genuine democracy.

The proposal for parity democracy is aimed at ensuring the balanced participation of men and women in political bodies. Moreover, it not only means women must play a more active role, but it also constitutes a broader and more ambitious proposal, one entailing a profound social transformation. It involves a thorough change that would make possible a more egalitarian society and more balanced participation in all spheres of decision making in society, the economy and cultural life. It is intended to help lay the foundation for a new social contract.

Parity democracy also represents a new beginning which will make it possible to overcome situations of subordination and discrimination that affect society. However, to achieve it, merely including a female perspective on public affairs is a necessary but not a sufficient condition.

The emergence of women's discourse in the public arena is, perhaps, one of the most important characteristics of the new century. Endowed with meaning, a result of all that was not expressed, that was blocked off and rendered invisible for centuries, women's discourse renews voices in a society of words without meaning and a social fabric being torn asunder. In response to the voice of instrumental rationalism, expressed by positivist, scientific and macho men, women prioritize the sphere of communicative action, to which they bring values and feelings, without losing the rational element. Women's discourse, which can no longer be contained, will not only bring about a new way of doing politics; it will also construct a form of communication that makes it possible to re-establish social ties.

Notes

[1] As Marcela V. Rodríguez indicates, affirmative action recognizes that at times it is necessary to provide certain groups with unequal instruments in order to guarantee real equality of opportunity and treatment. In effect, when social inequality is the prevailing norm in the initial context prior to the distribution of goods, resources or tools, we cannot expect mere formal equality to be capable of ensuring real equality. This is especially relevant for the purposes of evaluating the legitimacy of the system of quotas for women, in a context in which gender discrimination and social hierarchy are the norm. See Rodríguez, Marcela V., 2000. 'Igualdad, democracia y acciones colectivas' [Equality, democracy and collection action], in Alda Facio and Lorena Fries (eds). *Género y Derecho* [Gender and rights]. Chile: Lom Ediciones, pp. 249ff.

[2] The expression 'glass ceiling', created in the 1970s, symbolizes the invisible barriers that keep women from reaching the highest decision-making positions in both public and private organizations. Both at work and in politics, this artificial barrier, considered by the International Labour Organization (ILO) as 'a transparent yet solid wall, made from organizational attitudes and prejudices', remains in place despite decades of social development and the strides made towards gender equality.

[3] See note 1.

Case Study: South Asia

Reserved Seats in South Asia: A Regional Perspective

Shirin M. Rai

The implementation of reservations, or reserved seats in a legislature for certain under-represented groups, has a relatively long history in South Asia. As early as the 1940s, India began implementing caste-based reservations in the parliament. This case study[1] traces the evolution and current implementation of reserved seats for women primarily in the local governments of Bangladesh, India and Pakistan. National-level debates are ongoing, and some countries have adopted quotas at the parliamentary level. However, legislation introducing reservations for women in local government institutions has been in force for some time, generating empirical data on their functioning in all three countries.[2] This study also assesses the importance of reservations for enhancing the representation of women in political institutions,[3] but shows that they need to be supported by other initiatives that address poverty and its consequences for the majority of women.

The Evolution of Reservations for Women

There are three distinct phases in the debates that have led to different provisions of reservations in the region.[4]

The Origins of Reservations

Phase one was that of constitution-making after the achievement of independence in 1947. In India, caste-based reservations were introduced under the 9th Schedule (articles 330 and 331)[5] of the Indian Constitution in the first instance for 50 years, but under the 62nd Amendment Act of 1989 were extended for another 40 years, demonstrating the political sensitivity of the removal of reservations once they have been established. However, there were no quotas for women at any level of government.

In Pakistan, reservation of seats for women in the national and provincial assemblies, the Senate and local government was agreed in the first constitution of 1956, at a minimal level of 3 percent at all levels. Women were always granted reserved seats through indirect election. The revised constitutions of 1962 and 1973 also provided reserved seats for women at similarly low levels, of 2.75 percent and 5 percent, respectively, in the national and provincial assemblies.

In Bangladesh, the first constitution, promulgated in 1972, provided for 15 indirectly elected reserved seats for women in the national parliament for a period of ten years. This gave women a minimum representation of 4.7 percent. Members elected to the general seats constituted the Electoral College for electing candidates for the reserved seats.[6]

The Second Phase

The second phase of quota politics for women began in the 1970s and 1980s when international organizations such as the United Nations highlighted the importance of women in public life through such high-profile initiatives as the first UN Conference on Women held in Mexico in 1975 and the subsequent UN Decade for Women. Women's groups as well as the states in South Asia were affected by these developments.

In India, the first Commission on the Status of Women in India, established in 1972, recommended the constitution of statutory all-women panchayats (village councils) at the village level to promote the welfare of women, although this recommendation was not implemented by most provincial governments. The National Perspective Plan for Women (1988–2000) recommended the reservation of at least 30 percent of the total seats for women in the local government institutions. The provision of reserved seats in local government for women under the 73rd and 74th amendments to the Indian Constitution was a key initiative during this phase. The Women's National Commission was established in 1995 and has overseen the expansion of the quota system in India.

In 1985 the number of reserved seats for women in the Pakistan National Assembly was raised from 2.75 percent to 10 percent for a ten-year period or three general elections, whichever came first. The Report of the Commission of Inquiry for Women (August 1997), the National Plan for Action (NPA) (September 1998) and the National Policy for Development and Empowerment of Women (March 2002) attempted to respond to Pakistan's treaty commitments to promote women's free, equal and full political participation.[7]

In Bangladesh, international donor agencies, working with or within the UN framework of Women in Development (WID), were instrumental in developing the discourse of gender equality, mobilizing women at the local level, and funding their support and training.[8] The 1986 constitution did not provide for quotas but, with regard to local government institutions, its article 9 stated that 'The state shall encourage local government institutions [to give]… special representation…as far as possible to peasants, workers and women'. Reservation of seats was re-incorporated into the constitution in 1990, valid for ten years, which expired in 2000. In May 2004, the national parliament passed the 14th constitutional amendment to reintroduce quotas for women. The number of seats in parliament is to be raised to 345, of which 45 (13 percent) will be reserved for women.

Current Trends

The third, current, phase can be characterized by several key elements. Economic liberalization has led to the further erosion of the welfare state in India and Pakistan.[9] There has also been a worldwide consensus emerging about the relevance of state feminism, especially after the Fourth World Conference on Women in Beijing in 1995. This phase has seen the debate on the extension of reservations for women to the national parliament in India and the extension of quota provisions in Pakistan and Bangladesh.

The systems in place in the three countries differ. In both Pakistan and Bangladesh reserved seats have been introduced at both national and local levels, while in India they were introduced at the local level and the bill to introduce quotas at the national level still languishes in the parliamentary system.[10] In India there is a system of ward rotation for the reserved seats (the constituencies reserved for women are changed at every election in order to circulate the benefits of reservations geographically, although arguably this also leads to problems of continuity for women representatives), which is not present in Pakistan and Bangladesh. In Bangladesh the 'wards [districts] for the reserved seats for women are three times bigger than the "general seats". This is not the case in the other two countries. In Pakistan the union is not divided into different wards—as in India and Bangladesh—but serve as a single constituency for all the candidates'.[11]

However, there are also some similarities in these different quota regimes. All three countries have constitutional histories bound up with the British colonial past, have majoritarian electoral systems, and are also party-based political systems (even given the interruptions to democratic practice in Pakistan).

Table 14: Types of Quota in Bangladesh, India and Pakistan

Country	% Women in Lower House	Quota Provision		Electoral System National Level
		National	Local	
Bangladesh	2.0 (2001 election)	45 out of 345 seats (13%) are reserved for women (2004 constitutional amendment)	At least 25% of seats are reserved for women in union councils (1996 legislation)	First Past The Post (plurality system)
India (2004 election)	8.3	N/A	Not less than 33% women and other marginalized sections of society in all local bodies (1992 constitutional amendment)	First Past The Post (plurality system)
Pakistan (2002 election)	21.1	60 of the 342 (17%) seats in the National Assembly are reserved for women (2002 legislation)	33% of the seats are reserved for women in legislative councils at the union, tehsil (municipality) and district level (2000 Devolution of Power Plan)	Parallel Mixed System (First Past The Post combined with lists)

Reserved Seats in Local Government: How They Work

Bangladesh

In Bangladesh, urban local government is composed of two tiers: (a) *pourshavas* (90 municipal bodies) where there is a provision of a quota for at least three women members who are to be elected by the commissioners of the *pourshava*; and (b) city corporations (there are six of these). Rural local government is composed of four types of *parishad* (council)—*zila* (district), *upazila* (a subdivision of a district), union and village. Although women have the right to vote as well as to stand for election in these local bodies, during the last decade few women have been successful in winning seats. In 1993, direct election of reserved seats for women in the union *parishad* was provided for in legislation by the Parliament. Article 9 of the constitution, under 'Fundamental Principles of State Policy', stipulates the representation of women in local government institutions. The first election to the union *parishad*, under the new provision, was held in 1997.

India

In India, *panchayati raj* institutions (PRIs) function at three tiers—village *panchayat*, block *panchayat* and district *panchayat*. The size of a *panchayat* depends on the population of an area and varies across the different regions from 18,000–20,000 to 500–1,000. The 73rd and 74th constitutional amendment acts from 1992 strengthened the role of the PRIs as well as introducing reservations for women in urban and rural local government.[12] The *panchayats* have five-year tenures, have direct elections, and must include not less than 33 percent reserved seats for women and other marginalized sections of society. The election of the chairpersons of block and district *parishads* is indirect, with the mode of election at the village *panchayat* level left to the states to decide. The reservation of seats for women was done on a rotation basis, which means that those seats that were reserved in the first term were 'de-reserved' in the second term, thus causing discontinuities for women representatives, their development of experience and their building up a power base.

Pakistan

In Pakistan the military regime of Pervez Musharraf adopted the Devolution of Power Plan in 2000 to establish an identical set-up of local government bodies in all four provinces of Pakistan. This guaranteed a 33 percent quota for women at all three levels of the local government—*zila* councils (district level), *tehsil* councils (sub-district level) and union councils (village level). Members of the union councils are elected directly but the *tehsil* and *zila* council members are elected indirectly by an electoral college formed by the elected councillors on the union councils. The union council covers between eight and ten villages. It is composed of 21 members—one *nazim* (chairman), one *naib nazim* (vice-chairman), eight general Muslim seats, four women Muslim seats, four Muslim peasant/worker seats, two women peasant/worker seats and one religious minority seat. This means that six out of 21 seats are reserved for women. Thus the actual quota percentage is 29 percent and not 33 percent, which is the figure that is usually quoted. This is due to the fact that there were no quotas allocated for the *nazims* or the minority seats.[13]

Quotas in Practice: Do they Make a Difference?

The impact of reserved seats has been varied in the three countries, being influenced by the requirements of the law, process and outcome, and individual experiences with implementation. While the reserved seats have guaranteed women's access to local government, albeit in relatively low numbers, it is debatable whether quotas have really addressed the issue of women's empowerment in the countries concerned.

Impact of Quotas on Local Government
Arguably, one of the indicators of the success of the reserved seats is that women's presence has increased within local government and is resulting in their greater

participation in the work of the local bodies. As a result of the reservations, women's representation in local government has increased in all three countries.

In Bangladesh, in the union council elections of 1997 a total of 13,000 women candidates were elected to fill the reserved seats for women. A total of 63 women commissioners were elected in the country's four city corporations.

In India, reserved seats have allowed more than 1 million women from all strata of society to participate in decision making at the grass-roots level.

In Pakistan after 1979, local government elections were held in 1983, 1987, 1992 and 2001. The local government elections of 2000–2001 brought 42,049 women into local government.

There is some evidence of the qualitative impact that women representatives are making at the local level. In India women representatives are working better in those areas where they have been successful in micro-credit programmes, literacy campaigns or other social movements.[14] In Bangladesh the direct election of women to local bodies has raised questions about the terms of reference and spheres of activity of these bodies, as well as the need for continuing training programmes.[15] In Pakistan, women electors belonging to the poor strata of society are approaching female councillors as they are accessible and have pinned their hopes of solving their problems on the female councillors.

The Experience of Women in Local Government

The experience of women in local government in South Asia is mediated by gender and class regimes, the type of local institutions, formal and informal networks, and customary laws that influence women's full participation in local government. Their participation can also be affected by a lack of education, training and resources. Additionally, women representatives' dependence on male members of the household and their inability to access economic resources (there are, for example, no salaries for local government representatives) also affect their performance. The following examples illustrate the particular experiences of women at the local level.

In Bangladesh, women commissioners have been restricted from performing four major duties: the registration of births and deaths and the issuing of various certificates, including for nationality and character; examining the designs of buildings; assisting in census and all other demographic surveys; and monitoring law and order.[16] Women commissioners of city corporations and municipalities have been entrusted with responsibilities relating only to the prevention of women and child repression, while the male commissioners play the leading role in performing all other duties. In addition, the government is yet to finalize the remuneration for the women commissioners, and above all they do not have access to facilities such as specific office space, transport and other facilities.

In Pakistan, there are frequent complaints by women councillors that they do not receive invitations to council meetings, and less than 50 percent of women councillors attended only one meeting where the election of chairman took place. Often papers

179

are sent to their houses for their signature or thumb impression without women being consulted on development planning at the district and union council levels. Nor are they given an equal share of development funds, as women are often perceived as having no direct constituency to represent. Nearly all the women who stood for election after the introduction of quotas in 2000 did so because their male relatives or members of the community put their names forward for the position. This obviously undermines their position as independent actors in local government.

In India, successful self-help groups have boosted the self-image of women representatives in the villages: social mobilization has been one of the important by-products of the quotas for women.[17] However, there is continuing concern about the influence of male relatives over women representatives (the *biwi* brigade or the 'proxy women' discourse).

Challenges to Effective Participation

This section reviews some of the key challenges facing women in local governments in South Asia.

1. *Constituency representation.* In Bangladesh, 'Women members at the local bodies are not aware of their role and functions as a member of the Councils. Even most of the women voters do not know who their representatives are in the city corporations and what their actual functions are'. According to a study on the last union *parishad* polls held in 2003, several women were interested in competing for the general seats instead of the reserved seats.[18] This may illustrate that they see themselves as being empowered by the quota system to be able to aspire to the general seats, or it may highlight the problem of lack of constituency representation for women who are elected through a quota. One of the important issues that face both women and men is that central government control over resources undermines their autonomy. Women candidates also face the hurdles of money-based politics, issues of security as they travel over large constituencies, and the continuing influence of patriarchal social relations, which support segregation and purdah, limiting women's ability to participate fully in the political life of the local community.

2. *Relative influence at the local level.* In India, women are expected to adjust to the imperatives of party structures for their political survival. One of the structural challenges is the weak position of the *panchayats* vis-à-vis the state government, which erodes the autonomy of the *panchayats* and those who are elected to them. Several women have pointed out that without a proper salary[19] the *panchayat* is more open to corrupt practices and to being dominated by upper-class individuals who can afford not to be paid. So, in terms of process, the induction of women into politics requires attention to the expectations of members, their training and remuneration issues.

3. *Who do women represent?* In Pakistan women representatives are struggling to create space for themselves within the system. A study of six districts of Punjab showed

that women councillors had extremely limited knowledge and information about the powers and functions of local government.[20] They are confronting the traditional mindset where their male colleagues reject them as equal partners in politics. They are seen as representing only women and they are given responsibilities related to gender-specific projects and programmes. Councillors who were elected in reserved seats were not offered any honorarium, while it is difficult for women councillors to meet transport costs out of their own pocket, as most of them are economically dependent on the male members of their families.

Differences among women (as among men) on the basis of class, caste, religion and ethnicity are played out in different ways in the representative and party politics of the three countries. In Bangladesh, most of the elected women are elite women in terms of both class and education.[21] In India, while there is a considerable presence of poor farmers and agricultural labourers within the *panchayat* membership, Buch points out that the *sarpanch* (chairpersons) of *panchayats* are of higher class.[22] In Pakistan, nearly three-quarters of women councillors were illiterate and the majority were from a rural background.[23] The challenge here is to democratize the processes of selection for both men and women in such a way that class and caste do not play such a critical role in the selection of candidates, although the deep inequalities affecting the region will militate against this.

Conclusion

This case study, focusing on Bangladesh, India and Pakistan, suggests that reserved seats have indeed addressed issues of the under-representation of women, as increasing numbers are joining local government institutions. There is some evidence that their involvement may lead to an increased participation of women in provincial and national-level politics. We have also seen that women representatives do attempt to address women's basic needs, and are approached by women's groups to address their problems, and there is even some evidence that on the whole women representatives are less corrupt and therefore bring to local governance some degree of credibility in the eyes of the people.

However, women representatives face many challenges—structural, personal and party-political. They are often not taken seriously by their male colleagues, the level of training and information is poor, the party bosses continue to dominate local government, thus stymieing women representatives' attempts to bring about change, and the uneven gender balance within the family continues to deter women from taking an independent stand on issues. We also see that, despite some shifts, the continuing dominance of the middle and upper classes in local politics means that the differences between women are played out in particular ways. This means that low-caste women find it difficult to represent their own communities satisfactorily, while at the same time they are unable to represent any generalized interests of women.

Second, because of status differentials, the risks that poor, low-caste, minority women take in standing up to dominant privilege interests are very high. Finally, the rotational reservation of seats as used in India means that women representatives joining politics cannot nurture their constituency over a period of time, and therefore struggle to build a base for themselves in local politics.

Notes

[1] This chapter is based on a longer paper prepared for Dahlerup, Drude (ed.). *Quotas for Women Worldwide.* London: Routledge.

[2] While there has been some empirical work done on the process by which reservations for women were introduced and implemented and on the outcome for both women representatives and local government institutions in each of the three countries (Buch 2000, Mahtab 2003, Bari 1997: see below), this is the first comparative study on the issue.

[3] Women in South Asia (including Nepal and Sri Lanka) occupy only 7 percent of the parliamentary seats, 9 percent of the cabinet seats, 6 percent of the positions in the judiciary and 9 percent in the civil service. United Nations Development Programme (UNDP), 2000. *Human Development Report 2000.* Oxford: Oxford University Press.

[4] The first quotas were part of the British administrative regime in South Asia under the Government of India Act of 1935, which established quotas for women and minority groups.

[5] Article 331 stipulated a reservation of seats for the Anglo-Indian community for two years if the president thought it to be under-represented in Parliament.

[6] Chowdhury, Najma, 2003. 'Bangladesh's Experience: Dependence and Marginality in Politics', in International IDEA. *The Implementation of Quotas: Asian Experiences.* Quota Workshops Report Series. Stockholm: International IDEA, pp. 50–8.

[7] Ali, Shaheen, 2000. 'Law, Islam and the Women's Movement in Pakistan', in Shirin M. Rai (ed.). *International Perspectives on Gender and Democratisation.* Basingstoke: Macmillan.

[8] See Goetz, Anne-Marie, 1996. 'Dis/organizing Gender: Women Development Agents in the State and NGO Poverty-reduction Programmes in Bangladesh', in Shirin M. Rai (ed.). *Women and the State: International Perspectives.* London: Taylor & Francis; Goetz, Anne-Marie (ed.), 1997. *Getting Institutions Right for Women in Development.* London: Zed Books; Kabeer, N., 1994. *Reversed Realities: Gender Hierarchies in Development Thought.* London: Verso; and Kabeer, N., 1995. 'Targeting Women or Transforming Institutions? Policy Lessons from NGO Anti-poverty Efforts'. *Development and Practice.* Vol. 5, no. 2, pp. 108–16.

[9] The Human Development Index rankings for the three countries in 2003 are 139 for Bangladesh, 127 for India and 144 for Pakistan. United Nations Development Programme (UNDP), 2003. *Human Development Report 2003.* Oxford: Oxford University Press.

[10] Rai, S. M. and Sharma, K., 2000. 'Democratising the Indian Parliament: the "Reservation for Women" Debate', in S. M. Rai (ed.). *International Perspectives on Gender and Democratisation.* Basingstoke: Macmillan.

[11] Frankl, Emma, 2003. 'Quota as Empowerment: The Use of Reserved Seats in Union Parishad as an Instrument of Women's Political Empowerment in Bangladesh', unpublished paper, Stockholm University.

[12] In 2000 there were 532 district *panchayats*, 5,912 block or *tauluk panchayats* and 231,630 village or gram *panchayats*, and there are more than 3 million elected *panchayati raj* representatives, of whom women constitute one-third. See Ford Foundation, 2002. 'From Public Administration to Governance'. New Delhi.

[13] Graff, I., 2003. 'Women's Representation in Pakistani Politics: The Quota Systems under the Musharraf Regime'. Paper presented at the International Conference on Women and Politics in Asia, Halmstad, Sweden, 6–7 June.

[14] Buch, Nirmala, 2000. 'Women's Experience in New Panchayats: The Emerging Leadership of Rural Women'. Occasional Paper 35, Centre for Women's Development Studies (CWDS), Delhi.

[15] Reyes, Socorro L., 2002. 'Quotas in Pakistan: A Case Study'. Paper prepared for a workshop hosted by International IDEA.

[16] Mahtab, N., 2003. 'Women in Urban Local Governance: A Bangladesh Case Study'. Paper presented at the International Conference on Women's Quotas in Urban Local Governance: A Cross-national Comparison. New Delhi, February.

[17] Mohanty, Bidyut, 2003. 'Women's Presence in Panchayats (Village Councils) in India: A New Challenge to Patriarchy'. Paper presented at the International Conference on Women and Politics in Asia, Halmstad, Sweden, 6–7 June.

[18] Mahtab 2003, op. cit.

[19] The remuneration varies from 10 rupees (INR) per sitting to 50 INR. The *sarpanch* can get up to 100 INR.

[20] Bari, Farzana, 1997. 'Discovering Female Representatives in Local Government', unpublished report.

[21] Frankl 2003, op. cit., p. 42.

[22] Buch 2000, op. cit.

[23] Bari 1997, op. cit.

Further Reading

Bari, Farzana, 2004. 'Voices of Women Councilors'. Pattan Development Organization

Baxi, Upendra, 1995. 'Emancipation as Justice: Babasaheb Ambedkar's Legacy and Vision', in Upendra Baxi and Bhikhu Parekh (eds). *Crisis and Change in Contemporary India.* London: Sage

Blacklock, Cathy and Laura Macdonald, 2000. 'Women and Citizenship in Mexico and Guatemala', in S. Rai (ed.). *International Perspectives on Gender and Democratisation.* Basingstoke: Macmillan

Bystendinzky, Jill M. (ed.), 1992. *Women Transforming Politics: Worldwide: Strategies for Empowerment.* Bloomington and Indianapolis: Indiana University Press

Chatterjee, P., 1993. 'The Nationalist Resolution of the Women's Question', in K. Sangari and S. Vaid. *Recasting Women, Essays in Colonial History.* New Delhi: Kali for Women

Kabeer, Naila, 1999. 'Resources, Agency, Achievements: Reflections on the Measurement of Women's Empowerment'. *Development and Change.* Vol. 30, pp. 435–64

Lister, Ruth, 1997. *Citizenship: Feminist Perspectives.* London: Palgrave

Parpart, Jane, Shirin M. Rai and Kathleen Staudt, 2003. *Rethinking Empowerment.* London: Routledge

Rai, S. M., 1997. 'Gender and Representation: Women MPs in the Indian Parliament', in Anne-Marie Goetz (ed.). *Getting Institutions Right for Women in Development.* London: Zed Books

Sharma, Kumud (no date). 'From Representation to Presence: The Paradox of Power and Powerlessness of Women', in *PRIs,* Occasional paper, CWDS

Chapter 5

Chapter 5

Azza Karam and Joni Lovenduski

Women in Parliament: Making a Difference

Although women remain significantly under-represented in today's parliaments, they are now looking beyond the numbers to focus on what they can actually do while in parliament—how they can make an impact, whatever their numbers may be. They are learning the rules of the game and using this knowledge and understanding to promote women's issues and concerns from inside the world's legislatures. In so doing, they are not only increasing the chances of their own success, but they are also paving the way for a new generation of women to enter the legislative process. How can women maximize their impact on the political process through parliament? What strategies are most useful in increasing their effectiveness? What lessons can women MPs share with those aspiring to enter the field? In what ways have women impacted on political processes? This is our focus in this chapter, as we move from the road to parliament to making inroads in parliament.

1. Making Inroads in Parliament

In the Beijing Platform for Action (1995), more than 180 governments agreed that 'Achieving the goal of equal participation of women and men in decision-making will provide a balance that…is needed…to strengthen democracy and promote its proper functioning'.[1] When women in different parts of the world struggled to win the right to vote, they expected that this would inevitably lead to greater women's representation. Their expectations were not always met, as chapters in this volume have illustrated. Instead, women embarked on another long and difficult struggle to actually get women elected to parliament. Part of this effort involves convincing women voters to support women as their representatives. In most countries, much of

> The actual impact women parliamentarians can make will depend on a number of variables, including the economic and political context in which the assembly functions, the background, experience and number of the women who are in parliament, and the rules of the parliamentary game.

the work centres on political parties, the typical channels of entry to national legislatures. Women inside and outside political parties organize and mobilize themselves to change long-established party methods of political recruitment.

Once women enter parliament, their struggle is far from over. In parliament, women enter a male domain. Parliaments were established, organized and dominated by men, acting in their own interest and establishing procedures for their own convenience. There was no deliberate conspiracy to exclude women. It was, in most cases, not even an issue. Most long-established parliaments were a product of political processes that were male-dominated or exclusively male. Subsequent legislatures are, for the most part, modelled on these established assemblies. Inevitably, these male-dominated organizations reflect certain male biases, the precise kind varying by country and culture.

Until recently, this 'institutional masculinity' has been an invisible characteristic of legislatures; it is embedded, pervasive and taken for granted. Only recently have legislatures' masculine biases come under scrutiny. Indeed, in most countries, the political role of women in legislatures became a public issue only in the second half of the 20th century.

In 2005, women constitute 16.0 percent of members of parliaments (MPs) worldwide. In the Nordic countries, their numbers are highest at 40.0 percent, while in the Arab states their representation (as of January 2005) was only 6.5 percent.[2]

As with previous efforts to try to get women elected to parliament, today women inside parliament are organizing, mobilizing, motivating and advancing women from inside the world's legislatures. They are devising strategies and taking action to promote issues relevant to women and facilitate changes in legislation.

The actual impact women parliamentarians can make will depend on a number of variables that vary from country to country. These include the economic and political context in which the assembly functions, the background, experience and number of the women who are in parliament, and the rules of the parliamentary process. Each of these factors has a significant bearing on the extent to which women MPs can make a difference once elected. Because these factors vary significantly from country to country, it is difficult to make generalizations that are universally relevant regarding how women MPs can maximize their impact.

In addition, there is relatively little research and information available on what sort of impact women have made. Underscoring the need for more knowledge and understanding in this particular field of women and decision-making, the United Nations' Beijing Platform for Action, together with the Commission on the Status of Women (CSW), call for more documentation on 'women making a difference' in politics.[3] Extrapolating from what is available in this field and on the basis of interviews and discussions with women MPs around the world, we have identified some of the strategies and mechanisms women are using and can use to impact on the process. We have formulated a strategy, what we refer to as the 'rules strategy', to organize and present these ideas. The case studies that follow illustrate some of these strategies in action.

1.1. Presence

The extent of women's impact will depend very much on the number of women in parliament who are motivated to represent women's issues and concerns.

Feminists often argue that pioneer women parliamentarians became surrogate men—that they were socialized into the legislature and became indistinguishable from the men they replaced. We doubt this. Men are known to behave differently when women are absent. Because it upsets gender boundaries, the presence of even one woman will alter male behaviour; the presence of several women will alter it even further. West European experience shows that where women MPs have a mission to effect change even small numbers can produce significant results.

While the presence of even one woman can make a difference, it is most likely that long-term significant change will only be realized when there is a substantial number of women in parliament who are motivated to represent women's concerns. Buoyed by their colleagues, women MPs may then elicit the active partnership of their male counterparts. However, change does not simply result from numbers; rather it is a complex process of overcoming resistance to women in which presence is only one part of the necessary mixture. According to Drude Dahlerup, the test that a critical mass of women is present is the acceleration of the development of women's representation through acts that improve the situation for themselves and for women in general. These actions are critical acts of empowerment.

Once present in larger numbers, and willing to act together on behalf of women, women MPs can overcome the 'tokenism' phenomenon, that is, move beyond the perception they are subjected to, as well as be enabled to form interactive and strategic partnerships both within the legislatures and outside them. Within the legislatures, a critical mass makes it easier to cross party lines, and particularly to reach out to their male colleagues—the other half of an important equation for social transformation. Their presence as a critical mass also multiplies the possibilities and extent of their outreach to civil society organizations, which, in turn, enhances the momentum required in impacting on the legislature and its policies. In her studies of women MPs in Scandinavia and elsewhere, Dahlerup found that women politicians worked to recruit other women and developed new legislation and institutions to benefit women. As their numbers grew it became easier to be a woman politician and public perceptions of women politicians changed.[4] In 2005, Mercedes Mateo Diaz found in her study of Belgian and Swedish legislators that as the presence of women MPs increases so does their social representativeness.[5] When the numbers of women were low, at around 15 to 20 percent, women MPs were less like women voters than male MPs are like male voters. The differences are due to distortions caused by recruitment procedures that were designed to select suitable men. To succeed in such processes women have to display 'male qualifications'; hence they are more likely to have characteristics associated with male MPs. For example, they may have careers in male-dominated professions such as business or law. To display such characteristics they may have sacrificed domestic lives, and hence are less likely than men or women in the general population to have children. However, as the proportion of women in parliament nears parity it becomes more likely that they will reflect the social characteristics of women in the electorate.

1.2. Rules Strategy

In this chapter, we have formulated a strategy to help maximize women's impact on the legislative process. The full development of this rules strategy requires a critical mass of women working on and promoting women's concerns.

Simply put, the strategy consists of three parts: **learning the rules, using the rules and changing the rules.** By rules we mean the customs, conventions, informal practices and specific regulations that govern the way a legislature functions. These include law-making processes, the division of labour in the assembly, hierarchy structures, ceremonies, disciplines, traditions, habits and the norms of the assembly including its internal functioning and its relationship to other parts of the government and to the nation it has been elected to serve.

This strategy of learning, using and changing the rules is based on the belief that there is a need for change and that an objective in electing women MPs is to secure change. There are essentially four types of change that will make a difference to women. They can be categorized as institutional/procedural change, representation change, influence on output and discourse.

1. Institutional/procedural change refers to measures that alter the nature of the institution to make it more 'woman-friendly'. Greater gender awareness should be accompanied by procedural changes designed to accommodate women members. This is a product of an increased sensitivity to the fact that class, age, ethnicity, race, physical ability, sexuality, parenting and life stage have a determining effect on women's lives, in much the same way as they do on men's lives.

2. Representation change involves specific actions to secure women's continued and enhanced access to the legislature. These include the encouragement of women candidates; conscious use of role model capacities when applicable; the promotion of sex equality legislation, or parity or equality regulations; and appropriate changes in electoral and campaigning laws. Representation change also includes actions in parliament that are designed to place women in important parliamentary positions and to secure their presence in government. It must also include changes in political parties that bring more women to legislatures. Women MPs often use the power their representative status gives them to support the improvement of political opportunities for women in their parties, as well as organizing to support women for higher office. Parliaments constitute a crucial pool of recruitment to higher office.

3. Impact/Influence on output refers specifically to the 'feminization' or re-gendering of legislation and other policy outputs, that is the extent to which laws and policies have been altered or influenced in women's favour. This includes both putting women's issues on the agenda and ensuring that all legislation is woman-friendly and gender-sensitive.

4. Discourse change involves changes both inside and outside parliament. Not only should efforts be made to alter parliamentary language so that women's perspectives are actively sought and normalized; it is also necessary to make use of the parliamentary platform to alter public attitudes and to change the discourse of politics so that a political woman becomes as frequent a fixture of the political space as a man. Such 'speaking out the window' uses the parliamentary opportunity of greater access to the mass media and to the general public to raise awareness of women's issues and of women's political capacities in public debate.

Table 15: Four Areas of Change that will Impact on Women's Participation

Institutional/Procedural	Making parliament more 'woman-friendly' through measures to promote greater gender awareness
Representation	Securing women's continued and enhanced access to parliament, by encouraging women candidates, changing electoral and campaigning laws and promoting sex equality legislation
Impact/Influence on Output	'Feminizing' legislation, by making sure it takes into account women's concerns
Discourse	Altering parliamentary language so that women's perspectives are sought and normalized, and encouraging a change in public attitudes towards women

Table 16: Women: Making Impact through Parliament

	Institutional/Procedural and Representation	Influence on Output and Discourse
Learning the Rules	Participate in training and orientation exercises on internal parliamentary codes of conduct (e.g., how to ask for the floor); develop public speaking and effective communication; and relate to and lobby male colleagues. Network with women's organizations. Mentoring and shadowing by more senior MPs. Understand and handle the media.	Distinguish between women's perspectives, women-specific needs, and gender issues. Caucus with media, national and international organizations. Draw attention to sexist discourse. Establish a presence within different committees (e.g. budget, defence, foreign affairs). Clarify the value and importance of 'soft' committees.
Using the Rules	Make a point of nominating and voting for women in internal elections and within parties. Draw attention to absence of women in key positions. Invest in committee work. Push for and establish government equal opportunity positions and women's ministries. Campaign to expand existing structures to include women's concerns. Set up networks to train in more convincing and less adversarial types of debate.	Influence parliamentary agendas: introduce women-sensitive measures (e.g. changes in parliamentary work schedules to suit working mothers). Establish public enquiries on women's issues and use findings to place issues on government agendas and within legislative programmes. Speak for, co-sponsor and sponsor bills. Seek partnership with male colleagues. Make public issue out of certain concerns by cooperating with the media (e.g. on ways of referring to women in parliament, sexual harassment issues). Link gender inequalities to other inequalities. Form alliances with other excluded groups to seek representation. Use the media as a part of the effective outreach strategy to widen women MPs' constituencies and public support bases.
Changing the Rules	Change candidate selection rules for the entire party, especially for leadership positions. Introduce quota systems on certain committees or issue of proportionality for men/women representation. Establish a women's whip. Establish gender equality committees. Establish national machinery to monitor implementation and ensure accountability; institutionalize regular debates on progress into the parliamentary timetable.	Encourage the providing of financial incentives to programmes/projects designed to facilitate women's decision-making endeavours (e.g. for leadership-training schools, increasing government subsidies to political parties with more women in leadership positions/ candidates; introducing a specific women's budget earmarked for enhancing women's decision making). Cooperate with the women's movement and the media to change the image of women as 'only' housewives, to portray them as effective and efficient politicians and to normalize

| Changing the Rules | Establish mechanisms to encourage female speakers (e.g. giving them priority over male colleagues). Participate in institutional and procedural reform and modernization processes to ensure the resulting changes are women-friendly. | the image of a woman politician. Be proud of identity as a woman, instead of attempting to imitate men and hide or deny womanhood. Expand legislation to include emerging issues of importance to women (e.g. conflict resolution and peace-making, human rights, special women's budgets). |

2. Learning the Rules

Legislatures debate policies, make laws, examine their implementation and effects, provide a recruitment pool for government and scrutinize the activities of government. Most legislatures have a budgetary function; they are responsible for both the formal allocation of the budget

> **The first step is for women MPs to understand how the legislature works in order to be able to use this knowledge to operate more effectively.**

and auditing government spending. They are organized into front and back benches, government and opposition, and functional and procedural committees. Through such structures, debate, monitoring, interrogation and interpolation are organized. MPs tend to specialize in particular issue areas and make their parliamentary reputations on the basis of their performance in the various structures and processes of the legislatures.

For women to be effective parliamentarians, they must clearly understand the functions of the legislature and they must learn the rules of the game—both the written and unwritten codes, and the procedures and mechanisms for getting things done in parliament. They must first learn the internal practices of parliament in order to equip themselves to utilize these rules better and to devise effective strategies to change the rules to advance women's interests and goals. These ideas are elaborated below, grouped under each of the four main areas of change, namely institutional/procedural, representation, influence on output and discourse. In the margins, to facilitate easy access and readability, we highlight some of the specific strategies that we suggest within each area.

2.1. Institutional/Procedural

The first step is for women MPs to understand how the legislature works in order to be able to use this knowledge to operate more effectively within the legislature. MPs can acquire this knowledge in a variety of ways, including

> **Learn about the legislature through orientation programmes and through training by political parties.**

specific training and orientation programmes as well as more general socialization processes. For example, it is common for legislative leaders and other officials to offer orientation to new members on how the assembly works. Often, political parties also provide such training.

Training by political parties is particularly useful since it offers insight into how the MP's party understands the procedures and how the party itself fits into the procedures. Since the organization of legislative work often depends on party composition, parties have a significant influence on procedures. In some parts of the world political parties offer special skills training especially for women, since they may be less experienced in legislative procedures than men. However, in many parts of the developing world most parties do not have the resources, or the willingness, to offer such training. In fact, as many of the case studies point out, very often party allegiance can handicap the development of political discourse in general and of any assistance to women MPs in particular. Political parties in some of the Arab and Latin American countries, for example, do not allow for any structural improvements and still operate on the assumption that women's perspectives and women's issues do not deserve any specific priority. This has repercussions within parties both in and out of the legislature.

Networking is a crucial training and socialization mechanism for women MPs. Networking provides quick access to knowledge that may otherwise take years of experience to acquire and enables women MPs to come together to discuss their concerns and share their knowledge and expertise, thus greatly enhancing their potential for effectiveness. Such networking takes place both within and

> Network with women MPs and mentoring (shadowing) by more experienced women MPs.

(less frequently) across party lines. Cross-party alliances of women MPs have been successful in a number of countries including Sweden, France, the Netherlands, South Africa, Croatia and Egypt. The issues are as diverse as rape laws, electoral reform, institutional reform, personal status and other country-specific issues (such as women's rights to apply for passports without their husbands' permission in Egypt, and social, political and economic rights for Dalits (or scheduled castes, formerly called 'untouchables') in India). Also noteworthy is the formation of 'support groups' composed of women professionals and MPs, a phenomenon especially apparent in European countries. In the words of one Finnish MP, Riitta Uosukainen, 'The fact that these women are able to get together across party lines, across professional areas and support each other not only personally, but also seek to do so professionally, is invaluable'. Mentoring (i.e. supervising, befriending and giving advice and guidance) by more experienced women MPs is another important way of providing special training for women MPs. In the Netherlands, for example, a system of 'shadowing' was developed whereby women who were hesitant to be nominated for elected office were assisted by elected members to gain confidence.

One global structure that seeks to provide a space for women to exchange ideas and strategies across nations is the Inter-Parliamentary Union (see the case study that follows this chapter). This body works to enhance the visibility and effectiveness of

Participate in joint training sessions for men and women.

women locally, regionally and internationally and also provides women MPs with mentoring, capacity-building support and information.

In addition to programmes specially geared for women, orientation exercises involving both men and women are important. In joint training sessions, women are encouraged to address their areas of interest and to network with male counterparts, as well as to learn how to break through established 'codes of conduct'. At the same time, male MPs are made aware of women's issues and the importance of enabling women MPs to act effectively in the legislature. The latter in particular is an important step in overcoming the sense of threat that many male deputies feel vis-à-vis women colleagues, since it provides an opportunity not only to raise awareness of gender issues, but to indicate the extent to which they are interlinked with most other social, economic and political concerns. Thus training and orientation of male parliamentarians play an important role in the mainstreaming of women's issues and perspectives.

In addition to information about both the written and the unwritten rules and procedures of parliament, women may also find training in voice and image projection and public speaking particularly helpful. Many women have difficulty speaking authoritatively and arguing convincingly, and some find it difficult to make themselves heard in large legislative chambers. New entrants, in particular in developing democracies, confess that they find it difficult to be given the opportunity to speak and to know the ins and outs of parliamentary speaking procedures. The effectiveness of former actress Glenda Jackson in the British House of Commons, for example, proves that a trained woman's voice can have as much impact as a man's.

Some women MPs in established democracies have also organized media training sessions. This involves, among other things, seminars and workshops where MPs are informed about 'media-speak' (i.e. what kind of information the media are interested in and how best to deliver it) and advised on how to network with media personalities and on which ones are more sympathetic to women's issues.

Learn how to handle the media.

2.2. Representation

Institutional rules, customs and procedures (in addition to party politics) are key to determining the legislative positions and functions, such as committee assignments and participation in debates on the floor. Recruitment to these important positions may depend on any one or a combination of factors including party position, seniority, faction, ability, support for the government, national or local profile and

Identify key positions in parliament and develop channels to get women in.

issue expertise. While the appropriate strategy will depend to some extent on the number of women in the legislature, at a minimum women should identify key interests, positions and functions and strategize about ways to get women into the relevant forum. If existing channels are not open to promoting women into key positions, new avenues should be developed.

2.2.1. Gender Equality Committees

In some countries, such avenues could be parliamentary or governmental women's committees or broader equality committees that include women's rights in their mandate. Formal and informal gender equality committees were successfully established in Sub-Saharan Africa and the Netherlands, while the assemblies of Scotland and Wales have broadly-based equality committees which, under pressure from women representatives, take a close interest in equality. Also effective are committees of women legislators such as those found in New Zealand, Australia and the USA. In other cases, nationwide umbrella organizations (non-governmental) or strong grass-roots organizations can act as catalysts to get women into key areas. Further avenues could be opened through training and educational programmes, or through pressure for representation by the media. International pressure could also be used to encourage governments to include women at all levels of power and decision making.[6] Knowledge about these positions and about ways to get women in can be shared by mentoring, caucusing and networking both among women and with male colleagues.

Women in key positions not only enhance their own ability to make an impact; they also facilitate opportunities for other women to speak out. For example, a study of the Colorado State legislature measured differences in the speaking behaviour of members of legislative committees by sex, seniority, interest and party. It was found that women did better at controlling the dialogue and making themselves heard when other women were present, visible (sitting where they could be seen) and in positions of authority.[7] This research also showed that male dominance of conversation, discussion and meetings enhanced men's power and undermined that of some women even where the formal positions of men and women legislators were equal.

One way of building women's careers and thus their advancement into key positions is by learning how to use the media to increase the visibility and confidence of women parliamentarians. Since women employed in the media have their own problems of self-establishment and advancement they may be sympathetic to MPs interested in women's concerns. In fact, one of the key problems in most media is the lack of women in decision-making posts, which effectively means that decisions concerning editorial content and

Use the media to increase women's visibility.

production issues are largely controlled by men. As the presence of women in the media expands, so do the possibilities for women MPs and politicians, journalists and other broadcasters and writers to network on the basis of common interests and concerns.

Typically, women's interests have led them to what is still perceived as the less prestigious (and possibly less powerful) social policy areas of specialization, that is, committee assignments such as education, health and family affairs. Many women MPs believe it is necessary to establish women's presence in traditionally influential sites within parliaments, such as finance, defence and foreign affairs. Others argue that the distinction itself cannot be justified. European political scientists have made the important point that describing social issues as 'soft' caricaturizes them as unimportant and ignores the facts that these areas, in which European women are most active, account for the largest share of public expenditure—education, health and social services at local and regional levels. Women choose these areas because they prefer them and they accept making the very difficult decisions such as whether to prioritize care of the elderly or day care.[8] The traditional distinction between 'hard' and 'soft' issues is old-fashioned and inaccurate and should be contested by women representatives. Ideally a twofold strategy must be developed: on the one hand, the importance of such areas needs to be continually stressed; on the other hand, simultaneous efforts should be made to ensure women's active participation in all policy areas.

> **Stress the importance of 'soft' committees, while working to establish the presence of women in all committees.**

2.3. Impact/Influence on Output

To discuss the impact of women representatives it is useful to make a distinction between women's issues and women's perspectives. Women's issues are issues that mainly affect women, either due to largely physical concerns (e.g. breast cancer screening, reproductive rights) or for social reasons (e.g. sex equality or childcare policy). Women's perspectives are women's views on all political concerns. Some research indicates that, although broadly the same issues are significant for both sexes, women's perspective on issues differs from that of men. For example, research carried out in Britain in 1996 showed that, although both women and men prioritized economic issues, women were more concerned about part-time work, low pay and pension rights, while men were more concerned about unemployment.

> **Distinguish between women's perspectives and women's issues; and educate MPs about both.**

MPs need to have knowledge and understanding of both women's issues and women's perspectives—if only, as most contributors to this volume have expressed, to see the other half of reality—in order to produce output that has a favourable impact on women. The kind of impact MPs will wish to have will inevitably vary by party.

Stay informed about women's issues, by maintaining close links with the women's movement and women's organizations.

In her research on Sweden (in this volume) for instance, Lena Wängnerud reports that women representatives from different political parties tend to emphasize women's issues and concerns.

But the need for knowledge and information exists regardless of party perspective. Women MPs have successfully used various means of becoming informed about women's issues and perspectives. Most important in this regard is what contributors to this volume have repeatedly highlighted—maintaining close links with women's organizations of all kinds and drawing on their expertise and resources. Such linkages with women's movements also enhance the legitimacy of MPs and keep them in touch with changing, often varying, women's concerns and policy needs. European parliamentarians have made use of the goodwill and knowledge of academic experts to draft policies on such matters as domestic violence, female bondage, trafficking in women, care of children and the aged, pensions and women's health issues. Research on policy issues is a major political tool and can be gathered and used by MPs by participating in conferences organized by women's organizations, experts and politicians and by caucusing with other MPs who have similar interests. Caucusing is part of both learning and using the rules. MPs interested in a particular issue, for example employment or women's health, might meet to identify important upcoming votes and committee discussions and decide on tactics and strategies to influence the outcome. Another strategy is to facilitate the access of women voters to their legislators. In Scotland a crèche was established for visitors to the assembly to ensure that those with childcare responsibilities (usually women) can seek out and meet their representatives.

2.4. Discourse

Parliaments have their own distinct language, a product both of their specialized tasks and functions and of their culture and their traditional male membership. In the United Kingdom (UK), for example, the House of Commons had a discourse characterized by a formal set of titles, modes of address and rules of debate, as well as a barracking, sexist and scatological 'humour', from many years of male domination, that women MPs found offensive, especially when it was used on them. Familiarity with speaking and debating techniques can help to curtail such 'yahoo' heckling. British women have successfully used the media to draw attention to the sexism in the House of Commons by revealing these practices to women in the media and to other journalists eager to criticize ill-behaved MPs. The result has been a series of

Reveal sexist discourse; and learn speech and debating techniques to quell it.

press and broadcasting items about the childish and sexist behaviour of male MPs. The public, previously unaware of this, disapproved of their MPs' behaviour.

3. Using the Rules

By learning how to use the rules, women can seize opportunities to participate on key committees and positions, make themselves heard in discussions and debates, and fully utilize their skills and abilities.

Gaining familiarity with the rules is the first part of a longer-term process to enhance women's position and to highlight women's issues and perspectives. The next step is to learn how to use the rules for maximum impact. One of the problems many women parliamentarians face is that they are not allocated time in discussions and debates and they find it difficult to be selected for participation on key committees and in key positions. Thus they are not able to fully utilize their skills and abilities and their contribution cannot be accurately assessed. By learning how to use the rules, together with other women deputies and the media, women can break this vicious circle. Many of the tactics for using the rules, discussed below, can be shared across national boundaries.

Intergovernmental organizations such as the Council of Europe, the Commonwealth Secretariat, the European Union and the United Nations and international non-governmental organizations (NGOs) can and do play a vital role in helping women learn how to use the rules by facilitating the sharing of information. Their meetings bring together experts and politicians to network and exchange ideas and their publications make these discussions about women's needs, strategies and achievements available to a wider audience.

3.1. Institutional/Procedural

Formal and informal parliamentary roles are often allocated by established rules and procedures. There is, nevertheless, some room for influence and intervention which women should maximize. For example, women MPs should make a point of nominating and voting for women in internal elections, of suggesting women's names for informal positions, and of drawing attention to the absence or relative absence of women in key positions. Particular attention should be given to opportunities available in committee work, as there is considerable evidence from the long-established democracies that women do better in committee work than in debating chambers. Having said this, women

> **Make a point of nominating and voting for women in internal elections.**

should not abandon debating chambers since this is where parliamentary reputations are often made and where the media often direct their sustained attention. The skill of debating in general is a particularly important one and can be encouraged and sponsored through parliamentary networks linked up to schools, that is, through the curricula, as well as through leadership institutions. Women's parliamentary networks can also play a crucial role in supporting women speakers and in changing to less adversarial styles of debate.

Since government careers tend to follow from legislative careers, the advancement of women through the range of committees and through the legislative hierarchy is an important component in their qualification for high office. Equal opportunity positions in government and ministries for women's affairs and their shadow counterparts in opposition parties are other positions that have been well used by women politicians to advance their interests and their careers.

For example, between 1992 and 1997 four Labour women MPs in the UK were shadow ministers for women. All four were appointed to important government positions (two at cabinet level) when Labour won the election in 1997. They proved reliable advocates of gender equality and were supporters of women's concerns in their departments. Their numbers expanded in 2001. This indicates (a) that such positions need not be a ghetto for women, but may instead be a means of advancement, and (b) that they can facilitate the mainstreaming of gender sensitivity across government.

3.2. Representation

Rules have been used to increase women's representation in a number of ways. In this area, a three-track strategy has proved effective:

- pressure political parties to ensure that women are nominated for winnable seats in the legislature;
- design procedural mechanisms to ensure the presence of women in the full range of parliamentary positions; and
- design legislation that creates new structures to ensure that women's interests are represented.

The expansion of political structures, whether by creating new ministries or expanding the size of the cabinet for instance, has proved a useful means of securing women's representation. Modernization and reform of existing legislatures or the creation of new legislatures offers opportunities to secure or enhance women's representation. A good example is Scotland where feminists intervened in the process of constitutional change to secure a Scottish legislature in which women were fairly represented. Under the umbrella of the Scottish Women's Co-ordination Group they lobbied the Constitutional Convention and the political parties to gender the debate on devolution. They became involved in debates about institutional design and the recruitment of legislators. When the first Scottish Parliament was elected in 1999, 37 percent of its members were women, as were 30 percent of ministers, and 41 percent of committee members, including six out of 17 chairs. All the numbers increased in the subsequent election in 2003. However, constitutional change is an opportunity, not a guarantee, as experiences in

Campaign to expand existing structures to include women.

Eastern and Central Europe and with the European Convention indicate.[9]

In Costa Rica, a practice that the vice-president should be a woman has been established. The experience of the Netherlands shows that the creation of parliamentary committees on women's issues is one way of making positions available for women. Such committees scrutinize all legislation for their gendered content and thereby aid the extension of women's agendas. They also enhance awareness of the gendered nature of many political issues. The committees feed into the legislative process and also play a part in generating public discussion on such issues.

Concern has been expressed by women deputies in many countries that such devices may serve only to separate and 'ghettoize' women's issues and the politicians who support them. Although 'ghettoization' may be a risk in the short term, experience indicates that over time such work becomes accepted and, in fact, affirms and legitimizes broader gender issues. Moreover women gain valuable experience by serving on women's committees, in reserved places and in women's ministries. They may then extend their influence by working with other committees on different issues, for example by monitoring the implementation of the Beijing Platform for Action or other international treaties. Women's committees need not be seen as permanent structures, but while in existence they can enable women to display their skills and thus serve as launching platforms for careers in other political areas. Moreover women who have experience of sex equality portfolios carry this increased awareness and knowledge of women's issues to other ministries, thus advancing the process of mainstreaming women's concerns.[10]

> **Serve on women's ministries to gain valuable experience. Carry this increased awareness to other positions.**

3.3. Impact/Influence on Output

Knowledge of the procedural rules has frequently been used to influence the parliamentary agenda by introducing women's concerns into otherwise gender-blind debates—forcing debates on issues such as reproductive rights, equal pay, childcare and child rights—as well as by proposing sex equality legislation and amendments. Parliamentarians have established public enquiries into women's status and condition, and then used the results to push through legislative programmes. Once the issues are on the agenda, the behaviour of other politicians changes. After all, it is more difficult politically to come out against equality for women than it is to prevent equality issues from getting onto the agenda in the first place. An example in the UK is the Sex Discrimination Candidates Act of 2002 which permits political parties to use affirmative action to increase the number of women MPs and candidates. The bill was passed with all-party support and almost no dissent because its opponents were silent, unwilling to oppose women's representation in public. For

> **Influence parliamentary agendas by introducing women's issues into debates.**

similar reasons many male opponents abstained from participating in the French parité debate in the National Assembly in 2000.

In some cases, activities such as co-sponsorship, speech-making and sponsorship of bills by women have been much more effective than their actual votes. One study looking at the support for women's issues in the French legislative structures found that women were more likely than men to co-sponsor feminist bills, to make speeches on behalf of feminist legislation and to sponsor feminist legislation. A study of early day motions, which are devices for drawing attention to issues in the UK House of Commons, found women MPs much more active than their male colleagues in supporting women's concerns.[11]

There are many instances in some parts of the developing world, however, where women MPs shy away from any association with bills on women. This is largely

Speak in favour of, sponsor and co-sponsor bills.

due to their sense that such arguments would lack support and endorsement from their fellow colleagues and may contribute to their marginalization, as well as to a certain stigma associated with being 'feminists'. This further underscores the need for mainstreaming women's concerns, or raising awareness about the interlinkage between women's issues and every other issue handled by parliament. Budget and economic interests, for example, are not and should not be seen as only male concerns since they affect everyone. Similarly, health, social welfare and education do not only affect women.

3.4. Discourse

In certain countries, cultural norms of equality between men and women, or discourse on rights, meritocracy and conventions about representation, may be avenues that can be used to alter parliamentary balances. For example, Danish women MPs have succeeded in altering the parliamentary discourse. Drude Dahlerup notes how, prior to the entry of significant numbers of women into the Scandinavian parliaments, most politicians did not have the vocabulary to speak about issues such as discrimination, inequality, sexual harassment or sexual violence. Most had problems even using the word for women and preferred to use euphemisms. Over time in the Nordic states the increased presence of women has altered the style of campaigning, bringing in expressions of warmth and compassion as well as references to the family.[12] This does render campaigning less adversarial. In the Netherlands, study of legislative debates reveals how women's interventions have been associated with changing the way in which abortion policy is debated, notably its shift from a medical or religious issue to an issue of choice.[13] Research from the UK shows that the interventions of women MPs are more likely than

Make a public issue of concerns, such as sexual harassment.

those of men to refer to examples of how policies and decisions affect individuals and families, while male MPs invoke abstract concepts such as citizens or constituents.[14]

The participation of women politicians in major international conferences has also had an important effect on challenging public notions of what women can do. One example is the way in which perceptions about the women's movement in Egypt and in other Arab countries changed following the International Conference on Population and Development (ICPD) that was held in Cairo in September 1994. Prior to this conference, many Egyptian women MPs, and indeed the general public, had at best been ignorant of the women's movement and at worst been downright disdainful of its capabilities. Those involved in the women's movement held a similar view of women parliamentarians. The ICPD was an opportunity for women MPs to actually witness what women's NGOs had managed to accomplish and to network with them on issues of common interest. It also enabled the women's movement to realize that they could have potential allies in women MPs since they shared many interests and goals. Regardless of what may have actually happened later on, at least there was a perceptible change in awareness on the part of both the MPs and the women's organizations. Equally important was a shift in public awareness and perception of women as activists and as politicians. The ICPD and subsequent international networking opportunities demonstrated to the general public that women's issues (whether it was changes in family law, reproductive rights or female circumcision) were part of their general concerns and that, rather than a bunch of loose women clamouring for change, those articulating these concerns were capable and intelligent women who deserved to be listened to and taken seriously.

> Get involved in international conferences to highlight women's potential and capabilities.

4. Changing the Rules

The presence of women and the introduction of women's concerns will inevitably challenge existing arrangements and procedures. At a minimum, parliamentary timetables, places of meeting, childcare provisions, working hours and travel arrangements may be changed to make them more suitable for women.

One of the most significant changes that we have noted is the networking of women across party lines. This underscores the now more frequent cross-party cooperation by women legislators found in the European Parliament, South Africa, the USA, the Netherlands, France, Belgium and Italy on issues such as women's representation policy, forced marriage, domestic violence, reproductive rights, rape and employment equality.[15]

Women's experiences in a variety of parliamentary roles will build up political capital which can be used to secure further advancement, to help change existing rules and structures, and to assist new generations of women politicians.

4.1. Institutional/Procedural

Changes in parliamentary structures and procedures might include the introduction of proportionality norms for men's and women's membership in committees, the establishment of women's whips (responsible for organizing the parliamentary votes of women in a particular party) and formal or informal quotas for women in various legislative positions. Internal voluntary party quota systems have been used effectively in Germany at the local and national levels, and have been introduced in France by means of legislation. In countries where compulsory quotas are politically difficult, voluntary targets can be set. At their most effective such policies include deadlines and realistic timetables for implementation.

Mechanisms to monitor the implementation of quotas that are accountable to the assembly should be established. This ensures that regular discussions on progress are part of the parliamentary timetable. Setting up committees on women's issues and national women's policy agencies that are also accountable to parliament have similar effects. Accountability to parliament ensures that their work is scrutinized, debated and publicized, providing numerous additional opportunities for discussion of women's concerns. For example, the South African Government has implemented a national gender machinery which proposes changes in legislation and supervises and ensures implementation. The case of South Africa reveals how simultaneous functions, both inside and outside parliament, can operate: in South Africa a new constitution was drafted, a woman's empowerment programme was set up in consultation with women parliamentarians and an Office for the Status of Women was created to mainstream women's concerns and ensure follow-up. A Commission on Gender Equality was also established in 1997 to promote gender equality and to advise and make recommendations to the legislature about how proposed legislation affects gender equality and the status of women (see the case study). An important challenge is to ensure that these institutional mechanisms maintain their links with grass-roots activists, so that MPs are aware of what takes place outside the parliamentary walls.

> **Introduce proportionality norms or quotas for the representation of women and men.**

Changes in procedure can be effective in and of themselves and can also have a wider impact on society. One such practice is in place in the German Bundestag: when a woman raises her hand to speak in discussions she is automatically shifted to the top of the list of male speakers. This practice seeks to overcome women's diffidence about speaking in male-dominated groups by maximizing their opportunities to participate. It has become so ingrained in MPs that they repeat the practice even when they are outside parliament.

More fundamental changes involve changing the way in which certain issues, namely those closer to women's concerns and in which women have an expertise (e.g. education, welfare policy, family policy), are viewed in the parliamentary hierarchy. As we have mentioned, the distinction between 'hard' and 'soft' issues is difficult to sustain and is likely to break down. This process will develop from increased interest in 'soft' issues by all politicians, as women deputies become more successful in pushing them up the parliamentary agenda. Agenda changes are closely related to output changes.

Break down distinction between 'hard' and 'soft' issues.

4.2. Representation

Networks of women MPs have been successful in changing candidate selection rules to assist women's access to political office. Special measures such as quotas or minimum proportion rules for both sexes on candidate lists, reserved places for women and earmarked public funds for political parties have been operationalized. Political parties have been at the centre of most of the effective strategies to enhance women's representative capacities. Parties have developed strategies to promote women internally into decision-making positions in the party organization and externally into elected assemblies and public appointments. Generally they have been more radical, committed and imaginative in devising policies to bring women into internal party positions than to nominate women as candidates for elected office. Their most effective action has been the introduction of various kinds of quotas.

Quotas are, in most cases, temporary measures designed to overcome imbalances that exist between men and women. They are an effort to change the political equilibrium between women and men. The different types of quotas, and their consequences, are detailed by Drude Dahlerup in chapter 4 of this Handbook.

Another important representation strategy is to expand definitions of representation to include all public decision-making bodies, and to campaign for women's inclusion in the senior civil service and the judiciary. Such campaigns have been undertaken in Austria, Finland, the Netherlands, the UK and elsewhere. A difficult but necessary further step will be the extension of such demands to the private sector, as has happened in Finland.

Change candidate selection rules to assist women's access to political office.

4.3. Impact/Influence on Output

One clear indication that women have influenced output is the fact that quotas exist for women in political parties and parliament. Output changes are inevitable as women become more and more effective in promoting women's issues and concerns. Once women's issues are raised and sustained on the agenda, they rapidly secure the interest of all politicians. This interest can apply to a wide host of issues—political, economic, social and even cultural.

Recent research indicates that the most effective way to influence output and promote women's equality is to provide financial incentives to programmes geared towards women. For example, to enhance the education of girls, the Indian

Government pledged to match and double any contribution made to the building of girls' schools. The Dutch Government previously used the system of public funding of political parties to earmark special funding for the promotion of women candidates by all parties. South Africa introduced a women's budget to fund projects that cater to the particular needs and interests of women. Financial incentives may be targeted directly at women's representation by tying the public funding of political parties to their numbers of elected women legislators. This policy has been implemented in Italy, for elections to the European Parliament, and France, for elections to the National Assembly so that parties which do not nominate or return a certain number of women legislators forgo some of their public funding.

> **Encourage financial incentives for programmes geared for women.**

4.4. Discourse

The most important change affecting discourse has been the overturning of implicit rules limiting appropriate topics of debate to matters in the 'public' sphere. In cooperation with women's movements, parliamentarians in some countries have extended the agenda of legislatures to discussions of domestic violence, stalking, rape, forced marriage, female genital mutilation, consent in marriage and the rights of lesbian mothers.

Further change in the area of discourse can come about once women themselves become increasingly proud of their identities as women. Former member of the European Parliament (MEP) Hedy D'Ancona surveys some of the most influential women MEPs of the 1990s and argues that by not being shy of their 'womanhood', but rather being proud of their identity as women, they have enhanced their work, impact and performance.[16] Women are often apologetic about rather than proud or assertive of their identity as women. A change in a woman politician's self-perception, Nadezhda Shvedova maintains, remains key to changing public perception and reaction to women and their contributions.

A woman's sex identity and her 'outsider' status can even enhance electoral attractiveness, particularly in times of constitutional crisis. As relatively new political entrants, women are often not associated with the corrupt and autocratic practices of collapsing regimes. Instead they can become symbols of modernity, honesty, democracy and caring, all images that are invaluable to reform movements.

The process of increasing the proportion of women in legislatures is part of a larger phenomenon of changing political images so that politics starts to be regarded as a normal activity for women. To take hold, such an attitude shift requires significant reinforcement in the mass media, and support from within the women's movement.

5. Criteria for Measuring Success

'I am convinced that when we have established and are working with a system based on real equality, then the quality of women's participation will be raised.'

Birgitta Dahl, former Speaker of Parliament, Sweden

To claim that women representatives make a difference in political processes, it is necessary to establish clear criteria to measure their impact. A fundamental component of such criteria is that women parliamentarians act, at least some of the time, in women's interests. In formulating such criteria, it should also be recognized that: (a) there are many, sometimes conflicting, women's interests to be represented; and (b) the very presence of women in a traditional male environment creates gender awareness and alters expectations.

As we have mentioned, what women can actually achieve will vary according to their numbers in parliament. Numbers form an important, necessary if not sufficient condition for sustained impact. It takes a substantial minority of women to ensure that critical acts of representation are undertaken. As the numbers of women grow we should expect increased participation by women in all aspects of parliamentary life, including interventions in debate, the proposing and sponsoring of legislation, access to parliamentary resources and occupancy of leading positions.

Another criterion for determining success is that women's impact must be detectable in legislation on women's issues. With women's growing effectiveness, and enhanced representation, all legislation will increasingly take women's perspectives into account as a matter of course. An especially telling indication of women's impact will be an increase both in men raising women's issues and in men's deferring to women's voices on all legislative debates which would exhibit a concern for women's perspectives.

An important facet of success will involve interaction between the different agents of change—governments, women MPs, women's organizations and other members of civil society, locally, regionally and internationally. It should always be remembered that partnership between women and men is a key ingredient in the process of change and impact. Many women MPs openly acknowledge that to attempt to work alone, without men, is not feasible.[17]

6. Strategies to Enhance Impact

The following are some of the main strategies to help women maximize their power and effectiveness as representatives.

1. Raise awareness. Campaigns with the media should focus public attention on the importance of balanced participation and representation of women and men. Political parties or women's organizations could be financed to mount such campaigns and related activities. NGOs interested in encouraging the participation of women in political life have often been active in awareness raising. To encourage such campaigns, women and men politicians must be proactive in identifying and establishing relations and promoting these issues with key members of civil society as well as with media producers and presenters. An example of this is the Movement for Equal Rights–Equal Responsibilities in Cyprus which aims to promote public awareness that women can be politicians.

2. Work in partnership with men. This entails designing programmes, whether inside or outside specific political forums, that take into account men's concerns and perspectives with respect to solidarity with women politicians. This idea is now gaining credibility with the growing realization that women need the support of their male colleagues, partners and electorate to enhance the effectiveness of their strategies and increase the value of their social and political message.

3. Enlarge the pool of eligible, aspirant women. This means enhancing women's interest in becoming politicians as well as increasing their involvement in politics. Eligibility for and involvement in politics are partly a matter of access to general resources such as education, income and time, and partly a matter of specific resources such as knowledge and information about politics and political experience. Policies to enhance women's access to higher education, to paid employment and to various social and economic organizations provide a context for political participation that is increasingly hospitable to women. However, even where they lack adequate resources to participate politically, women are devising creative strategies to mobilize resources that would facilitate their access. For example, in India some women draw upon transitional networks of extended family, neighbourhood links and other 'women-centred' spheres to enable them to gather the resources they may require.

4. Take positive action. Quotas have been particularly effective in increasing women's presence in legislatures. Both incremental and 'fast-track' models have been used effectively. An example of the incremental model is Sweden, where women used several means to press their parties to nominate women candidates and place them in favourable positions on party lists. One way was to simply put forward women's names, a tactic that was very important in the early stages. They also conducted campaigns to promote women candidates and issued proposals to get women into better positions on party lists. Finally, they acted as watchdogs and protested whenever reversals occurred. This process of securing substantial increases in women's electoral fortunes was achieved without recourse to formal compulsory quotas. Recommendations, arguments and the threat to press for quotas succeeded in setting targets requiring women to get 40 percent of the nominations. Once these targets were set, considerable progress was achieved.[18] Fast-track models have been more commonly used in transitional or democratizing countries.

5. Amend laws to allow positive discrimination. Such practices were once rare in politics. In the past governments did not use the law to compel parties to promote women, not least because such policies often ran against other legal principles. But this is an area of change as governments have legislated to compel (Belgium), to provide incentives (France, Italy) or to permit (the UK) measures to guarantee better representation of women legislators. Moreover, some countries have introduced laws requiring that women hold a certain proportion of seats on government-appointed bodies. Such laws were introduced in Denmark in 1985, Finland in 1987, Sweden in 1987, Norway in the 1980s, the Netherlands in 1992 and Germany in 1994. Published statistics in these countries indicate that women's participation in such bodies has risen steadily since. Governments can also use incentives. This is particularly easy where there is state funding of political parties. For example, the Dutch Government was able to make financial support for political parties dependent on their efforts to increase the proportion of women in their electoral bodies.

6. Raise the general standard of living and access to resources of all women. The high achievements of Scandinavian women stem from a combination of government policy, party initiative and demographic changes. The remarkable position of women in Scandinavian politics rests on social/demographic foundations involving considerable changes in the structure of women's family, economic and social lives. These are probably irreversible. The policies on equality of representation have included government equality reforms operating in conjunction with the influence of the women's movement, functioning both autonomously and through the political parties. To some extent there is feedback between demographic and political change as policies have included explicit attempts to change demographics and the gendered division of labour both in the family and in paid employment.

7. Build and maintain links with women's organizations and civil society institutions as a whole. The maintenance of ties to the women's movement is crucial both for their support and for information on issues; similarly, the women's movement needs bases in political parties and in the legislature.

8. Caucus and network. This allows women MPs to share information, ideas, resources and support. Networks may be party-based, cross-party (very rare), local, regional and international. Meetings, conferences, seminars, newsletters and electronic mail links are useful networking devices. Consultations with women's organizations and research gauging the needs of women (demand) and their practical constraints (supply) enable women MPs to target their efforts to activities that will be most useful and effective. In this regard training on the use of information and communication technology, and eventually also on an introduction to and efficiency in emerging e-government practices, will become increasingly necessary to place women firmly at the cutting edge of governance as a whole.

9. Use the mass media effectively. Women MPs must use the mass media, particularly the resources offered by women broadcasters, editors and journalists, to communicate their concerns and highlight relevant issues. As well as enhancing the image of women MPs and promoting their political ideas, the mass media are instrumental in educating and mobilizing voters, particularly in rural areas—an important concern particularly in developing countries where women, with limited resources, may have difficulty reaching out to these voters.

10. Establish women's committees and other machinery accountable to the legislature. This provides opportunities for women deputies to gain experience and for women's issues and perspectives to be debated and publicized.

11. Collect, monitor and disseminate statistics and facts about women's political participation and representation. This enables women's advocates in parliament to analyse the position of women in decision making and to define problems, devise appropriate solutions and seek political support for their preferred solutions. In particular, a collation of data on how women MPs have actually managed to make a difference through their legislatures is an ongoing need.

12. Mainstream gender issues. Ensure that gender issues are integrated within different political, social and economic concerns, in order to reveal the interdependence and linkages with other issue areas.

The ultimate objective of enhancing the quality of women's political participation is a goal that must be worked towards constantly. In much the same way as men's political input is in constant need of improvement, women should not be complacent about their contributions to the political process; nor should they take whatever gains are achieved for granted. Political participation is a process that is evolving and developing. The actors involved in this process should be prepared always to strive to keep ahead of the changes. The women and men involved in this process should work together to be agents of change, constantly aware that obstacles are but means to realize new and evolving strategies. Women and men politicians have achieved a great deal in the area of women's participation. Politicians of both sexes have contributed to advancing women's political participation in general and within legislative structures in particular. Although the road ahead is long, the lessons learned from the accumulation of experiences can, and will, significantly illuminate and smooth the many paths ahead.

Notes

[1] United Nations, 1995. 'The Beijing Platform for Action: Women in Decision Making', para. 181, available at <http://www.un.org/womenwatch/daw/beijing/platform/decision.htm>.

[2] Inter-Parliamentary Union, 2005. 'Women in National Parliaments: Situation as of 31 July 2005', <http://www.ipu.org/wmn-e/world.htm>.

[3] Excerpted from the moderator's summary published as UN document ECN.6/1997/lL.2/Add.2.

[4] Dahlerup, Drude, 1988. 'From a Small to a Large Minority: Theory of Critical Mass'. *Scandinavian Political Studies*. Vol. 11, no. 4, pp. 275–98. See also Lovenduski, Joni, 2005. *Feminizing Politics*. Oxford: Polity Press.

[5] *Mateo Diaz,* Mercedes, 2005. *Representing Women? Female Legislators in West European Parliaments.* Colchester: ECPR Press.

[6] See also chapter 4 on how quotas can help this process.

[7] Kathlene, L., 1995. 'Position Power versus Gender Power: Who Holds the Floor?', in G. L. Duerst-Lahti and R. M. Kelly (eds). *Gender Power, Leadership and Governance.* Ann Arbor, Mich.: University of Michigan Press, pp. 167–94.

[8] Raaum, N. C., 1995. 'The Political Representation of Women: A Birds Eye View', in L. Karvonen and Per Selle (eds). *Women in Nordic Politics.* London: Dartmouth Press.

[9] Lovenduski 2005, op. cit., pp. 85–8.

[10] Skjeie, Hege, 1991. 'The Rhetoric of Difference: On Women's Inclusion in Political Elites'. *Politics and Society.* No. 2.

[11] Childs, S. and J. Withey, 2005. 'Sex Equality and the Signing of Early Day Motions in the 1997 Parliament'. Political Studies. Vol. 52, issue 3.

[12] Karvonen, L., G. Djupsund and T. Carlson, 1995. 'Political Language', in Karvonen and Selle (eds), op. cit.

[13] Outschoorn, J., 1986. 'Women in Nordic Politics. The Rules of the Game: Abortion Politics in the Netherlands', in J. Lovenduski and J. Outschoorn (eds). *The New Politics of Abortion.* London: Sage.

[14] Lovenduski 2005, op. cit.

[15] Lovenduski, Joni with Claudie Baaudino, Marila Guadagnini, Petra Meier and Diane Sainsbury (eds), 2005. *State Feminism and Political Representation.* Cambridge: Cambridge University Press.

[16] D'Ancona, Hedy, 1997. 'Politieke diva's rekenen af met de haantjestcultuur in Brussel' [Political divas reckon with the working culture of Brussels]. Opzij. December.

[17] See the Inter-Parliamentary Union's references to this in the case study that follows.

[18] Sainsbury, Diane, 1993. 'The Politics of Increased Women's Representation: The Swedish Case', in Joni Lovenduski and Pippa Norris (eds). *Gender and Party Politics.* London: Sage.

References and Further Reading

Childs, S. and J. Withey, 2005. 'Sex Equality and the Signing of Early Day Motions in the 1997 Parliament'. *Political Studies.* Vol. 52, issue 3

Dahlerup, Drude, 1988. 'From a Small to a Large Minority: Theory of Critical Mass.' *Scandinavian Political Studies.* Vol. 11, no. 4, pp. 275–98

— and Freidenvall, L., 2005. 'Quotas as a Fast Track to Equal Political Representation'. *International Feminist Journal of Politics.* Vol. 7, no. 1, March, pp. 26–48

Dodson, Debra L., 1991. *Gender and Policy Making: Studies of Women in Office.* New Jersey: Centre for the American Woman and Politics, Eagleton Institute, Rutgers University

Karvonen L. and Per Selle (eds), 1995. *Women in Nordic Politics: Closing the Gap.* London: Dartmouth Press

Krook, Mona Lena, 2003. 'Gender Quotas: A Framework for Analysis'. ECPR General Conference, Marburg

Lovenduski, Joni. 2005. *Feminizing Politics.* Oxford: Polity Press

—, with Claudie Baudino, Marila Guadagnini, Petra Meier and Diane Sainsbury (eds), 2005. *State Feminism and Political Representation.* Cambridge: Cambridge University Press

Matteo-Diaz, Mercedes. 2005. *Representing Women? Female Legislators in West European Parliaments.* Colchester: ECPR Press

Case Study: The IPU

Promoting Partnership between Men and Women in Parliament: The Experience of the Inter-Parliamentary Union

Sonia Palmieri and Kareen Jabre

Partnership and Democracy

The Inter-Parliamentary Union (IPU) works for the enhancement and strengthening of democracy through the institution of parliament. It does this based on the understanding that there is a fundamental relationship between gender equality in politics and democracy, and that more precisely the involvement of women in all aspects of political life is key to a more just and equitable society, as well as to stronger, more representative democracy. In 1997, the IPU consolidated these views in its Universal Declaration of Democracy, article 4 of which explicitly endorsed the link between democracy and a 'genuine partnership between men and women in the management of public affairs'.

Accepting that genuine democracy cannot exist without the equal participation of men and women in politics, the IPU has been at the forefront of efforts to support women in this field. More specifically, in working positively towards the promotion of women's participation in parliament, the IPU has also taken on board a number of the key strategies discussed by Karam and Lovenduski (see the preceding chapter). This case study presents the work of the IPU in enhancing the participation of women in parliament, and is divided into three sections, each mirroring different aspects of this work. Continuing the IPU's tradition of 'raising awareness' and 'collecting data', the case study begins with a brief empirical analysis of the progress made and setbacks encountered by women parliamentarians over the past ten years. This is followed by an examination of the ways in which the IPU has used its *own* structures to establish best practices for parliaments in facilitating the participation and particular contribution of women. The final section reflects on a number of capacity-building efforts in national parliaments, and outlines the strategies employed by the IPU in encouraging these institutions to address the question of gender equality.

'We believe that true equality between the sexes can only be achieved if both women and men pull forces together to break the barriers of age-old belief that women and men have different roles to play and therefore have an unequal stand in society ... A man of quality should not fear women who seek equality.'

*Mose Tjitendero, former chair of the IPU Gender Partnership Group
and speaker of the National Assembly of Namibia*

Women in Parliament 1995 to 2004: A History of Gradual Progress

An International Framework Conducive to Change

The history of women in parliaments over the last ten years is one of steady, gradual progress. In many ways, this progress has been underpinned by a greater prominence of gender equality issues on the international agenda.

When women met in Mexico City in 1975 for the First United Nations World Conference on Women, the question of women in decision-making bodies was hardly raised. At the time, women accounted for only 10.9 percent of parliamentarians worldwide. Ten years later, at the Third World Conference on Women held in Nairobi, the question of women in decision-making bodies raised more interest. There, participants were confronted with a lack of adequate data and a greater consciousness of the existing gender gap in this field. Women's representation in parliament had increased by just 1 percentage point in the preceding ten years. Despairing of this situation, the conference in Nairobi marked the beginning of more sustained action and growing awareness. Governments and parliaments began to make a series of commitments to promoting gender equality in all areas of political life.

In 1995, with the proportion of women in parliament actually having decreased (see table 17), the commitments of governments were consolidated in the Beijing Platform for Action, which paid particular attention to the question of how women were involved in decision making. In this regard, states were called on to take measures to ensure women's equal access to and full participation in power structures and decision making, and to increase their capacity to participate in decision-making and leadership.

One of the most significant expressions of action has been the nearly universal endorsement of the 1979 Convention on the Elimination of All Forms of Discrimination Against Women (CEDAW). One hundred and seventy-nine countries are now party to the convention and one other state has signed the treaty, binding itself not to contravene its terms.

In 2000, the United Nations also recognized the fundamental role of women in the development process when it established the empowerment of women as one of its Millennium Development Goals. The proportion of seats held by women in national parliaments is now considered one of the key indicators in measuring progress towards this goal.

World Trends

Having perceived the need to fill a gap in terms of research and data collection, the IPU set out to collate and analyse information on the status of women in parliaments worldwide. Its earliest research effort in 1975 synthesized the experiences of women in 32 countries. Today, the IPU is the world's leading source of data on the proportion of seats held by women in 183 national parliaments. Using these data, the IPU has been able to monitor the trends in the participation of women parliamentarians and to present an accurate depiction of their situation.

Figure 7: World Average of Women in Parliament, 1995–2004

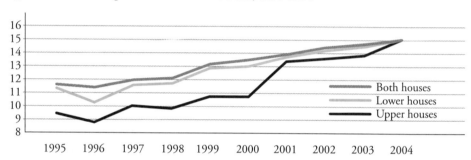

* Situation in January of each year, except in 1995 (July) and 1996 (April). Percentages do not take into account the situation of parliaments for which data were unavailable.

The rise from 11.3 to 15.2 percent across both houses of parliament over the ten years 1995–2004 is a sign of progress, not least because women's parliamentary representation today is at an all-time high.

For many years, the record for women's representation worldwide was that of 1988. With the collapse of communism in 1989, however, the proportion of women represented in the parliaments of the states concerned fell drastically. Not surprisingly, the world average followed suit: the percentage of women in lower or unicameral houses fell from 14.8 percent in 1988 to 10.3 percent in 1993. Whereas many communist governments and one-party states had effectively ensured the selection of large percentages of unopposed women (and men) candidates, the move towards multiparty democracies in the 1990s made the electoral process far more competitive for women.

The world average has only recovered to its 1988 level in the last two years. Each of the world's regions has seen some improvement in the proportion of women elected to national parliaments.

Regional Improvements and Contrasts

Progress has been marked, however, by interesting regional contrasts. Throughout the past ten years, the Nordic countries have maintained their exemplary position, with averages consistently over 38 percent. In constrast, women continued to be least represented in the parliaments of the Arab states, despite an encouraging incremental trend which has lead to the current average of 6 percent. Outside these two regions, averages have tended to stabilize at between 10 and 15 percent. The most significant progress has been evident across the Americas (+5.5 percentage points), in sub-Saharan Africa (+5.3) and in Eastern Europe (+4.9) (see figure 8).

Figure 8: Regional Averages of Women in Parliament, 1995, 2000 and 2004

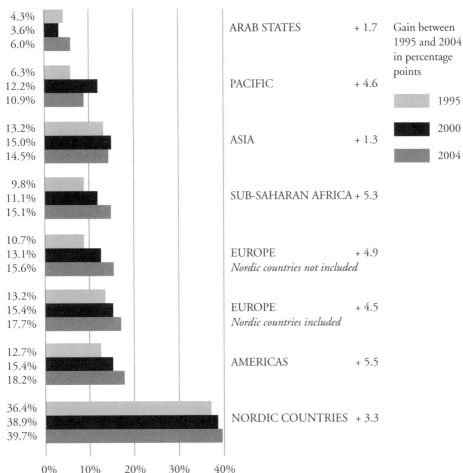

• Situation in July 1995, January 2000 and January 2004, both houses combined.

Ranking in ascending order of 2004 averages.

* Percentages do not take into account the situation of parliaments for which data were unavailable.

217

National Parliaments at a Glance

In the same period, there has been a significant change in the ranking of national parliaments that include the highest proportions of women. In 2003, Rwanda replaced Sweden as the champion in this respect, following the election of women to nearly half the seats in its National Assembly. In fact, over these ten years, women's parliamentary representation in Rwanda increased by almost 32 percentage points, to 48.8 percent. At the other extreme, the greatest setbacks were encountered in Chad and Bangladesh, where women's representation fell by 10.6 and 8.6 percentage points, respectively.

Positively, the percentage of parliaments with a substantial proportion (30 percent or over) of women members has increased threefold over the past ten years (from 2.4 percent in 1995 to 6 percent in 2004) while the percentage of parliaments where less than 10 percent of representatives are women has fallen by nearly half (to 37 percent from 63.5 percent in 1995).

Worldwide, the number of parliaments in which there are no women has not changed dramatically. Ten years ago, there were 12 countries with no women in parliament. Today (as of August 2005) there are nine, in just two regions, the Pacific and the Arab world.

Much of this is linked to the evolution of democracy in these two regions. Women in Kuwait were only granted the right to vote in May 2005. While men in Saudi Arabia voted for the first time ever in 2005 to elect local representatives, women were excluded from the exercise. As of August 2005, elections for the members of the consultative councils in Saudi Arabia or the United Arab Emirates have never been held. Similarly, in the relatively new legislatures of the Pacific Island states (many of which were established only after independence, between 1977 and 1993), women have only recently been granted the right to vote. In 1960, Tonga was the first country in the Pacific to give women the right to vote and stand for election. It would take another 30 years for all women in this region to secure the same voting rights.

Introducing Quotas: The Need for Political Will

In circumventing the absence of a 'gender-sensitive culture', a number of countries have introduced affirmative action measures. These measures have been used not only to ensure women's presence in parliament, but also to implement commitments made under international instruments, including CEDAW.

In the process of democratization, many nations emerging from internal conflict have succeeded in increasing the percentage of women in their new or restored parliaments. Recognizing the importance of including women in reconstruction processes and in cementing women's participation in new democratic institutions, various affirmative action measures were introduced. The reviewed national constitutions—of Rwanda and Burundi, for example—now include provisions to reserve seats for women; in South Africa and Mozambique, quota mechanisms have been introduced by political parties. At a regional level, the Southern African

Development Community (SADC) countries have now set a target for women's representation in parliament of at least 30 percent by 2005. These efforts have meant that, alongside the Nordic states, post-conflict countries now rank among those with the highest levels of women's representation in the world. In South Africa, Mozambique, Namibia, Uganda and Eritrea, women's representation in parliament now ranges from 22 to 33 percent.

The impressive 5.5 percentage point increase in women's parliamentary representation in the Americas over the past ten years is in large part attributable to the enthusiasm with which many countries in the region have implemented affirmative action measures. Various legislated quotas now exist in 11 countries of the Americas. In several of these, over 20 percent of parliamentarians are women (Argentina, Costa Rica and Mexico). Additionally, several political parties have adopted voluntary party quotas.

Driven mostly by political elites, efforts in the Arab world were first made in Morocco when an agreement was made between political parties whereby the electoral law was amended to reserve 30 seats for women in parliament prior to the 2002 elections. Thirty-five women were subsequently elected to the Moroccan parliament. Since that time, Djibouti and Jordan have followed suit. In Djibouti, a quota law was adopted in December 2002 stipulating that among the candidates presented by each party, at least 10 percent must be of either sex. The results of the 2003 elections there saw the unprecedented arrival of seven women in parliament, accounting for more than 10 percent of the newly-elected parliamentarians. In Jordan, the electoral law was amended prior to the 2003 elections to reserve six seats for women in the Lower House of the Majlis. Since the approval of a referendum held in 2001 in Bahrain, women can vote and stand for office in that country.

In the Absence of Quotas: The Need for Political Awareness
The case of Bangladesh, conversely, illustrates the particular difficulty women can face in gaining acceptance as legitimate political actors in the absence of quotas. In 2001, women's representation fell from 9 percent to 2 percent when a quota law reserving 30 additional appointed seats for women expired. The paucity of that result, however, actually led to the recent introduction of a stronger constitutional provision, reserving 45 additional parliamentary seats for women. The measure is valid for ten years.

This case points to a certain weakness in the adoption of special 'temporary' measures: 'fast-tracking' women into parliament is not necessarily accompanied by sufficient sensitization among parties and voters to the need for women in political life. For their part, political parties play an ever-increasing role in the management of parliamentary politics, and it is therefore at the party level that the principle of equality must be put into practice. Political parties, which are traditionally male bastions, need to be further encouraged to revise their statutes, admit more women into their internal structures and include them as candidates in elections (see in particular chapter 3).

The examples of France and Belgium are illustrative. From a paltry 5.6 percent in 1995, women now represent 17 percent of the French Senate (an increase of 11.4 percentage points). Over the same time period, women's parliamentary representation in the Belgian House of Representatives increased from 12.2 to 35.3 percent (23.3 percentage points). In both countries, the electoral laws were amended (France's in 2000; Belgium's in 2002) to oblige political parties to present an equal number of men and women on their electoral lists.

Some political parties in France showed tremendous resistance to complying fully with the law. In some instances, they even preferred to pay a fine rather than include women on their electoral lists. While change has come gradually, the results of the latest elections to the French Senate, which saw women's representation improve from 11 to 17 percent, give cause for some optimism. These results suggest that political parties in France may yet understand the fundamental importance of including women in prominent positions on electoral lists. (The situation of France is further elaborated in the case study in this Handbook.)

Electors too must be sensitized to the importance of facilitating women's entry into parliament and access to this institution. To this end, a noticeable trend has developed in a number of countries holding elections over the past few years: awareness-raising campaigns have been run among voters to highlight gender issues, and among women to encourage them to exercise their right to vote. In the lead-up to the 2002 elections in Pakistan, it was particularly important to encourage women to stand as candidates and to vote in more conservative parts of the country, where female participants had to defy local rulings that prohibited them from voting. For the 2002 elections in Lesotho, special campaigns and workshops were held to sensitize women and men to adopt a more gender-balanced political approach.

Ultimately, both affirmative action measures and inclusive, gender-sensitive social norms have a role to play in promoting a more equitable representation of women in national parliaments.

Making Women Count at the IPU

'The IPU provides a good example of the change towards more democratic institutions: cooperation between women of different persuasions and back-grounds is one of the real plusses of this organisation of world parliaments.'

Mrs Rita Süssmuth, former president of the German Bundestag (1988–98)

Table 17: Women in Parliaments and at the IPU

A. Women in Parliament: 1945–2000

	1945	1955	1965	1975	1985	1995	2000
Number of parliaments	26	61	94	115	136	176	177
Percentage of representatives who were women (lower house or unicameral)	3.0 %	7.5 %	8.1 %	10.9 %	12.0 %	11.6 %	13.4%
Percentage of representatives who were women (upper house)	2.2 %	7.7 %	9.3 %	10.5 %	12.7 %	9.4 %	10.7%

Sources: Inter-Parliamentary Union (IPU), 1997. Men and Women in Politics: Democracy Still in the Making, Study No. 28; and IPU, 'Women in National Parliaments', available at <http://www.ipu.org> (regularly updated statistical data on women in parliament, worldwide, by region and by country).

B. Women at IPU Conferences: 1947–2000

		No. of parliamen-tarians	No. of women parliamen-tarians	Percentage
1947 Cairo	(36th Conf.)	241	3	1.2%
1950 Dublin	(39th Conf.)	209	10	4.8%
1961 Brussels	(50th Conf.)	419	29	7 %
1965 Ottawa	(54th Conf.)	390	25	6.4%
1970 The Hague	(58th Conf.)	469	33	7%
1975 London	(62nd Conf.)	502	39	7.8%
1980 Berlin	(67th Conf.)	560	40	7.1%
1985 Lomé	(73rd Conf.)	386	28	7.3%
1990 Nicosia	(83rd Conf.)	444	57	12.8%
1995 Madrid	(93rd Conf.)	600	115	19.2%
2000 Amman	(103rd Conf.)	648	139	21.5%

Source: IPU. See the web site at <http://www.ipu.org/wmn-e/dlgtns.htm>.

Today, women account for almost 30 percent of the parliamentarians who take part in IPU statutory assemblies. Some 50 years ago women represented a mere 1.2 percent. How can this change be explained?

One of the IPU's biggest successes has been its proactive stance on the need to ensure gender equality in politics, and more particularly in parliament. This early commitment was followed by a series of measures and actions that were first implemented at the IPU itself. Very early on, the IPU stated its commitment to ensuring partnership between men and women in politics. Today's Statutes ensure that gender equality is the IPU's utlimate objective for participation by men and women.

Women have benefited from a strong current of favourable political will within the IPU and a growing awareness of the need for, and benefits of, gender equality within its member parliaments. This was the background to the establishment of the Meeting of Women Parliamentarians (see box 3). The insitution of the meeting at the IPU bears witness to both the ability of women to make positive change and the commitment of the IPU to accept that change. It is the result of women's intensive lobbying for a space of their own so as to make a greater impact on the overall work of the organization.

The sustained growth of women's participation corresponds to the increasing prominence attributed to the Meeting of Women Parliamentarians. From 1985 to 1995, the increase in women's presence at IPU assemblies was exponential. However, despite the structures now in place and a clear political will within the organization to see a greater presence of women parliamentarians, the participation of women began to plateau. Meeting the set objectives would clearly require stronger action.

The IPU is one of the first international organizations to have adopted affirmative action measures within its own structures to ensure stronger participation of women. Implementing these measures mainly came as a result of a three-year consultative process initated by the Gender Partnership Group, itself comprising two men and two women from the IPU Executive Committee. Ultimately, a series of measures effectively amounting to quotas and targets were included in the IPU Statutes and Rules. These relate to the IPU's three main bodies: the Executive Committee, the Governing Council and the Assembly.

- A straightforward quota system was introduced for elections to the Executive Committee: 20 percent of its elected members now must be women (article 23.2 of the Statutes).
- For the Governing Council, a gender-neutral target was adopted which, if strictly applied, would ensure that at least 30 percent of its members would be of each sex: each delegation of three members is called on to include both men and women. Where this target is not respected, the member of parliament's voting rights are reduced by a third (Rule 1.2 of the Governing Council).
- Another gender-neutral target was adopted for the Assembly: where delegations attend IPU assemblies without representatives of both sexes three times in a row, their voting rights and officially registered numbers are reduced (articles 10.3 and 15.2(c) of the Statutes).

Over the past years the IPU has tackled the question of women's participation within its own structures from both quantitative and qualitative perspectives.

'The single greatest success of this Assembly will be hard to determine. But I can say … that one of its most outstanding achievements has no doubt been the fact that nearly all the discussions held here, whether in plenary, in Standing Committees or at other specialized meetings, have shown consummate interest in gender issues. I mention this because I feel that this is the best way of celebrating 20 years of work by the Meeting of Women Parliamentarians. For over and above the ceremonies there is no greater reflection of the inherent value of the Meeting than its practical effect.'

*Philippine Senator Pia Cayetano, President of the Manila session
of the Meeting of Women Parliamentarians, 112th Assembly*

Box 3. The Experience of the Meeting of Women Parliamentarians in Changing the Rules

It has taken time and sustained dedication on the part of women, but today the IPU Meeting of Women Parliamentarians is a success story in 'changing the rules'. The meeting ensures women's participation, visibility and influence in the decision-making processes of the IPU and allows women to play a decisive role in the development of the IPU's programme on the status of women.

Ambitious Beginnings
The idea for a Meeting of Women Parliamentarians came from a small but active group of women, determined not only to become acquainted with one another and discuss their experiences as members of parliament but also to encourage women to participate more actively in the work of the IPU. Women delegates from Italy and the Federal Republic of Germany held a first meeting in Bonn in 1978, during the 65th Inter-Parliamentary Conference, to discuss mechanisms to put gender equality on the IPU's agenda and to ensure that women participated in its conferences in greater numbers. While this group recommended that as many women parliamentarians as possible who were present in Bonn should be included in the delegations to the next IPU Conference, subsequent conferences saw the level of women's participation drop from 7.8 percent to 5.9 percent.

Learning the Rules (1978–82)
This first initiative effectively marked the beginning of a 'women's movement' at the IPU. Women continued to meet informally during IPU statutory sessions. Often held during lunch breaks, these events were coordinated by women parliamentarians from the conference's host country or by women delegates to the Inter-Parliamentary meetings. They were held without any fixed agenda

simply to allow women parliamentarians to exchange experiences and learn about each other. Inevitably, this period gave women an opportunity to learn the rules of the IPU.

Using the Rules (1983–90)

With a better understanding of the IPU's structures, in 1983 women parliamentarians expressed a desire to establish, under IPU auspices, an association of women parliamentarians. A nine-member preparatory group was tasked with studying the question and coming up with recommendations. Consultations between the group and the IPU secretary general took place, and it was decided that the participation of women would be promoted by establishing a group that would meet at the start of each IPU conference. The underlying idea was that the Meeting of Women Parliamentarians would influence the organization's working groups, plenary discussions, policies and decisions.

The IPU's governing bodies approved this decision in 1984, thereby ensuring that the Meeting of Women Parliamentarians would have adequate funding, technical coordination and support, including the provision of premises and secretarial and interpretation support from the IPU Secretariat.

The first Meeting of Women Parliamentarians coordinated by the IPU Secretariat was held in Lomé during the 73rd Inter-Parliamentary Conference in 1985, seven years after the first informal meeting of women parliamentarians. Since then, traditionally, the host parliament has organized a luncheon for the meeting's participants so as to facilitate dialogue among women and the development of personal contacts.

Changing the Rules (1991 to the present)

The creation of the Meeting of Women Parliamentarians provided women with a forum though which they could voice their opinions and apply pressure within the IPU to push their agenda. One of their objectives was and still is to ensure that gender issues are addressed by the IPU as a whole and mainstreamed in all of the organization's work. For example, following its own constructive debate on HIV/AIDS in April 2005 during the 112th IPU Assembly, the meeting was able to contribute gender-related elements to the IPU's unanimously adopted resolution on the issue. This process has seen women contribute to a wide range of debates, from financing for development to migration to conflict resolution. Upon the initiative of women parliamentarians, the following institutional changes have taken place, each aimed at ensuring a greater role for women within the IPU:

- the establishment of a formal mechanism through which the Meeting of

Women Parliamentarians reports on its work and presents recommendations to the Governing Council of the IPU;

- the amendment in 1995 of the language of the IPU Statutes and Rules to eliminate any wording likely to convey a message of superiority of one gender over the other;
- the creation of a Gender Partnership Group in 1997 to ensure that in all its activities the IPU takes into account the need to act in a spirit of partnership between men and women;
- the amendment in 1999 of the union's Statutes and Rules, to officially recognize the Meeting of Women Parliamentarians, assisted by a Coordinating Committee, and the adoption, in 2000, of the Rules of the Meeting and of its Coordinating Committee; and
- the amendment in 2004 of the Rules of the Assembly, allowing the Meeting of Women Parliamentarians to submit amendments to draft resolutions during IPU assemblies so as to ensure that the work of the meeting and gender issues in general are reflected in the organization's work. The amendment establishes the meeting as the only body with this right.

From its humble beginnings, the Meeting of Women Parliamentarians has thus succeeded in increasing significantly the number of women taking part in IPU assemblies. In 1947, women comprised only 1 percent of all delegates to the Conference. While slight progress was made by 1975, when 8 percent of all delegates attending the 62nd Conference were women, the overall percentage skyrocketed to 29 percent of delegates by the time of the 111th Assembly in 2004. Today, women parliamentarians are in fact better represented at IPU meetings than they are in national parliaments.

What has been the impact for women parliamentarians worldwide?

In addition to changes in the rules, the Meeting of Women Parliamentarians has provided:

- a forum for the exchange of experience among women members of parliament;
- an opportunity to showcase development for women MPs at the national level; and
- a think-tank for strategies to improve women parliamentarians' presence at IPU meetings and in parliaments more generally.

Applying Changes at Home: Assisting Women Parliamentarians at the National Level

If the changes made at the level of the IPU's own structures serve as a case study in terms of establishing international precedents and regional and national mechanisms, it is also true that focused action was required at the national level. For this reason the IPU has also extended its work in this field.

Over the past few years, the IPU's strategies have evolved to address specific needs of women at the national level and to enhance the capacities of parliaments to address gender issues. Gender issues are understood as those which impact upon, and concern, society as a whole, rather than women specifically or individually. Violence against women, for example, is seen as a gender issue rather than a women's issue in that addressing it requires addressing roles women and men might play in a society and looking at the impact on both men and women. In a sense, most issues could be analysed from a gender perspective and be seen to have a differential effect on different groups of men and women.

In addition, the research carried out by the IPU on the situation of women in parliament, their difficulties and successes, has provided useful insight into the development of national support strategies. Along these lines, several main strategies can be highlighted.

Enhancing the Capacities of Women Members of Parliament
One leitmotif in the history of women in politics is their initial lack of experience when entering the parliamentary arena. Building women's confidence and strengthening their capacity to fulfil their mandates appropriately is thus crucial at both the pre-electoral and the post-electoral stages. Recently, the IPU's attention has focused on countries emerging from conflict. A seminar for Rwandan women candidates enabled women parliamentarians and future candidates to exchange information with other women parliamentarians from the region, as well as representatives of the media and political party leaders, on campaigning mechanisms and strategies.

Activities carried out in Burundi and Rwanda were aimed at strengthening contact with the electorate, and more particularly with women. Women parliamentarians benefited from donor support to organize field trips in their constituencies and to participate in popular debates. In many instances this made them sensitive to their constituents' concerns and helped them to explain the political processes under way: in Burundi, for example, women parliamentarians were able to explain the intricacies and implications of the Arusha peace agreements to women.

In Burundi, Rwanda and Timor-Leste, newly-elected women expressed a wish to develop their leadership and communication skills. IPU training activities subsequently focused on public speaking, the preparation and delivery of campaign speeches, and the development of communication strategies and techniques.

Training on parliamentary procedures was also provided. In Djibouti, IPU training seminars were organized on the role and mandate of parliamentarians. These seminars were attended by both men and women parliamentarians. In Timor-Leste, a seminar on the role of parliament in the budgetary process, including from a gender perspective, was organized prior to the opening of the budget session in parliament so as to help parliamentarians prepare for the second budget review in Timor-Leste's history.

Caucuses and Networking, Including with Women's Organizations
The strength of newly-elected women legislators can lie in their solidarity and capacity to unite, beyond their party structures, to tackle specific gender issues. Generating such unity among women from all parties is not, however, an easy task. In Rwanda and Burundi, these structures already exist: the Forum of Rwandan Women Parliamentarians (FFRP) and the Association of Women Parliamentarians from Burundi (SOFEPA) serve to mobilize women around specific gender issues. IPU support has served merely to strengthen the legitimacy of these associations and their capacity to generate change.

IPU activities have also focused on ensuring that contact is made between different national partners working on gender issues. In the case of Rwanda, a seminar organized during the constitutional process brought together members of the Forum of Rwandan Women Parliamentarians, members of the Legal and Constitutional Committee of the Transitional National Assembly, members of the Ministry of Gender Issues and representatives of civil society organizations. One of the positive outcomes of this activity has been to consolidate cooperation between these different national actors.

Enhancing Parliaments' Capacity to Address Gender Issues
The sharing of expertise on gender issues of particular concern to newly-elected women is often necessary to assist women legislators in addressing specific national gender priorities. To respond to this need, experts were fielded to assist women members of parliament in dealing with these concerns. Training seminars on specific gender issues, bringing together men and women parliamentarians and experts from other countries, were also organized. The pooling of experience between members of parliament of different origins has proved very constructive and useful.

Access to adequate background information on specific gender issues is key to parliamentarians' legislative and oversight functions. In all parliaments which have benefited from IPU assistance, documentation centres on gender issues have been established. While this particular type of activity benefits women parliamentarians first and foremost, it also contributes to the strengthening of the parliament's research capacity as a whole. Where the parliamentary library is open to the public, the documentation centre also serves civil society organizations working on gender issues.

IPU training activities have often included segments for parliamentary staff, with a view to enhancing the insitution's capacity in addressing gender issues.

Mainstreaming Gender

Advocated in a number of key international instruments, the concept of gender mainstreaming has become increasingly important. The IPU has applied this concept most succesfully to the budgetary process. In fostering the need to promote the role of women in parliament and in processes leading to good governance, the IPU has organized a series of seminars on parliament, the budget and gender. Organized together with the United Nations Development Programme (UNDP), the World Bank Institute and a host parliament, five regional seminars have now been held in Africa, Asia and the Arab region.

Work in Partnership with Men

The IPU has long held the view that consolidating a sense of partnership between men and women on gender issues contributes to an appreciation that they are not and should not be the exclusive domain of women. For this reason activities aimed at supporting women parliamentarians have often included segments designed to sensitize men to gender issues and establish alliances between men and women in favour of gender equality, thus avoiding the marginalization of gender issues.

In those parliaments where women's entry in high numbers has changed the initial or traditional gender balance, seminars for men and women have provided an opportunity for all parliamentarians to work together in their new environment. In Djibouti, for example, women were elected to parliament in significant numbers for the first time in 2002. Together, the IPU and the United Nations Development Fund for Women (UNIFEM) organized a seminar for both men and women, to familiarize new members of parliament with the idea of working together.

Conclusion

Equality in Politics: Not a Question but a Necessity

It cannot be assumed that women's increased representation in parliament will necessarily lead to a positive change for women in the electorate and that women will bring a different approach to politics. Parliaments are not gender-neutral institutions; they have their own cultural norms and rules. Women parliamentarians are expected to work within these norms and rules, and any change they may bring will inevitably involve a great deal of effort and time.

Women's involvement in political institutions, however, remains crucial. Women constitute over 50 percent of the population of most countries and on that basis they should be represented in all legislatures and decision-making bodies. It is also clear that women's presence in parliament broadens priorities on the political agenda to include a range of previously unconsidered issues. At their initiative, issues such as childcare, women's health, violence against women and sex discrimination, to name but a few, have been given far greater prominence. To varying degrees, women have also been quite successful in pointing to the inadmissibility of sexist or demeaning language in the parliamentary environment and changing the mores of parliamentary life.

Ultimately, the need for women in politics remains unquestionable. What can be questioned is the existence and operation of a parliament without women: how can politics possibly be defined without women; how can decision-making bodies effectively address the needs of a society without the participation and involvement of half of its population? A gender-balanced approach to politics is what the IPU believes in and defends. Anything less can only amount to a democratic deficit.

Promoting Partnership between Men and Women in Parliament:
The Experience of the Inter-Parliamentary Union

Case Study: South Africa

South Africa: Beyond Numbers

Sheila Meintjes

Quantitatively, women's representation in the South African Parliament has hovered around the 30 percent 'critical mass' mark since 1994. This level of representation remained constant in the two subsequent elections, in 1999 and 2004. This significant proportion of women was largely due to the informal quota of the African National Congress (ANC), the ruling party. This case study explores the significance of women's presence and the impact it has made on the political process and on the decision making and policy making in parliament during the first decade of democracy.[1]

A Decade of Electoral Politics

In 2004, South Africa celebrated ten years of democracy after more than 40 years of apartheid rule.[2] It was a democracy that had been hard fought for during a 30-year period of armed resistance and low-level civil war against white supremacy between the years 1960, when armed struggle began, and 1990, when the ban on the ANC and other liberation movements was lifted. Women had participated in the struggle for democracy in a multitude of ways, including as militant activists. How would this participation be translated into electoral politics and representative democracy? Would women's presence be reflected in political and material gains for women in society?

In April 2004, the country held its third democratic election, with overwhelming support given to the ANC, led by Thabo Mbeki, who began his second term as president. The first democratic parliament, led by President Nelson Mandela, had seen a remarkable array of parliamentarians from all sectors of society, from all race groups, and from a multitude of party political affiliations. A Government of National Unity opened the democratic phase, led by the ANC, but including the National Party (NP) that had ruled South Africa uninterruptedly since 1948. To symbolize a new era, the NP developed new logos, renamed itself the New National Party and opened its doors to black members. However, it was never able to establish a place for itself. Ironically, in 2004 it formed an election alliance with the ANC and a few months later it disbanded, its members flocking to the ANC or joining the opposition Democratic Alliance.

Of the 400 seats in the National Assembly, 131, or 33 percent, were held by women after the 2004 election, a marginal increase from the 28–29 percent in the second democratic parliament. Eight of 27 cabinet ministers were women (29.6 percent), and eight of 13 deputy ministers were women (61.5 percent). The use of closed lists in the proportional representation (PR) electoral system had clearly been good for women's presence in parliament. Moreover, their presence at the highest levels of decision making—the cabinet—suggested that women's status was significantly higher under democracy than it had been under apartheid, when less than 3 percent of representatives had been women. The PR system, the ANC quota, and the commitment of the governing party to gender equality were among the main reasons for this significant showing.

Background to Women's Participation in Parliament

South Africa's 40-year struggle against the racist edifice that came to be known as apartheid, between 1949 and 1990, involved a wide spectrum of civil society—trade unions, civic associations, youth movements—and included all race groups, in South Africa then classified, under the 1950 Population Registration Act, into whites, coloureds, Indians and blacks. Women organized separately, and joined the non-racial movement opposing apartheid from the 1950s onwards. A march of 20,000 women opposed to passes and inferior Bantu education, on the Union Buildings in Pretoria on 9 August 1956, is commemorated every year in South Africa in recognition of the contribution women made to the political struggle against apartheid. The tradition of separate and independent organization of women was a thread that ran through the mobilization of popular opposition during the 1970s and 1980s.

During the negotiations for a new constitution, between 1992 and 1994, women's organizations played a pivotal role in ensuring that the idea of women's needs and interests should become part of the debate about rights. A Women's National Coalition (WNC) was formed that crossed racial and ideological divides to influence the constitution-making process. After a two-year national campaign involving more than 2 million women, the WNC produced a Charter for Women's Effective Equality, a document that represented the hopes and dreams of South African women. The involvement of women from every political party in the WNC had also created a cohort of women political leaders whose joint concern was to promote gender equality. Their participation in the Charter campaign had created a broad consensus within different political parties not only about the need to integrate the needs and interests of women into their mandates, but also to include women candidates in the parliamentary elections. The Charter became the blueprint for the gender policy direction of the new state. Included in its 12 articles was the demand for full and equal participation of women in representative politics.

Politics of Civil Society Mobilization

The WNC Charter campaign signalled that women were active political agents, deeply engaged in forging substantive civil and political equality for women citizens. When the traditional chiefs tried to suggest that customary law, which defined women as minors, should override the constitution, women throughout the country mobilized to protest against any attempt to prevent their enjoying equal citizenship rights. The WNC proposed that the new state should include a 'package' of institutions to promote and protect gender equality: in parliament, a women's caucus; in the state, an Office on the Status of Women; and an independent Commission for Gender Equality (CGE). These were later established.

From 1994, not only was women's political activity in South Africa characterized by the formal party political activities common to developed democracies; it was also, even more, linked to the mobilization of movements around particular issues that affected the everyday productive and reproductive interests of women. These issues included land distribution, anti-privatization, health, including reproductive health, HIV/AIDS and gender-based violence, among other more local demands such as housing and the provision of electricity to millions of people.

Gender-based violence and the very high prevalence of HIV/AIDS in South Africa proved to be one of the most challenging aspects of the transition to democracy. The new democratic era had produced a more acute awareness of women's rights in the context of the United Nations World Conference on Violence Against Women (1993), at which the concept of 'women's rights as human rights' had been widely accepted and adopted internationally. In 1995, the year following South Africa's first democratic election, the Fourth United Nations World Conference on Women held in Beijing provided the context for debate on gender equality and the idea of gender mainstreaming within state institutions globally. Research into political violence in South Africa acknowledged the high levels and endemic nature of gender-based violence. The HIV/AIDS pandemic also became a highly contentious issue as the state belatedly confronted the issue of its treatment. These issues became the centre of political activism and discourse.

Thus in South Africa there is little possibility of conceiving of electoral politics alone as 'the normative space' for politics. Politics exists in a wider sphere. A majority of the political activists involved in social movements were women. Despite high levels of illiteracy, women form the majority of active participants in social movements such as the Treatment Action Campaign (which deals with HIV-related issues). Women's political activism was reflected, too, in the fact that more women than men were registered as voters on the first voters' roll compiled during 1998, just before the second general election.

Apart from the mobilizing of social movements around the issues mentioned above, there was also a strong women's and gender non-governmental sector involved in a range of action that embraced advocacy, litigation, research and information dissemination, which coexisted alongside the activities of grass-roots social movements and institutional political pressure groups. The transition to democracy, though, meant a new professionalization of interest-led non-governmental organizations (NGOs). The state itself was particularly receptive to these groups, and public–private partnerships became a hallmark of state–society relations despite some of the tensions mentioned above. Efforts by civil society and the state to deal with gender violence were particularly strong—and continue to characterize their relations at the time of writing.

At the 2004 elections the overall majority of the ANC alliance significantly increased. Part of the reason for this seems to lie in the responsiveness of the ruling party to the demands of different constituencies. The women's agenda is one example. In few other countries have women been able to influence the national policy agenda in quite the same way as they have in South Africa. Part of the reason lies in the history of women's separate organization in civil society. Moreover, because of the nature of the struggle against apartheid, and indeed the support of apartheid by many women's organizations themselves, women's organizations were affiliated to different political parties. The depth of the women's organizations also challenged the political parties to take up women's interests as part of their manifestoes in order to get their vote. The fact that the ANC Women's League retains its separate organization, for instance, is a constant challenge to the party in general to take up women's issues as part of its general mandate.

Main Achievements of Women Legislators

The presence of large numbers of women in parliament has been an important aspect of engendering the institution. This included such material needs as crèches and women's toilets. Evidence from South Africa and elsewhere shows that the presence of women in electoral systems and in parliaments has made a significant difference to both the procedural aspects of parliamentary politics—sitting times are an example—and the legislative agenda, which has become more gender-sensitive. Formal experience was lacking among a majority of parliamentarians, but women faced particular constraints related to the inequality and the secondary status of women in society generally. One of their greatest contributions has been on the legislative front.

After the 1994 election a cross-party women's caucus was formed to coordinate what came to be seen as a 'women's agenda', the outcome of the WNC's Charter campaign. It soon became apparent that the driving force for legislative change was the ANC. New institution-building, however, has proved a complex matter, partly because of the lack of appropriate committed leadership at ministerial level, despite public commitment. Free health care for pregnant women and children under six years was instituted by the first Minister of Health, Dr Nkosazana Dhlamini Zuma, who also spearheaded the legislation on reproductive rights and the right to abortion, despite opposition in the ANC. It was largely because of the strong women's lobby within the ANC that the act was passed in 1996.

An ad hoc committee to promote the 'quality of life and status of women' was established (at first without a budget) which within three years became a Joint Standing Committee of Parliament, known as the Joint Monitoring Committee on the Quality of Life and Status of Women (JMC). The task of this committee was to monitor legislation and to promote research into the key areas that prevented women from enjoying full equality. The JMC was chaired by Pregs Govender, an ANC MP and former manager of the WNC. She championed the issues raised by women in civil society and drove the legislative agenda relating to women. In 1998, she was responsible for ensuring that the Domestic Violence Act (no. 116 of 1998), the Maintenance Act (no. 99 of 1998) and the Recognition of Customary Marriages Act (no. 120 of 1998) were passed. One of the lessons learned, though, was that it was all very well to promote legislative change. More important was that adequate budgets be provided and that training of officials who implemented the acts be undertaken. This did not take place adequately, and the implementation of these acts has been the subject of considerable advocacy.

Within the state, the Office on the Status of Women was established to lead the process of gender mainstreaming. It also developed the national policy on gender equality. However, its role has been limited largely because it has no authoritative role in relation to the line departments in government and because it is under-resourced. Its influence is thus limited. It does, though, play a role in bringing the gender institutions together every quarter to share ideas and evaluate progress.

In 1997, in fulfilment of the constitutional prescriptions, the independent Commission on Gender Equality was established. The commission's role was to protect and promote gender equality in state and society, undertake research, investigate complaints and ensure that the country fulfilled its international commitments. Its contribution has been uneven, however, partly because of organizational tensions and its alignment with the other new state institutions.

Challenges to Policy Development

While policy development was the focus of the first democratic parliament, the period from 1999, after the second election, was driven by a commitment to the implementation of the new legislative frameworks. But it was more difficult to translate commitment into reality. Part of the challenge related to the lack of transformation within various departments. The Department of Health, for instance, had to contend with lack of primary health care services in general in the context of a lack of basic infrastructure—electricity supply, telecommunications, transport and even water. In the case of the criminal justice system, the Domestic Violence Act required levels of sensitivity and commitment from the South African Police Services that were almost impossible to achieve. Efforts to overcome the act's deficiencies required considerable coordination and cooperation between different departments. This too, proved difficult to follow through. Moreover, the Treasury failed to provide an adequate budget for the act to be properly implemented. Thus the act was not entirely effective. The major challenge that faced the South African Government was the disjuncture between progressive planning and policy development and the necessary capacity to implement them.

The Domestic Violence Act replaced an earlier act, the Family Violence Act, which was passed quickly, and perhaps cynically, without widespread consultation, by the last National Party government in 1993. The revisions in the 1998 act were the work of the South African Law Commission (SALC) in concert with NGOs and legal academics with experience of the needs of survivors of intimate family violence. But its progress is also instructive in providing evidence of how easy it can be for legislation to be undermined by the limited understanding of the drafters of legislation. When the draft was first produced, it was rejected by the Chairman of the SALC for its 'lack of neutrality' and a revised draft was sent to parliament. Fortunately, the vigilance of civil society and the JMC forced the Justice Portfolio Committee to consider the first version of the bill, which then became the basis of the final act. The role of the committee was critical in ensuring that the act was passed.

In addition, there was also the promotion of a Woman's Budget process that was the outcome of a civil society–JMC partnership. The initiative came from a Commonwealth group that was keen to promote the idea in a few countries: Australia had been the pioneer of the process. South Africa was one of the first countries to implement the process, championed by Pregs Govender and assisted by technical experts from Australia and Britain. In 1998 and 1999 the national budget specifically acknowledged its adoption of a 'gender mainstreaming' approach, although during the subsequent three years this tended to fall into abeyance. The androcentic culture within politics and in parliament continued to bedevil the institution despite avowed changes in the role that women have played in altering the rules and forcing debates on gender equality, including participating in the legislation passed in 1997 setting up the CGE. Reports of continuing sexism and sexual harassment testified to the difficulties of transforming the environment.

How Has the Participation of Women Changed Politics?

Women's specific interests—sexuality, reproduction, violence and customary law—were translated into law through the strategies adopted by organizations in civil society in conjunction with the JMC, which in turn forged alliances with certain progressive male members of parliament, including President Thabo Mbeki.[3] What seems clear from the South African case is that, while a critical mass of women in parliament is important, a necessary aspect of the effectiveness of the numbers is what Anne Phillips calls the politics of ideas.[4] The presence of women leads to change within parliament on such issues as meeting times or providing childcare. But the political agenda around gender issues more widely relies on an understanding of what gender transformation really means.

Gender mainstreaming can simply mean integrating women at the top without confronting the fundamental issues of gender equality. Political will within the political parties has to be fostered by feminist politicians who in turn must be both accountable to and supported by civil society lobbies. The transformation agenda of a cluster of feminist politicians is what ensures that policy and legislation transcend the mere presence of a critical mass of women. The danger is that these feminist politicians do not stay the course. The important factor seems to be the relationship between parliamentarians and the women's movement and NGOs committed to gender transformation. This calls for a commitment to ensuring that women's organizations continue to work together. The challenge is to ensure that this happens.

Evaluations of the gender machinery have clearly shown that the JMC's role has been critical in driving the process of legislative change. While the CGE made submissions to the committee and developed relationships with stakeholders in civil society, it has been less effective than was hoped. It became embroiled in internal conflicts that for some years hindered its institutional development. Although it has had some successes in undertaking public education and calling government departments to account, its public profile has not been very significant. It has monitored internal elections and with the Electoral Institute of Southern Africa (EISA) called on political parties to explain their gender policies. It is the activities of civil society itself that have been most effective in ensuring that women's issues were taken up by political parties. Indeed, women comprise the largest number of registered voters in South Africa—54.82 percent of registered voters—testament to the importance women attach to the vote and to the role of formal politics in their lives.[5]

Notes

[1] For a detailed study of the gender politics of the electoral system see Fick, Glenda, Sheila Meintjes and Mary Simons (eds), 2002. *One Woman, One Vote: the Gender Politics of South African Elections*. Johannesburg: Electoral Institute of Southern Africa. See also Albertyn, Cathi, Beth Goldblatt, Shireen Hassim, Likhapha Mbatha and Sheila Meintjes, 1999. *Engendering the Political Agenda: A South African Case Study*. Johannesburg: Centre for Applied Legal Studies.

[2] This case study takes for granted some understanding of South Africa's colonial and political history. For a useful overview see Lodge, Tom, Denis Kadima and David Pottie (eds), 2002. *Compendium of Elections in Southern Africa*. Johannesburg: Electoral Institute of Southern Africa (chapter 10).

[3] Albertyn et al. 1999, op. cit.

[4] See for example Phillips, Anne, 1995. *The Politics of Presence: The Political Representation of Gender, Ethnicity and Race.* Oxford: Oxford University Press.

[5] Independent Electoral Commission, 'Registration statistics as on 26 Feb 2004', available at <http://www.elections.org.za/Statistics1.asp>.

Further Reading

Agenda, 1999. *Agenda Monograph: Translating Commitment into Policy and Practice: Three Case Studies.* Durban: Agenda

Ballington, Julie, 1998. 'Women's Parliamentary Representation: The Effects of List PR'. *Politikon.* Vol. 25, no. 2

Beinart, William, 1994. *Twentieth Century South Africa.* Cape Town: Oxford University Press

Cock, Jacklyn, 1997. 'Women in South Africa's Transition to Democracy', in J. Scott, C. Kaplan and D. Keates (eds). *Transitions, Environments, Translations: Feminism in International Politics.* New York: Routledge

Hassim, Shireen, 1999. 'From Presence to Power: Women's Citizenship in a New Democracy'. *Agenda,* 40

— 2005. *Contesting Authority: Women's Organisations and Democracy in South Africa.* Madison: University of Wisconsin Press

Lowe-Morna, Colleen, 2004. *Ringing up the Changes: Gender in Southern African Politics.* Johannesburg: Genderlinks

Meer, Shamim, 1998. *Women Speak: Reflection on our Struggles, 1982–1997.* Cape Town: Kwela Books

Meintjes, Sheila, 1998. 'Gender, Nationalism and Transformation: Difference and Commonality in South Africa's Past and Present', in R. Wilford and R. L Miller (eds). *Women, Ethnicity and Nationalism: The Politics of Transition.* London: Routledge

Case Study: Sweden

Sweden:
A Step-wise Development

Lena Wängnerud

In 1971 the proportion of women in the Swedish Parliament was 14 percent. Since the last election, in 2002, the proportion is 45 percent. The difference is remarkable; in 30 years there has been a threefold development. The increase is also visible in government where in 2005, 11 out of 22 cabinet ministers are women. This case study will focus on the story behind the figures and discuss how women have effected change in parliament.[1] Since 1985 the proportion of women in the Swedish Parliament has exceeded 30 percent. Even though it is hard to say what would constitute a critical mass, the number has been comparatively high for a long period of time.

If changes occur as a result of women's representation, traces of this should be visible in Sweden.

Increase in Sheer Numbers

To understand the process behind the increase in the numbers of women in parliament, we have to examine Swedish politics 40 years ago. Then women were clearly less involved in politics than their male counterparts: fewer participated in elections or became party members, and they were also heavily under-represented in leading positions within parties as well as within decision-making bodies.

The turning point occurred in 1972. The leaders of the two leading parties at that time, the Liberals and the Social Democrats, started to compete to win female voters. The strategic reasoning behind this was that winning women's votes would mean gaining more seats and hence increased power. Measures were taken to enhance the status of gender equality as an issue on the political agenda as well as to put up certain goals for women's representation. Two important factors in particular can be mentioned: in 1972 Socialdemokratiska arbetarpartiet (the Social Democratic Party), being in power at that time, introduced a central gender policy unit in government;

and in the same year the Liberal Party was the first party in Sweden to formally recommend that women should make up 40 percent of its internal leadership positions, as in the party's governing board.

The process that took place in Sweden can be characterized by two features: integration; and step-wise development. Integration means that, even though there have been, and still are, women's federations in Swedish politics, they have always worked inside the established party structures. It also means that measures concerning women's representation have been a subject for broad debate within parties. Women's federations have worked as a vanguard in this field; however, the final decisions have always been reached in each party's highest decision-making forum—the regular national party meetings. The consequence of this is that, with seven different parties represented in the parliament, as is currently the case in Sweden, we will find seven slightly different stories.

The issue of women's representation has thus been on the agenda in all parties; however, they have not all adopted numerical goals like a 40 : 60 gender balance on political party lists. The Conservative Party and the Centre Party are examples of parties that are still relying on more 'soft' strategies, like loosely formulated goals for equality.

However, step-wise development can be seen as a catchword for a more general picture. For most of the parties, more loosely formulated goals have over time been transformed into stricter recommendations, and three parties have implemented quotas. In the Swedish case quotas mean regulations voluntarily written into the statute of a party and not into the constitution of Sweden. The Green Party has adopted quotas from the start, since it was set up in 1981. For the Left Party the decision to use quotas came in 1987, and for the Social Democrats in 1993. In most cases measures focusing on internal party structures (boards etc.) have preceded measures focusing on party lists.

With or without quotas, the competition that once started between Liberals and Social Democrats now includes all parties. With few exceptions, Swedish party leaders today describe themselves as 'feminists'. Since 1994 the slogan of 'every second seat for a woman' is rooted within Swedish politics, symbolizing an ambition to alternate women and men on lists for election to different powerful positions and not just include women for the sake of window-dressing.

Transforming the Agenda

However, if we understand the processes behind the increase in women's representation as a purely strategic manoeuvre, we will not get a complete grasp of the whole picture. While it is obvious from the documentation of different parties that there have indeed been calculations as to how to gain more (female) votes, there has also been serious consideration of how to use this increased power—how to change the situation of women in society and reach gender equality in a deeper sense.

Studies indicate that women in Sweden today are better integrated into politics than they were in the 1960s. Since 1976 women's turnout in elections has been slightly higher than men's. The gender gap in both political interest (subjectively measured) and party membership has decreased, although it has not completely vanished. A strong indicator of change is the figures quoted earlier in this case study—the shift from 14 percent women in the Swedish Parliament in 1971 to 45 percent in 2004.

The tricky question, then, is how to capture qualitative changes stemming from shifts in gender balances and to move beyond examining sheer numbers. In attempting to make these assessments, there is a dual risk. On the one hand, there is the risk of over-expectation, or using vague criteria in the haste to prove impact of women's efforts and the change wrought by their political participation. On the other hand, underestimation can also take place, whereby harsh criteria are used that ultimately overlook contributions and interpret women's efforts as being limited to the domain of tokenism.

To be able to draw valid conclusions we have to understand the political process. What is taking place in the parliament, at least in the chamber, can be compared to the tip of an iceberg. When a final decision is about to be reached each political issue has been through a period of processing. Most of the time this process is stretched out over many years and involves meetings in many different settings such as parliamentary committees and different groups within parties.

To capture what is going on beneath the surface without actually being there, we have to rely on indicators that reflect the process. One way of doing so is to use questionnaires and personal interviews with central actors. In the following section I will use some examples of questions posed to Swedish members of parliament (MPs) about their political work. The samples focus on campaign issues and areas of personal interest. In no question is the issue of gender raised outright. Instead the answers have been subjected to gender analysis afterwards (what are the answers among women, what are the answers among men?). The questions have been open-ended and each politician could mention whatever issue they wanted.

In analysing the answers I have used a broad definition of the concept of 'women's interests'. On a theoretical level the aim has been to capture policies that can be expected to increase the autonomy of female citizens. Even in Sweden there is a division of labour between women and men, with women more frequently engaged in different sorts of care work, both privately within the family and publicly in the professional care sectors such as health and the care of the elderly and children.

The assumption is that, to be able to increase gender equality in a society, women's interests have to be voiced. The empirical question then is: do women MPs have an agenda that differs from that of their male colleagues? Are women MPs giving women's interests a voice? Figure 9 shows the number of male and female MPs who mentioned social policy, family policy, care of the elderly or health care as a campaign issue or an area of personal interest in 1985, 1994 and 2002. These four items can be seen as a broad way of conceptualizing women's interests.

Figure 9: Women's Interests on the Agenda of Swedish MPs, 1985–2002

Figures are percentages.

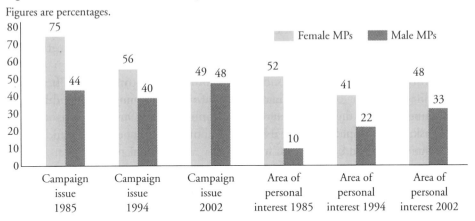

Note: The figure shows the responses to two open questions which read, in the following order: 'Which issue/s or problem/s did you emphasize most in your campaign work before this year's election?' (up to five issues could be mentioned); and 'Which political issue area/s are you personally most interested in?' (up to three issues could be mentioned). The responses were coded according to a detailed coding scheme. The numbers shown are the percentages of female and male MPs who included women's interests among either set of issues. Included in the category 'women's interests' were responses referring to social policy, policy on the family, health care and care of the elderly. The numbers of respondents (women : men) were: in 1985, 96 : 218; in 1994, 132 : 190; and in 2002 142 : 175. The total number of MPs in the Swedish Parliament has been 349 since 1976.
Source: Parliament Studies of 1985, 1988 and 1994. The Swedish Election Study Program at the Department of Political Science, Gothenburg University.

Figure 9 shows several important results. The first is that there is a connection between the sex of politicians and the extent to which they pursue women's interests. In 1985, 75 percent of female MPs addressed issues of social policy, family policy, care of the elderly or health care in their election campaigns. The corresponding figure among male MPs was 44 percent. In that same year, 1985, 52 percent of female MPs stated care policies as an area of personal interest, while the proportion of male MPs who did so was 10 percent.

The second important result is that, although there gender differences were found upon the two subsequent survey occasions, the gap has closed over time. I will come back to this below.

The third significant result shown in figure 9 has to do with comparison of the various arenas. Gender differences were consistently greater when it came to politicians' personal agendas—those that show up when they state their own areas of interest—than on the agenda that appears in the election campaign. This is important to notice because different arenas can be exposed to different levels of outside control. The election campaign, for example, is an arena that is centrally controlled to a considerable extent by the parties. One can assume that the 'personal interest' indicator is the measure that best corresponds to what is happening in the everyday world of politics, that is, who is putting forward women's interests in meetings, in committees and so on.

Before drawing any further conclusions we should also consider specifically the dimension of gender equality. What happens if we take a more narrow definition of women's interests and only include policy priorities that are exclusively directed towards changes in gender balances? Figure 10 shows the number of male and female MPs who mentioned gender equality explicitly as a campaign issue or an area of personal interest in 1985, 1994 and 2002.

Figure 10: Gender Equality on the Agenda of Swedish MPs, 1985–2002

Figures are percentages.

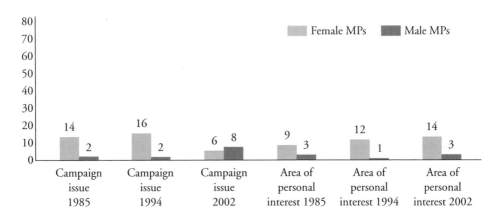

Note: The figure shows the responses to two open questions which read, in the following order: 'Which issue/s or problem/s did you emphasize most in your campaign work before this year's election?' (up to five issues could be mentioned); and 'Which political issue area/s are you personally most interested in?' (up to three issues could be mentioned). The responses were coded according to a detailed code scheme. The numbers shown are the percentages of female and male MPs who included gender equality among either set of issues. Included in the category 'gender equality' were responses referring explicitly to shifts in gender balances (promoting women). The numbers of respondents (women : men) were: in 1985, 96 : 218; in 1994, 132 : 190; and in 2002, 142 : 175. The total number of MPs in the Swedish Parliament has been 349 since 1976.

Source: Parliament Studies of 1985, 1988 and 1994. The Swedish Election Study Program at the Department of Political Science, Gothenburg University.

A cursory overview shows that, when defined in this way, women's interests are a much less visible issue on the political agenda in Sweden. But the main result is that women MPs are more heavily engaged in this field than their male colleagues, the only exception to this being the election campaign in 2002.

By relying on a wider range of indicators than those presented above, there are two important conclusions that can be drawn from the research among Swedish MPs.

The first is that there are some areas which are very seldom promoted by men in politics. Gender equality is one example. My conclusion is that this is an issue that women have placed on the political agenda. Without female politicians there is a risk that there would be silence on issues of gender equality. Women to a large extent initiate the discussions here.

The second conclusion is that there are some areas where we can notice a shift in emphasis when we get more women elected. These areas have to do with the politics of care, like social policy, family policy and care of the elderly. What do I mean by a shift in emphasis? Effectively, men promote these kinds of issues, but the difference is that women give them an even higher priority. There is clearly a male and a female dimension to politics in Sweden. I thus maintain that the high number of women in the parliament has meant that the female dimension has become stronger.

Division of Work or Real Transformation?

The conclusions presented above can be viewed from two different angles: as a classic gender-based division of labour, or more dynamically as a real transformation. Reading between the lines, I tend to favour the interpretation that this is dynamic transformation. However, this cannot be taken for granted. Analyses such as those presented so far in this case study are significantly reinforced by studies of gender awareness or gender sensitivity, as well as by surveys of MPs' contacts with women's organizations outside the parliamentary arena. To be able to change things, women politicians need a platform.

Table 18 shows the degree of contact between Swedish MPs and women's organizations. It indicates that female politicians are in more frequent contact with women's organizations than male politicians. Taken as a group therefore they have a platform outside the parliamentary arena. I will not provide any figures on this but our statistics also indicate that women are gender-sensitive in the sense that they are more strongly in favour of changes in the direction of more gender equality in the future. An additional way of supporting the assessment that there has been a dynamic transformation is to ask the politicians themselves. In 1994 we asked the following question to the MPs: 'In the past 20 years, the proportion of women has increased in most parties in the Riksdag (the Swedish Parliament). Are there concrete issues where you believe the position of your party has changed because of the increased representation of women?'. A majority of Swedish MPs (75 percent among women and 50 percent among men) agreed that there have been changes, and the areas most frequently mentioned were gender equality, family policy and social policy.

Table 18: Degree of Contact between Swedish MPs and Women's Organizations
Figures are percentages.

Year	Frequent contact (percentage)			No contact (percentage)		
	Women MPs	Men MPs	Difference	Women MPs	Men MPs	Difference
1985	55	9	+46	4	14	− 10
1994	51	4	+47	4	18	− 14
2002	40	6	+34	3	14	− 11

Note: The question read: 'This question deals with your contacts as a politician with various organizations, groups and authorities in the past year. Disregarding how the contact was made, how often have you in the past year, personally or by letter, been in touch with any of the organizations, groups or authorities listed below?'. The MPs were asked to state their degrees of contact with about 20 different organizations, among which were listed women's organizations. They could state in their responses whether contact took place at least once a week, once or twice a month, a few times, occasionally or never. The table shows those who answered once a week or once or twice a month (frequent contact) and the percentage who answered never (no contact). The number of respondents (women : men) was: in 1985, 99 : 229; in 1994, 134 : 191; and in 2002, 142 : 175.
Source: Parliament Studies of 1985 and 1994. The Swedish Election Study Program at the Department of Political Science, Gothenburg University.

Different Phases

The results presented here challenge the unreflective or naive 'gender neutrality' which one has to remember still characterizes much of the research on representative democracy. But one also has to remember that, even if gender matters, this does not happen consistently or universally. The main conclusions presented above are visible even if we take party affiliation, age, education, parliamentary experience and so on into account. However, this does not mean that women in all parties behave or think in the same way; party ideology, as well as a number of other considerations, must also be taken into account, as other chapters in this Handbook indicate.

There is, naturally, a risk that the patterns described here confirm rather than change existing power relations. However, it is likely that what we have at hand is a development that can be described in terms of different phases. The fact that women have historically contributed to greater emphasis being put on the social welfare aspects of politics does not necessarily mean that they should confine themselves to this area for all time. Seen from a longer-term perspective, it would in fact be rather odd if women and men did not eventually exercise power and influence in all political domains to roughly the same extent. However, I believe it is almost impossible to go from a low proportion of female parliamentarians to a high proportion without going through a stage in which patterns of 'masculine' and 'feminine' appear with respect to the content of politics.

In recent years efforts have been made to try to bridge gender gaps. One of the most visible arenas for this is the composition of the standing committees in the Swedish Parliament. Altogether there are 16 standing committees dealing with different areas. During the 1980s and early 1990s women were strongly *over-represented* (compared to the average in parliament) in committees dealing with social welfare, such as the committees on social insurance, health and welfare, education and the labour market. Simultaneously they were *under-represented* in committees dealing with economic or technical issues such as taxation, finance, industry and trade, and transport. However, since the election of 1994, when the slogan 'Every second seat for a woman' really became rooted in Swedish politics, the picture has been more balanced. The explanation behind this is to be found on an institutional level: the leadership in different parties decided to make changes. This was a result of dual pressure—pressure both from inside (women's federations and others) and from feminist networks outside the parties.

How Have Changes Been Made?

One of the main findings emerging from this case study is that changes often occur in 'hidden' arenas and at a slow pace. It is hard to give exact answers to questions like 'What are the main achievements?' or 'How have changes been made?'. However, many indicators point in the same direction: studies of speeches made in parliament or on motions or bills put forward also reveal the importance of gender. What is somewhat missing, however, is studies on the output side, meaning the 'real' effect of politics (or policies) on citizens.

On the other hand, one of the frequently mentioned important gains for women is the comparatively generous system for parental leave in Sweden. The parental leave system also tries to enable both women and men to take an active part in the responsibilities of caring for children. Moreover, Sweden, like many other countries, also has legislation against sex discrimination and for abortion rights.

Equally under-researched is the area of precise strategies used to affect change. However, a few more features can be mentioned here.

1. Partnership and collaboration with men is an important factor.
2. Integration was mentioned earlier, and it is important to underscore that women in Sweden have to a great extent chosen to work inside the established party structures.

3. At the same time they have formed their own federations and networks and also been in touch with women outside parliament.

This way of working has been termed a *double strategy* which can be understood as women MPs working together with women's organizations but also working together with men.

A few more concrete examples of strategies include those adopted by the former speaker of the Swedish Parliament, Birgitta Dahl, who during the 1990s introduced a series of meetings in parliament inviting guests to discuss different aspects of gender equality but also democracy in a wider sense. A child care centre was also introduced in parliament, enabling MPs with small children from outside the capital to have their family, at least for a time, with them in Stockholm.

No Glorious World

When I use the expression 'step-wise development' I want to highlight that one cannot expect a linear development. Sweden is no glorious world for women, even though many things surely work quite well. Even women in Swedish politics will encounter challenges and be subjected to stereotyping. The question is whether we will ever achieve a truly gender-equal society, with no subordination for women. There have been setbacks for women in recent years when the economy in Sweden has been under pressure. What we can learn from the Swedish experience is that under these circumstances, when the political system is under stress, one has to be even more aware of women's interests.

Even if gender equality remains a utopian goal we have to believe in the possibility of reaching *more* equality between women and men. In the process of realizing that ambition, women MPs are important actors.

Note

[1] Most of this case study builds on research presented in the author's dissertation (Wängnerud 1998) and related work (Wängnerud 2000a and 2000b). However, a deeper study of the process within the parties is presented in Wängnerud 2001, and indicators relating to political participation among female citizens are presented in Oskarson and Wängnerud 1995. The Swedish Election Study Program sends questionnaires to voters as well as to MPs. Sören Holmberg, Peter Esaiasson and Martin Brothén have also been responsible for the investigations referred to in the text. Some figures have been updated for this case study and have not been published elsewhere.

References and Further Reading

Oskarson, Maria and Lena Wängnerud, 1995. *Kvinnor som väljare och valda: Om betydelsen av kön i svensk politik* [Women as voters and elected MPs: On the importance of gender within Swedish politics]. Lund: Studentlitteratur

Wängnerud, Lena, 1998. *Politikens andra sida. Om kvinnorepresentation i den svenska riksdagen* [The second face of democracy: Women's representation in the Swedish Parliament]. Gothenburg: Göteborg Studies in Politics

— 2000a, 'Testing the Politics of Presence: Women's Representation in the Swedish Riksdag'. *Scandinavian Political Studies*. Vol. 23, no. 1, pp. 67–91

— 2000b, 'Representing Women', in Peter Esaiasson and Knut Heidar. *Beyond Westminster and Congress. The Nordic Experience.* Columbus: Ohio State University Press

— 2001, 'Kvinnors röst: En kamp mellan partier' [Female votes: A competition between parties], in Christer Jönsson (ed.), *Rösträtten 80 år* [Eighty years of the suffrage]. Forskarantologi. Stockholm: Justitiedepartementet

Chapter 6

Chapter 6

Azza Karam

Conclusions

'Don't think of yourselves as being unfortunate because of having to live through these times. Think of it as fortunate, because you have an opportunity to work for justice and the welfare of other people. This sort of opportunity does not come to everybody all the time.'

Aung San Suu Kyi

The main objective of this Handbook was to provide a comprehensive overview of the processes relating to women's participation in parliament, and by so doing highlight some concrete strategies to enhance women's input and effectiveness in parliamentary structures, while referring to case studies that reflect on and assess women MPs' experiences thus far. To that end, each chapter has dealt with a different facet of the process—from the hindrances to women's participation, to the mechanisms for overcoming them, to the means of making an impact. The experiences culled here are a sum of experiential and scholarly insights which narrate the stories behind women's journeys into the corridors of power from each corner of the world.

These features are what is unique about IDEA's approach—drawing on facts, lived realities, combined insights and experiences, an emphasis both on the creation of a critical mass and on using the institutions and forging the necessary strategic alliances to make a difference to the broader political process—and to make sure that the information provided reflects the realities of women east, west, north and south.

1. The Issues and the Obstacles

We began by outlining why it was that women's participation and input are not a favour that is granted, nor are they about tokenism for the sake of looking good. Rather, we explained why it is that women's contribution to any political process is a fundamental human right, and a need that contemporary global societies, in the throes of radical technological, social, economic and political transformation, cannot do without. The argument is even more straightforward: women comprise half of the world's population. Their perspective on all issues—and thus their active and equitable involvement in politics—are an integral aspect of any process of civic engagement. And, since politics is ultimately about ruling people's lives, it is not possible to believe that it can be done without representative and just inclusion of those who are affected.

In considering some of the obstacles women face in entering politics in general, and parliaments in particular, **chapter 2** has highlighted the correlation between the problems women face and the aspirations they have. Hence, we presented a broad overview of these obstacles, categorized into political, socio-economic, and ideological and psychological hindrances. Briefly, the some of the main common obstacles can be described as follows:

- lack of political party support;
- lack of coordination and support networks between women MPs and other public organizations;
- the dominance of male-oriented norms and male-dominated structures which work against women's public participation;
- insufficient mobilization of media support;
- lack of large-scale leadership-oriented training and education for women;
- an electoral system that is not conducive to women's participation; and
- the lack of quota reservations.

The case studies on the Arab states, Ecuador and Indonesia highlight these common impediments to women's participation, despite socio-economic, cultural and significant geopolitical differences. For women in these areas, the prevalence of male-dominated institutions; political, legislative and electoral frameworks that work against the inclusion of women; political parties that hesitate to support or endorse women candidates; lack of media support; and inadequate networking strategies with civic organizations outside the direct political sphere, in addition to rapidly changing political topographies—all constitute ongoing challenges for women's representation.

2. Overcoming Obstacles

In **chapter 3** we address two of the obstacles mentioned above—political parties and electoral systems. Political parties are entrusted with perhaps the most strategic responsibility in democracy—to prepare and select candidates for election and to support them in positions of leadership and governance. As political parties are the gatekeepers to elected office, since they choose lists of candidates, they hold the key to the political advancement of women. In this process, it is argued that women must keep in mind the rules for selecting women MPs. The stage at which party gatekeepers choose the candidates is the most crucial for getting women into legislatures, as their inclusion and placement on party lists is of vital importance for getting elected. So long as political parties remain highly gendered institutions, women's access to leadership positions will be impeded.

While there is no guarantee that a proportional representation (PR) system will lead to an immediate increase in women's representation, the research increasingly indicates that it is a step in the right direction. Chapter 3 also indicates that not any PR system will work well for women's representation. On the contrary, the author stresses that some PR systems (i.e. those that guarantee high party magnitudes through a combination of high district magnitudes and electoral thresholds) are preferable to others. Still, we are cautioned that 'immediate results cannot be guaranteed'. However, the advantages of PR systems over plurality/majority systems are made clear in the French case study, which illustrates the wide variations in women's representation in different legislatures because of the electoral systems in operation. Regardless of the type of electoral system, there is a need for coordination and organization among women MPs and their political parties, as well as between MPs and other interest organizations outside parliament. In other words, 'changing the electoral system is only one part of what should be a comprehensive strategy to enhance women's representation in parliament'.

The following chapter, **chapter 4**, looks at another mechanism for enhancing women's representation—the quota system. Here, the pros and cons of quotas are discussed, the different types of quotas that are used are defined (with a brief overview of the experience of Nordic countries), and the relationship between political parties and quotas, as well as the dynamics of post-conflict societies and the implementation of quota systems, are assessed. It is argued that, in spite of the critical role actually played by quotas, quota rules alone are not enough. What makes a difference is that the quota 'must be embedded in the selection and the nomination processes of political parties from the very beginning'.

The author warns us that the more vague the regulations about quotas, the greater the likelihood that they will not be effective. And hence the need, she continues, to have some form of sanctions for non-compliance with the quota requirement.

Echoing what are fast becoming words of wisdom in the enterprise of women in politics, the author stresses that pressure from women's organizations is needed to ensure a successful implementation of quotas, and urges us to keep in mind that quotas alone do not remove all barriers to women's entry into legislative structures.

The regional case studies on Latin America and South Asia, together with the case studies on Argentina, Burkina Faso, France and Rwanda, provide additional experiential reflection on the interaction between electoral systems, political parties and quotas. In Latin America, the author acknowledges that, while electoral systems and quotas have led to gains for women in the legislatures of some countries, significant challenges, such as persisting sexist attitudes and the lack of achievement of parity with men in party leaderships, remain. But the case study also points to an issue of impacting beyond numbers that is less talked about—that 'even when women are present, they do not always act to promote a gender equality agenda'. Nevertheless, the author balances this critique by noting that 'perhaps it is unreasonable to expect that a group of newcomers could so quickly modify the logic of the political marketplace. It is one thing to put women in power. It is quite another to transform the way politicians behave'. While looking at the gains made through quotas in India, Bangladesh and Pakistan, the author of the South Asian case study also echoes a point raised by the Latin American and Burkina Faso experiences, when she implies that disparities in income and the economic disempowerment of the majority effectively translate into many women lacking basic capabilities, and thus remaining excluded from eligibility pools for leadership. 'Despite some shifts', the author notes, 'the continuing dominance of the middle and upper classes in local politics means that the differences between women are played out in particular ways ... low-caste women find it difficult to represent their own communities satisfactorily, while at the same time they are unable to represent any generalized interests of women'. The author of the case study on Rwanda, assessing the unique post-conflict context there, also agrees, noting that women MPs 'carry a double burden, as they must find ways to insert a gender perspective into a new range of issues—foreign affairs, for example—and yet remain loyal to their constituency of women in a country where the basic development needs are so great and women still lag behind men in terms of rights, status, and access to resources and education'.

3. Making an Impact

It is relatively easy to enumerate the various challenges regarding women's political participation, but it is much harder to appreciate the strengths of women and the positive differences they have made in their chosen professions. The second theme of the Handbook shifts the focus to how women can move 'beyond numbers' in parliament to make an impact on the political process. **Chapter 5** outlines how women can reform the inherent 'institutional masculinity' which characterizes most legislatures by implementing a 'rules strategy'. They identify three key areas: learning the rules, using the rules and changing the rules. The aim is to go 'beyond tokenism' and move towards adopting a woman's perspective and making changes on women's issues. Women seeking to make an impact need to keep three broad tactics in mind:

- learn the rules that apply to the parliamentary *mode d'emploi* or functioning;
- use these rules to bring about desired changes; and
- change the rules, which, in some instances, may be unhelpful in advancing women's concerns.

Each tactic embodies various strategies which fall under four broad categories: the nature of the institution of parliament, issues of representation, the discourse used about and for women MPs, and legislative or policy outputs.

One of the frequently mentioned aspects of learning the rules while impacting through the different categories is the need for training and orientation exercises for MPs, which would also enable them, among other things, to:

- distinguish between women's perspectives and women's issues;
- network with media and women's organizations on various levels—local, regional and international; and
- take an active role in a broad range of committees.

When it comes to changing the rules, women MPs need to consider:

- the establishment of national machinery to support women's causes and to monitor the implementation of policies and recommendations;
- changing the candidate selection rules for their parties, especially with regard to leadership positions;
- the establishment of mechanisms within parliament which would give women MPs priority in areas where they are under-represented or less vocal than their male counterparts—such as giving women MPs the opportunity to speak first, and instituting quotas in different committees in parliament;
- providing special incentives for initiatives outside parliament which sponsor and support women's issues and women's representation (e.g. women's leadership training schools, media programmes on women politicians); and
- expanding legislation to include emerging issues of interest to women.

In addition to the concrete suggestions to enhance impact outlined in this section of the Handbook, further general areas of need have also been highlighted, including:

- general awareness-raising and particularly the realization of the potential of rural women;
- impact-based research and training for women;
- understanding and targeting the critical role of the media in shaping discourse and action;
- constant positive discrimination which would enable women to increase their numbers in the political arena, as well as amend laws (or introduce new ones) to

encourage women's participation—such as quotas for women in different areas of public involvement and the allocation of specific funds to promote women's participation;

- concerted and impact-based positive action on the part of governments (e.g. through national machinery), women's organizations, and other public and interest-based organizations; and
- constant caucusing and networking between MPs and outside organizations and interest groups working for the enhancement of women's position generally.

The case studies on South Africa, France, Sweden and Rwanda illustrate the diverse conditions and areas in which women are making an impact. The changes, among many others, include:

- institutional and representational changes such as the specification of women's budgets, the specification of parity laws, and the creation of national machinery; and
- changes in discourse, such as cooperating and networking with the women's movement to change the way in which women are referred to, their participation is evaluated and sought after, partnerships with men are formed, and their efforts are assessed.

4. International Efforts

The experience of the major player in the field of parliamentary activity in general, and women parliamentarians in particular—the Inter-Parliamentary Union (IPU)—is noteworthy and learning from it will be critical to successfully meeting a number of needs, including one that the IPU focuses on—partnership between men and women as an essential factor in accomplishing change and impacting on politics. The IPU's work further validates the emphasis earlier chapters put on the crucial role international intergovernmental organizations can play in enhancing the capacities of women MPs in national parliaments, caucusing, responding to women's common needs, mainstreaming gender, and enhancing parliaments' capacity to address gender issues, to name but a few.

The discussion on the IPU's Meeting of Women Parliamentarians, for example, brings to light another relatively little-known and yet important reality. Caucusing is not only a forum of women MPs who come together and share experiences and strategies to enhance their representation; it is also of benefit to the organizational structures which service women's needs. This is particularly the case when there is a need to fine-tune the responsiveness to changing contexts, political realities and consequent needs of women parliamentarians. Coordinated efforts in this regard should be made at various levels—the local, regional, and international—and must build on, rather than replicate, the pioneering work that has already been carried out.

5. The Road Ahead

In sum, looking beyond numbers does not mean that numbers no longer matter. On the contrary, numbers are integral to making an impact on politics. After all, half the world's population cannot but be a critical constituency. One of the threads running throughout the past narratives of challenges and remaining challenges is that success *is* possible, a difference *has* been made, and there is more to look forward to.

IDEA enters its second decade of operation with the understanding that there is still much work to be done to increase women's political participation. Yet continuing to translate the power of numbers into the constructive transformation of whole societies, by women in partnership with men, is what this millennium is about. In each country the methods will be different. It is IDEA's challenge to examine the options, collect evidence of best practice, and encourage the reformers. As we strive to inform the debate on democracy we, in turn, learn from the many courageous, creative and active men and women who truly believe that it can only be achieved when all citizens are represented in all the political structures which affect their lives. We hope that with this Handbook we have helped to highlight the signposts along a critical road of ongoing democratic development.

Annex A.
About the Authors

Julie Ballington was the Programme Officer responsible for the Women in Politics project at International IDEA between 2001 and 2005. During this time, she managed and edited the production of regional-language versions of the *Women in Parliament: Beyond Numbers* Handbook in Indonesian, French, Spanish and an abridged Russian version. She also spearheaded International IDEA's ground-breaking work on electoral quotas for women, including managing the Global Database of Electoral Quotas for Women and editing five regional publications on the implementation of quotas around the world. Prior to joining IDEA in 2001, she headed the project on Gender and Elections at the Electoral Institute of Southern Africa (EISA) based in Johannesburg, South Africa. She is the author of numerous publications and articles, and her research interests relate to the political representation and participation of women, voter turnout and electoral politics. She is currently working for the Programme for the Promotion of Partnership between Men and Women at the Inter-Parliamentary Union (IPU) in Geneva, which aims to promote women's participation and input in parliaments.

Elisa Carrio is an Argentinian lawyer. She holds a postgraduate degree in public rights and is Professor of Constitutional Rights at the National University of the Northeast. She has been a member of the Constitutional Assembly (in 1994), a member of the Argentinean Congress (1995–2003), President of the Commission of Constitutional Affairs (1999–2001), President of the Anti-Money Laundering Commission (2001), and a member of the Commission of Political Impeachment. Author of more than 100 bills, among them important initiatives regarding the constitutional order and gender equality, and of books and articles in magazines specialized in rights and policy, in 2004 she also published *Hacia un Nuevo Contrato Moral*. She was President of the Parliamentary Bloc ARI—third majority in the Parliament from 2001 to 2003, and was a candidate for the presidency in 2003. In 2004 she set up the Instituto Hannah Arendt in Buenos Aires, which she now directs. In 2004 she initiated the Political Women's Leadership Network of Latin America (Red de Mujeres Líderes Políticas de América Latina), in collaboration with International IDEA. In addition, she is a member of the Argentinean Association of Constitutional Rights, the Argentinean

Association of Philosophy of Rights, the Women's Leadership Conference of the Americas (WLCA), the Society for International Development, and the Emerging Leaders of the Western Hemisphere Conference.

Nestorine Compaoré holds a PhD in development sociology from the University of Montreal, Canada. She is currently gender adviser for the Dutch Embassy in Ouagadougou, Burkina Faso, and lecturer at the Department of Communication and Journalism, University of Ouagadougou. She is also Gender Adviser to the Center for Democratic Governance, a leading NGO in Burkina Faso, on the topic of democracy and governance, and has carried out some exploratory and empirical research into women's political participation in the country. Since December 2004, Nestorine Compaoré has been coordinating a three-year programme funded by a consortium of donors to increase and improve women's political participation in Burkina Faso.

Drude Dahlerup is Professor of Political Science at Stockholm University, Sweden. She has undertaken extensive research on women in politics, social movements, the history of the women's movement, gender segregation of the labour market and feminist theory. She has published many articles and books in Danish, including, most recently, *Rødstrømperne: Den danske Rødstrømpebevægelses udvikling, nytænkning og gennemslag 1970–1985*. Bd. I-II, Gyldendal, 1998 [The redstockings: The rise and fall, the new ideas and impact of the Danish Women's liberation movement, 1970–1985]. In English, among other things, she has published *The New Women's Movements, Feminism and Political Power in Europe and the USA* (Sage, 1986); and 'From a Small to a Large Minority: Women in Scandinavian Politics'. *Scandinavian Political Studies,* Vol. 11, no. 4 (1988). She has also written a handbook on women's representation, which was published by the Nordic Council of Ministers in all five Nordic languages, and is the editor of *Women, Quotas and Politics: A Comparison of the Use of Quotas Worldwide* (Routledge, forthcoming 2006).

Frene Ginwala PhD is a member of the National Executive Committee of the African National Congress (ANC), Presiding Co-Chairperson of the Global Coalition for Africa and Chancellor of the University of KwaZulu Natal in South Africa. She is currently working of issues of development, in particular on good governance and human rights, and in 2005 was preparing a report on human security in Africa. She is a member of the International Women's Commission (IWC) for a just and sustainable Israeli–Palestinian peace. She was the first Speaker of the democratically elected National Assembly of South Africa for ten years, until she left the Parliament in 2004. On her return to South Africa from exile in 1990, she became a founder member and the first Convenor of the Women's National Coalition, formed to unite all women's organizations in campaigns to ensure that the new South African constitution would provide effective equality for women. In the early 1990s she was a member of the ANC's negotiation team and the Constitutional Assembly.

Mala N. Htun is Assistant Professor of Political Science at the New School for Social Research, New York, USA, and the author of *Sex and the State: Abortion, Divorce, and the Family under Latin American Dictatorships and Democracies* (Cambridge University Press, 2003). Her work on gender politics, women's rights, and race and politics has appeared in the *Latin American Research Review, Perspectives on Politics, Social Research, Current History*, and several other journals and edited volumes in English, Spanish and Portuguese. She recently held fellowships at the Kellogg Institute of the University of Notre Dame, USA, and the Radcliffe Institute at Harvard, USA, and her work has been supported by the National Science Foundation, the Social Science Research Council, and the National Security Education Program. She holds a PhD in political science from Harvard University and a BA in international relations from Stanford University, USA. Her current research focuses on the politics of gender and ethnic representation in Latin America and worldwide.

Kareen Jabre is the Manager of the Programme for Partnership between Men and Women of the IPU, where she is responsible for activities aimed at promoting women's participation and input in parliaments. She is also responsible for the development and production of research material and statistics on women in politics at the IPU and for activities at the IPU related to international humanitarian law and child protection issues. Before joining the IPU, Kareen Jabre worked at UNESCO in the Coordinating Unit on Gender Issues.

Azza Karam is Senior Policy Research Advisor in the Arab Human Development Report Unit Regional Bureau for Arab States of the United Nations Development Programme (UNDP). She joined UNDP after serving as Senior Adviser and Programme Director at the World Conference of Religions for Peace since 2000, where she worked with religious leaders and communities around the world. She came to this after serving as Programme Manager and Lecturer in Politics at the Centre for the Study of Ethnic Conflict at the Queen's University of Belfast, in Northern Ireland. After working and teaching in the human rights and development arenas both in the Arab region and in Europe for many years, she joined International IDEA as a Senior Programme Officer and was the architect of its programmes on gender and on the Arab world from 1996 to 1998. Apart from the first edition of IDEA's Handbook on *Women in Parliament* (1998), her publications include *Transnational Political Islam* (2004), *Islamisms, Women and State* (1998), *Religious Women as Public Actors* (2002) and *Religion, Women and Conflict: A Manual* (2004).

Joni Lovenduski is Professor of Politics at Birkbeck College, London University, United Kingdom. Her research is on the political behaviour of British and European women and especially women's representation in politics. Her main books are *Feminizing Politics* (2005), a reflection on what happens in politics when the numbers of women increase; *Women and European Politics* (1986), a comparative study of the impact of women and feminism in Europe; *Political Recruitment* (with Pippa Norris, 1995), a study of the British candidate selection process; *Contemporary Feminist Politics* (with Vicky Randall, 1993), a study of the British women's movement in the Thatcher years; and *Politics and Society in Eastern Europe* (with Jean Woodall, 1989). She co-edited *The Politics of the Second Electorate* (1981), *The New Politics of Abortion* (1986), *Gender and Party Politics* (1993), *Different Roles, Different Voices* (1994) and *Women in Politics* (1996), and is the editor of *Feminist Politics* (1996). She is lead editor (with Claudie Baudino, Marila Guadagnini, Petra Meier and Diane Sainsbury) and one of the authors of *State Feminism and the Political Representation of Women* (Cambridge University Press, 2005).

Richard E. Matland is a Professor of Political Science at the University of Houston, Texas, USA, and has had a long affiliation with the Department of Administration and Organizational Theory at the University of Bergen, Norway. His research interests include the fields of women and politics, comparative politics, and public policy. His work has been published in several leading political science journals, including the *American Journal of Political Science*, the *British Journal of Political Science,* the *Journal of Politics, Comparative Political Studies*, and the *Canadian Journal of Political Science*. A common theme in Dr Matland's work has been the effects of electoral systems on women's representation. He has done research on questions of electoral systems and women's representation in Canada, Costa Rica, Indonesia, Norway, Sweden, the United States and Eastern Europe, and is the co-editor of *Women's Access to Political Power in Post-Communist Europe* (Oxford University Press, 2003).

Sheila Meintjes is Assistant Professor in the Department of Political Studies at the University of the Witwatersrand, South Africa, and was a full-time Commissioner on the Commission on Gender Equality from 2001 to 2004. She teaches African politics, political theory and feminist theory and politics. She has a BA (Hons) from Rhodes University, Grahamstown, South Africa, an MA in African Studies from the University of Sussex, UK, and a PhD in African history from the School of Oriental and African Studies at London University, UK. She has published on the politics of gender and gender violence, and most recently has co-edited three books: *The Aftermath: Women in Post-conflict Transformation* (Zed Press, 2002); *One Woman, One Vote: The Gender Politics of South African Elections* (Electoral Institute of Southern Africa, 2002); and *Women Writing Africa: The Southern Volume* (Feminist Press and University of the Witwatersrand Press, 2003).

Nina Pacari is a Kichwa indigenous lawyer from Ecuador. She has served as Legal Adviser (1989–93) and Leader of Land and Territories (1993–6) of the Confederation of Indigenous Nationalities of Ecuador. In 1997 she was elected to the Constituent National Assembly, managing to incorporate in the political constitution the collective rights of the indigenous peoples as well as their recognition by the Administration of

Justice. She is the founder of the Pachakutik Movement, was an elected member of the parliament of Ecuador from 1998 to 2002, and was its vice-president from 1998 to 2000. Her legislative tasks have focused on economic and social issues as well as on the defence of the rights of indigenous people and women. Between 15 January and 6 August 2003, Ms Pacari held the position of Minister of Foreign Affairs of Ecuador, making her the first indigenous woman to hold such a high position within the government. She has participated actively in international events and several of her reports have been published at the national as well as the international levels.

Sonia Palmieri was the Researcher for Gender Issues at the IPU from 2003 to 2004, where she was responsible for producing various analyses of the progress and setbacks of women in national parliaments. Her doctoral thesis explored the question of women's impact in parliament and examined the gender dynamics evident in men and women MPs' interactions during two Australian federal parliamentary committee hearings. She has published a number of articles and conference papers on the subject of women in parliament, including 'Gendered Parliamentary Debates: The Case of Euthanasia', *Australian Journal of Political Science*, Vol. 34, no. 1 (1999).

Khofifah Indar Parawansa is a graduate of the Faculty of Social and Political Science at the University of Airlangga, Surabaya, Indonesia. She is the Chairperson of the Pucuk Pimpinan Muslimat of Nahdlatul Ulama (NU, one of the biggest Muslim organizations in Indonesia). She is also the Chairperson of the Lembaga Pemenangan Pemilu Partai Kebangkitan Bangsa (National Awakening Party). She was elected as a member of the Dewan Perwakilan Rakyat Republik Indonesia (DPR RI, House of Representatives of the Republic of Indonesia) for three separate terms, in 1992, 1997 and 1999. During her terms in the DPR, she served in the following capacities, among others: as Pimpinan Komisi (head of commission), Pimpinan Fraksi (head of fraction), and Pimpinan DPR RI (vice-speaker). She also served as State Minister for the Empowerment of Women and as Head of the National Family Planning Coordinating Board (1999–2001).

Elizabeth Powley directs the Rwanda project of Inclusive Security: Women Waging Peace and was previously the Associate Director of Women Waging Peace's Policy Commission in Washington, DC. In that capacity, she was the lead researcher and author of 'Strengthening Governance: The Role of Women in Rwanda's Transition', a field-based case study on women's political participation. Her technical experience is in conflict analysis, democracy and governance, civil society, transitional justice, and gender equality and women. An experienced trainer and educator, she has worked with peace-builders and civil society activists in Angola, Mali, Nigeria, South Africa and Rwanda. She has developed curricula on women's political participation and leadership, transitional justice, and civil society's involvement in peace negotiations. She holds a MA degree from the American University's School of International Service in Washington, DC.

Shirin Rai is Professor of Politics and International Studies at the University of Warwick, UK. Her research interests are in the area of feminist politics, democratization, globalization and development studies. She has written extensively on issues of gender, governance and democratization and is the author of several books, the most recent being *Gender and the Political Economy of Development* (Cambridge: Polity Press, 2002). She has also co-edited *Rethinking Empowerment: Gender and Development in a Global/ Local World* (Routledge, 2002) and edited Mainstreaming Gender: *Democratizing the State?* (published for and on behalf of the United Nations by Manchester University Press, 2003), and the special issue of the *International Feminist Journal of Politics* on Gender Governance and Globalization, 2004, Vol. 6, no. 4.

Amal Sabbagh was the Secretary General of the Jordanian National Commission for Women (JNCW), one of the first semi-governmental commissions established in the Arab world to promote women's issues, until October 2005. The JNCW leads Jordan's effort to formulate a national strategy for women by working to define policies and legislation related to women and identifying priorities, plans and programmes in both the governmental and the non-governmental sectors in order to carry them out effectively. Dr Sabbagh was formerly Director General of the Regional Centre for Agrarian Reform and Rural Development in the Near East (CARDNE), Jordan, and prior to that held a number of positions within the Jordanian Ministry of Social Development. She holds a PhD in social policy from the University of Nottingham, UK. Her research interests mainly focus on issues of social equity, the empowerment of marginalized groups, specifically rural populations and the poor, and gender equality.

Nadezhda Shvedova is a Fulbright Scholar and an international specialist on Russian women in Russian politics. She is a leading researcher at the Institute of the USA and Canada Studies at the Russian Academy of Sciences in Moscow, Russia, and has worked as a consultant to the State Duma of Russia, the Supreme Soviet, the Ministry of Health Care and the Ministry of Foreign Affairs, among other institutions. She is the Vice-Chairperson of the Gender Section of the Russian Association of Political Scientists and the author of numerous works related to women in politics in Russia, the former Soviet republics and the USA. Her publications include *The Code of Honour of the Russian Women Movement* (1993) and *The Abyss* (1988), and she is co-author of a chapter on women in Russian elections in *Women in Politics and Society* (1996). Her publication *Simply About the Complex: Gender Education* (Moscow: Antikva Press, 2002) has been translated into the Kyrgyz and Armenian languages. In 2003 she was a member of the team preparing the review report on Gender Status Issues in the Russian Federation by request of the World Bank. In 1999, Dr Shvedova was awarded a Certificate of Merit by the Russian Academy of Sciences in recognition of her pioneering research, and in 2003 the Russian Ministry of Labour and Social Development awarded her a Certificate of Merit in recognition of her efforts to improve the status of women in Russia.

Mariette Sineau is a political scientist and Research Director of the Centre National de la Recherche Scientifique (CNRS, National Centre for Scientific Research). She works in Paris, France, at the Centre de Recherches Politiques de Sciences Po. (CEVIPOF, Centre for Political Research). Her main research fields are women's political attitudes and behaviour, and women politicians. Her work is also concerned with family policy and the childcare system. Her recent publications include *Profession: femme politique. Sexe et pouvoir sous la Ve République* [Profession: Woman politician. Gender and power under the Fifth Republic] (Paris: Presses de Sciences Po., 2001); *Who Cares? Women's Work, Childcare and Welfare State Redesign* (with Jane Jenson, University of Toronto Press, 2001); and *Mitterrand et les Françaises: un rendez-vous manqué* [Mitterand and French women: A missed rendezvous] (with J. Jenson, Paris: Presses de Sciences Po., 1995).

Lena Wängnerud is Associate Professor at the Department of Political Science, Gothenburg University, Sweden. She has written several books and articles dealing with the issue of women's representation. Empirically she has focused on the Swedish Parliament, but also parliaments in other Nordic countries, where the number of women in parliament has been relatively high for a long time. Her current research is on the turnover of members within parliament, focusing on the increasing number of MPs who leave the Swedish Parliament at each election. She is also working on a project mapping different forums to discuss political issues within civil society.

INTERNATIONAL IDEA

Supporting democracy worldwide

Created in 1995, the International Institute for Democracy and Electoral Assistance – IDEA – is an intergovernmental organization that supports sustainable democracy. Working globally, but with a current focus on Africa and the Middle East, Latin America and South Asia, IDEA seeks to improve the design and effectiveness of democratic institutions, and to strengthen democratic processes through:

- assisting countries in developing and strengthening democratic institutions;
- providing researchers, policy makers, activists and media representatives a forum in which to discuss democratic principles;
- blending research and field experience, developing methodologies and providing training to improve democratic processes; and
- promoting transparency, accountability and efficiency in managing elections.

Its main areas of activity include:

- **Democracy building and conflict management.** IDEA's work in this area focuses on constitution building, reconciliation, inclusive dialogue and human security. It targets societies in transition, particularly those emerging from periods of violence and weak governance.

- **Electoral processes,** including ensuring the professional management and independence of elections, adapting electoral systems, improving access and building public confidence. IDEA develops training modules and materials for election officials and provides comparative data and analyses on both the political and the technical aspects of designing, organizing and running elections.

- **Political parties, political equality and participation** *(including women in politics)*. IDEA's work includes the review of political parties' external regulations, public funding, their management and relations with the public. It also includes identifying ways to build commitment to inclusive politics, especially those related to the inlcusion of women in politics, through for example the provision of comparative experiences on the application of special measures like gender quotas.

Membership

Membership of IDEA is open to governments and intergovernmental organizations. Currently IDEA has 24 member states: Australia, Barbados, Belgium, Botswana, Canada, Cape Verde, Chile, Costa Rica, Denmark, Finland, Germany, India, Mauritius, Mexico, Namibia, the Netherlands, Norway, Peru, Portugal, South Africa, Spain, Sweden, Switzerland and Uruguay. Japan has taken up observer status. In addition, associate membership is open to international organizations. There are currently four associate members: the International Press Institute, Parliamentarians for Global Action, Transparency International and the Inter-American Institute for Human Rights.

International Institute for Democracy and Electoral Assistance
(International IDEA)

Strömsborg, SE-130 34 Stockholm, Sweden
Tel: +46-8-698-3700
Fax: +46-8-20-24-22
E-mail: info@idea.int
www.idea.int